the
conflict
paradox

the conflict paradox

paradox

Seven Dilemmas
at the Core
of Disputes

Bernard S. Mayer

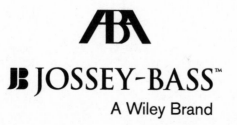

JB JOSSEY-BASS™
A Wiley Brand

Published by Jossey-Bass
A Wiley Brand
One Montgomery Street, Suite 1000, San Francisco, CA 94104-4594—www.josseybass.com

Jossey-Bass books and products are available through most bookstores. To contact Jossey-Bass directly call our Customer Care Department within the U.S. at 800-956-7739, outside the U.S. at 317-572-3986, or fax 317-572-4002.

Wiley publishes in a variety of print and electronic formats and by print-on-demand. Some material included with standard print versions of this book may not be included in e-books or in print-on-demand. If this book refers to media such as a CD or DVD that is not included in the version you purchased, you may download this material at http://booksupport.wiley.com. For more information about Wiley products, visit www.wiley.com.

Library of Congress Cataloging-in-Publication Data

Mayer, Bernard S., date-
  The conflict paradox: seven dilemmas at the core of disputes / Bernard S. Mayer.—First edition.
    pages cm
  Includes bibliographical references and index.
  ISBN 978-1-118-85291-0 (hardback)
  1. Conflict (Psychology) 2. Interpersonal conflict. 3. Conflict management. 4. Negotiation.
  I. Title.
  BF637.I48M387 2015
  303.6'9—dc23

                                         2014032312

Printed in the United States of America
FIRST EDITION
HB Printing   10 9 8 7 6 5 4 3 2 1

contents

Preface   ix

Acknowledgments   xv

1   The Art of Conflict   1

2   Competition and Cooperation   25

3   Optimism and Realism   61

4   Avoidance and Engagement   95

5   Principle and Compromise   131

6   Emotions and Logic   167

7   Neutrality and Advocacy   201

8   Community and Autonomy   237

9   The Conflict Dialectic: Better Paradoxes,
    Better Conflict   267

    References   295

    Index   307

To Hopey
Who handles life's paradoxes with honesty,
kindness, and wisdom

preface

How wonderful that we have met with a paradox. Now we have some hope of making progress.

Niels Bohr, Niels Bohr: The Man, His Science, and the World They Changed

T he most important, difficult, and complicated challenges we face in conflict are also the simplest and most straightforward. How do we guide destructive interactions in a more positive direction? How do we change a hostile, competitive relationship into a partnership for change? How do we find a way through seemingly intractable differences about values or resources? Although there are no easy answers to these challenges, there are simple ones. For example:

- When communication breaks down, adversaries need to listen more and argue less.

- When disputants are locked into a negative and competitive interchange, they should each try to identify possible avenues for cooperation.

- When stuck in opposing positions, disputants should explore underlying interests and concerns and look for integrative options.

- When two people are enraged at each other but depend on each other, they need to examine the source of their anger and find ways of being a bit less dependent.

- When opponents are sure they are right and the other side is wrong, they should entertain doubt.

The very simplicity of the answers to so many of conflict's challenges makes this kind of advice almost banal. But if the advice is simple, what is necessary to implement it is very difficult indeed. Much of the best wisdom about conflict offers practical advice about how to approach conflict differently, how to communicate better, or how to problem solve more effectively. But conflict takes place in the chaotic world of human society, fraught with intense emotions, complex interactional systems, long histories, and troubling power dynamics. So while the answers may seem simple, the path to them is very complex. To make our way down this path, we need new ways to understand conflict and the choices it presents. Whether we are trying to work our own way through a difficult dispute or help others to do so, the biggest challenge we face is finding new ways to think about conflict that open up new and practical approaches to engaging in it in the messy, unpredictable, complex world in which we live.

I present seven paradoxes in this book—all seeming contradictions that frame how we make sense of conflict. Each poses an essential dilemma for how we approach conflict, how we think about it, and how we can move forward in a productive way. In each, we seem to face a difficult choice between two alternatives, neither of which is entirely acceptable.

- Competition and cooperation

- Optimism and realism

- Avoidance and engagement

- Principle and compromise

- Emotions and logic

- Neutrality and advocacy

- Community and autonomy

We grow in our ability to handle conflict, and we help others to grow as well, when we realize that we do not have to *choose* between these stark alternatives. They are not mutually exclusive; each element of each polarity implies and indeed requires the other. We mature in our capacity to engage and intervene in conflict by developing a deeper understanding and comfort with these paradoxes—both by working on them for ourselves and honing our ability to help others. We may not do this consciously or intentionally, but this challenge is so essential to effective conflict work that is natural for us to grapple with it.

This book describes these paradoxes and discusses how we tend to pose them as intractable dilemmas or opposites—that is, as contradictions requiring a difficult choice—and argues that they are not contradictions at all, but codependent realities. I discuss these paradoxes always with an eye to both the conceptual and practical challenges we face: how do we understand this, and what does this mean for practice?

We can view each of these paradoxes independently, and some no doubt will resonate more with individual readers than others. But taken together, they present a powerful way of understanding the challenges presented by conflict.

The Conflict Paradox builds on previous works but also departs from them in significant ways. As with earlier writings, I try here to deepen our understanding of our role and purpose in conflict work and the conceptual frameworks that guide us. But I go a step further in this book by examining and challenging the fundamental way we think about conflict itself—and in particular the polarized, bifurcated view we tend to take of it. I came to this by reflecting on what appeared to be at the core of my own conflict work and my thinking about conflict, but also by considering what seemed to me to be at the heart of some of the most influential contributions to conflict theory and conflict intervention by leading scholars and practitioners. I hope that this book will contribute to a better understanding of how we can engage and intervene in conflict more effectively and that it will challenge readers to reflect on what they actually do that makes a difference in conflict.

I have addressed this book to conflict specialists such as mediators, advocates, coaches, facilitators, and collaborative practitioners, but also to conflict participants. I have used examples throughout from both perspectives, and each of the chapters can be viewed through the lenses of conflict engagement and conflict intervention. Readers of my previous books will not be surprised that I have avoided focusing on conflict resolution, because I believe that is only one part of our purpose in conflict—and concentrating on this often leads us away from the more important work we have to do. Instead, our goal as interveners and as participants in conflict is to promote more constructive approaches to conflict engagement.

I also have not focused on the professional role of the third party, although many of my examples come from situations in which I participated as such. While the work of mediators, facilitators, fact finders, and others who function as "third siders" is important, other conflict intervention roles are also crucial to constructive conflict engagement. Advocates, coaches, system designers, strategic advisers, substantive experts, and many others who are not in an ostensibly neutral role also fulfill essential functions, and this book is also addressed to them. I directly address this in chapter 7, "Neutrality and Advocacy."

I have been privileged to work across a wide range of disputes, and this has shaped my understanding of conflict. If a dynamic seems significant across multiple arenas of conflict, it seems likely that it reflects a fundamental truth about conflict. The seven paradoxes that I describe apply across all arenas of conflict, and I provide examples of how they operate from widely different contexts. I use family, organizational, interpersonal, small and large group, community, societal, and international disputes throughout as illustrations of the paradoxes in operation.

Some of the examples are drawn from specific conflicts that I have worked on. Some are amalgams of several different but similar disputes, and a few describe from a new perspective disputes presented in previous works. Some are public conflicts; others are confidential. In a few of them, I was a disputant, observer, or consultant and not an intervener. Unless a conflict was public, I have changed the facts to protect confidentiality but have tried to maintain the interactional dynamics. And where I report direct dialogue, this is reconstructed from memory.

This book is also more personal than my earlier works. I have included throughout descriptions of my own path and struggles in developing a constructive approach to conflict. Additionally, each chapter ends with a section containing personal and professional reflections in which I focus on how I developed the ideas described in the chapter and how I have applied these to my work and my life. These sections are intended to share my own ongoing efforts to be a reflective practitioner. I hope that they will help readers to engage in their own reflections about their approach to conflict.

November 2014   Bernie Mayer
                                                                                   Kingsville, Ontario

acknowledgments

My first exposure to conflict intervention as a field of practice was serendipitous. In 1977, I was encouraged to attend a workshop on nonviolent social change conducted by Chris Moore. This was a life-changing experience for three reasons. First, because the underlying wisdom of nonviolence (which I had been previously exposed to in my days as a civil rights activist) has guided my understanding of conflict, social change, and life ever since. Second, because the training was grounded in the relationship among values, theory, and practice—and that, too, has been a guiding principle in my professional work. Finally, and probably most importantly, because of Chris Moore himself, who became my lifelong friend, mentor, and partner at CDR Associates. His interest in conflict work was infectious, and I followed him right along as he became interested in mediation and dispute systems design. Chris was the catalyst who brought together Susan Wildau, Mary Margaret Golten, and the two of us to form the four original partners at CDR Associates. Our partnership started in the late 1970s, and ever since, Chris, Mary Margaret, and Susan have been my constant supporters, teachers, and friends. Other partners and staff at CDR have also been important to my personal and professional development, especially Jonathan Bartsch, Suzanne Ghais, Louise Smart, Peter Woodrow, Judy Mares-Dixon, Mike Harty, Mike Hughes, Paula Taylor-Howlett, and Joan Sabott.

For the past nine years I have been a professor at the Werner Institute at Creighton University. Werner has provided a creative and nurturing atmosphere that has fostered my writing and thinking. My colleagues there have offered useful, indeed critical, input on the ideas in this book. Jackie Font-Guzmán, Noam Ebner, Bryan Hanson, Mary Lee Brock, Theresa Thurin, Jessica Miller, and Pat Borchers have provided a collegial atmosphere, both honest and kind (perhaps another paradox to address!). I also want to acknowledge the kindness of many on the Creighton faculty, particularly Ron Volkmer and Marianne Culhane, for their long-term support of both the Werner Institute and of me. Theresa Thurin assisted with checking references and resources. Mitchell Brazell, my graduate assistant at Werner, not only provided invaluable help with references but also offered important lessons in philosophy as well.

Along the path that led to this book, I had many formative discussions that helped me develop my own thinking. I am particularly grateful to Richard McGuigan, Arnie Shienvold, John Manwaring, Sylvia McMechan, Karen Largent, Don Loney, David Hoffman, Fiona Hollier, Larissa Fast, Don Selcer, Howard Cohen, and Anne Sutherland-Kelly (to name just a few). My wonderful students at Werner and at the Kroc Institute for International Peace Studies at Notre Dame were subject to some of the earliest iterations of these concepts and provided much encouragement and feedback.

I am especially appreciative of those who reviewed and commented on my manuscript. My editors at Jossey-Bass, Christine Moore and Kathe Sweeney, as well as Noam Ebner, Julie Macfarlane, Mark Mayer, and Jackie Font-Guzmán. This book is being co-published by Jossey-Bass and the Dispute Resolution Section of the American Bar Association—a first. I want to thank both partners for their willingness to take the plunge into a cooperative venture with this book, and particularly Kathe Sweeney and Rob Brandt at Wiley and Daniel Bowling and Richard Paszkiet at the ABA.

My most powerful teachers have always been the many disputants who have been willing to let me into their lives and who have provided me the crucial insights and feedback that have informed my thinking and my personal and professional growth.

Most importantly I want to appreciate the wonderful support I have received from my family throughout my entire professional life. You know who are. I especially want to thank my son Mark Mayer, who took time out from writing his own book to review, critique, challenge, and encourage me throughout this project. My most powerful critic, supporter, and editor is my wife, Julie Macfarlane. She helped me develop the ideas in this book; she encouraged me when I was feeling uncertain; she told me boldly, clearly, and always with love when she thought I was off base; and she took care of business while I hid out in various corners of our house working on this project. Without her, this book would not have happened.

Finally, this book is dedicated to my remarkable stepdaughter, Hopey Moon, who will turn sixteen at about the time this book will be published. Hopey has been a wonderful presence in my life since she was three. She is a wise, courageous, good-hearted, and passionate soul (and a first-rate photographer). She embodies the values of good conflict work.

the
conflict
paradox

chapter one

the art of conflict

The test of a first-rate intelligence is the ability to hold two opposed ideas in the mind at the same time, and still retain the ability to function.

F. Scott Fitzgerald, The Crack-Up

When we intervene in conflict, whatever our role, we inevitably address how people think about their disputes. We may believe that we are trying to hammer out an agreement, change the way people communicate, or help them through a healing and recovery process. However, we do not really change the dynamics of a conflict unless we change how those involved see the challenges before them, the people they are in conflict with, or the way in which the conflict has arisen and developed.

This is also true for ourselves. Unless we change how we make sense of our own conflicts, we are unlikely to change the fundamental way in which we approach them. These changes may be minor or transformative; they may be conscious or unrecognized; and it may never be clear to anyone, including ourselves, just what happened to alter these narratives. But unless disputants understand and experience their situation in an altered way, they are unlikely to improve their approach significantly, and the impact of our intervention will not only be ineffective but will probably be unrecognized.

Although changing how people think may seem like a daunting task, it lies at the heart of how we repeatedly make a difference in conflict. Conflict professionals, as a field of practice, have equated

1

our impact on conflict with the intervention roles we play (mediation, facilitation, arbitration, advocacy, systems design, coaching), the tactics we use (reframing, active listening, looking for agreements in principle, identifying underlying interests, empowering participants), the forums we employ and create (negotiations, policy dialogues, consensus decision-making processes, restorative justice programs, settlement conferences), or the purposes we bring (resolution, transformation, healing, peace building, communication, decision making, engagement). All of these are important defining principles for how we approach our work in conflict, but none really gets at the heart of how we make a difference. Though important tactics, processes, and roles, exactly *how* do they move a conflict forward in a more productive direction?

In *Dynamics of Conflict* (2012), I discuss five essential elements that we bring to the table as conflict interveners that make a difference in the way people interact. In essence, we

- Create a new structure of interaction

- Bring a set of skills that help promote more constructive interchanges

- Introduce a specific approach to intervention

- Bring our values

- Incorporate our personal qualities

Each of these helps frame the way we work on conflict and is an important avenue for making a difference. But just how do they make a difference?

I suggest in this book that the core of what we do is to help disputants change their approach to seven fundamental paradoxes about the nature of conflict. We can understand each of these as a dilemma, polarity, contradiction, duality, or paradox that frames how people view conflict and that limits their ability to be flexible and creative. Everyone involved in a dispute, including conflict professionals, tends to stumble over these polarities or tries to find easy ways to rectify the very real contradictions they represent. The more people succumb to dualistic thinking in response to these polarities, the more they become trapped in a conflict. And the more we as interveners buy into these dualities, the less effective we are in helping others find a constructive way to move forward. However, if we're able to see these polarities as guideposts for finding a way through conflict—and that each element of them is an essential part of the larger truth that conflict presents—we can achieve profound and meaningful intervention.

We can view these polarities collectively as the *conflict paradox*—the inevitable and defining contradictions that we face when deciding how to approach a conflictual interaction. In essence, the conflict paradox is about the intellectual and emotional maturity that we bring to conflict. The higher the stakes, the greater our tendency to view these polarities in a more primitive or immature way—to believe that we must *choose* between one side or the other and to see one element as right and the other as wrong. For example, we may view the situation as either hopeless or as very resolvable. We may feel that we cannot trust the other side or that we should fully trust them. We may decide to engage fully in conflict or to avoid it entirely. We may believe that we take either a thoroughly cooperative stance or we zealously compete. In this way, conflict induces a dualistic and simplistic way of thinking. But effective conflict work requires a more sophisticated, nuanced, and complex approach that recognizes that in most instances, both sides of these polarities must be embraced, and we have to get past understanding them as contradictions. The central premise of this book is that these polarities are genuine paradoxes. They appear to offer either-or choices or divergent realities, but the higher truth is the one that embraces the unity of both elements.

This does not mean that we necessarily accept in a nondiscriminatory manner the truth or the validity of all approaches to conflict. We may continue to believe that one side has the moral high ground, the more reasonable approach, the greater need, or the more persuasive argument. But it doesn't serve us well to allow this belief to lead us into a primitive view of the conflict or the potential approaches that can be taken to it. And it is our job as interveners to help disputants see the situation they are in and choices they face in a more sophisticated way.

We do this by working on seven essential dilemmas that disputants face in approaching a conflict. Each of these is generally experienced as a polarity or dualism—a pair of opposites that require a decisive choice between them. The challenge we face is to help others—and ourselves—move to a more nuanced, more complex, and less bifurcated view. Of course, disputants seldom understand it in these terms. As a result, they often fail to recognize the process of choosing how to view a conflict or even the fact that we are choosing a view at all. However, in conflicts large and small, intense or mild, we must find a way of working with these dualities. The way we do this determines to a large extent how we think about conflict and therefore how we react to it.

We will discuss each of these conflicts in a separate chapter. Taken together, they constitute the conflict paradox:

- **Competition and cooperation**   We view these as opposite strategies that disputants must choose between. A more nuanced view may suggest a mixed strategy, combining cooperative and competitive moves, but it's even harder to grasp that competition requires cooperation, and without competition the motivation to cooperate is absent. Almost every move we make in conflict involves both cooperative and competitive elements; without one, we really cannot have the other.

- **Optimism and realism**   Optimism without realism is not meaningful; realism without optimism is a dead end.

A constructive approach to conflict can occur only when both are at play—when we are motivated by optimism and guided by realism.

- **Avoidance and engagement**   We cannot avoid or address all conflict. In addition, all conflict moves involve a mixture of conscious and unconscious decisions about how and what to engage and avoid. The decision to address one conflict inevitably involves a decision to avoid another.

- **Principle and compromise**   People tend to act as if compromising on important issues is unprincipled or cowardly. We believe we must decide whether to carry on a conflict in a principled manner (i.e., in accordance with our most important values or beliefs) or to compromise on something essential to us; yet we never want to forgo our essential principles, because they are the guideposts that help us through all of our decisions in conflict. But without compromise, we can do nothing to advance them.

- **Emotions and logic**   We frequently hear that the key to dealing with conflict or being effective in negotiations is to be rational and to hold our emotions at bay. However, emotions are an important source of power and an essential tool for moving through conflict constructively.

- **Neutrality and advocacy**   The line between these approaches to conflict is much thinner than we may think. Conflict interveners have to be effective advocates for disputing parties and for the process while bringing an impartial perspective.

- **Community and autonomy**   The dynamic tension between our need for community (interdependence with others in our lives) and autonomy (independence) infuses our thinking and action throughout conflict.

All disputants have to deal with these polarities, and all inter-veners have to find a way of helping parties find their way through them. Together, they define the conflict paradox; simultaneously, they are our greatest challenge as interveners and offer us the greatest potential to make a genuine difference. We can see every move that someone makes during conflict as an expression of at least a momentary choice about how to handle these dilemmas, and every intervention by a conflict specialist as an effort to help people approach them in a more nuanced and sophisticated way.

What We Bring to the Table and What the Table Brings to Us

As in all professional endeavors, what we as interveners think we are all about and what is important to us are not always the same as what our clients want or what the circumstances allow. For example, conflict professionals tend to believe that the purpose of our intervention is to find an outcome that meets everyone's needs as much as possible—a fair, reasonable, balanced way forward through a conflict. But this is often not even *close* to what disputants want or to what a decision-making structure may allow. Consider the following scenario:

> Pauline had worked for HZD Industries for three years. She had filed several grievances during this time, mostly against her immediate supervisor, Luis. None of these had led to a favorable finding for Pauline, who felt exploited and misunderstood by "the system." After a couple of unsatisfactory performance appraisals (both of which Pauline dismissed as yet another example of Luis's determination to "get her"), HZD's management terminated Pauline. Again she grieved, and came to mediation requesting reinstatement, a pay raise, and an apology from the company.

In a circumstance such as this, it may be that the company wants to agree on a reasonable severance package and that Pauline's most important goal is to receive guidance and financial assistance while moving on to a new job. If that is the case, there is at least some overlap between each party's goals and the purpose of the interveners. But it may also be that while management feels obligated to go through mediation, they also believe that they have already given all they can or "put up with enough" from Pauline. And perhaps Pauline is simply determined to give them a piece of her mind and to find a way to "publicly shame them." In that case, our goal as interveners may well be at cross-purposes with those of the parties. We may realize while working through these competing goals that this case has no business being mediated—or it may cause us to redefine our objectives in some way.

Every intervention poses this dilemma, in a sense, because interveners and disputants inevitably have different goals or needs. Where an intervener may want to lower the level of conflict or end it altogether, a disputant may want to have her say and to get her way as much as possible. And while interveners see the necessity of giving everyone involved a voice at the table and an opportunity to promote their legitimate interests, disputants are usually more interested in making sure their own voices are heard and their own concerns addressed. They do not necessarily care whether other parties are satisfied or have had a significant voice in the outcome.

These differences are not signs of poor faith, but they are important. They reflect the different roles that disputants and interveners play in conflict and the necessarily different values and goals that accompany them. One result of these differences is that disputants and interveners often come down on different sides of a paradox. Our response as interveners often is to try to balance an overemphasis on one element by promoting the opposite. Unfortunately, if we merely seek balance—instead of trying to move beyond the polarity—we may evoke resistance and can actually create a more entrenched view of the choices that people face. For example, consider the following possible approaches that interveners might take in Pauline's case:

- Pauline and HZD see themselves in a competitive relationship and feel the need to compete effectively. In response, interveners may want to urge them to cooperate and look for integrative outcomes.

- Pauline and HZD feel pretty hopeless about coming to any agreement, and as a result interveners feel that they should be encouraging and optimistic.

- Pauline and HZD view this as a matter of principle, whereas interveners try to encourage compromise.

- Pauline and HZD want to assert their independence (autonomy) from each other by denying that they are in any way dependent or vulnerable to the other, whereas interveners may want to encourage them to look at their interdependence (community) by focusing on potential areas of mutual interest.

Because of the difference between what we bring to the table as interveners and what the disputants want—or what the structure of the interaction demands—interveners are always negotiating our way through these polarities. This is the heart of our challenge. We do not meet this challenge, however, by asserting only one side of the polarity—usually in opposition to the element that we believe is perpetuating a conflict. We meet it by embracing both aspects—in Pauline's case, the need for her to compete effectively if cooperation has any chance to succeed. We must seek the truth that encompasses both sides of these polarities (remember that genuine optimism must be realistic). When we truly grasp that what we perceive to be polarities and mutually contradictory choices are not that at all—but are, in fact, paradoxically, essential aspects of the same reality—then we can begin to make a difference in how we approach a conflict.

How Contradictions Make Us Who We Are

Why is it that conflicts or disputes are the defining characteristic of our field? These terms are the central concept in the names of most major professional organizations in the United States (for example the Association of Dispute Resolution, the Dispute Resolution Section of the ABA, the International Association for Conflict Management) and elsewhere (for example, LEADR Association of Dispute Resolvers in Australia and New Zealand; Centre for Effective Dispute Resolution [CEDR] in the UK; the African Centre for the Constructive Resolution of Disputes [ACCORD] in South Africa). Most graduate programs also organize their names around the concept of conflict or dispute intervention. The major alternative is to invoke a *role* (mediation—International Academy of Mediators) or a *type* of conflict (Association of Family and Conciliation Courts) that references, conflict by implication. We have become so accustomed to this that we don't question it, but it is not completely obvious that we should be organizing ourselves around conflict as our defining focus. We could define ourselves in terms of communication, decision making, peace building, negotiation, or problem solving. However, though we often use these terms as secondary descriptors for our work, they are not usually at the forefront of our primary professional identification. Instead, we focus on conflict—which I think is a good thing.

The entire human experience is defined by conflict. We evolved through conflict. Conflict is a principle force governing the growth of social and communal organization; it is a driving force in our maturation and development. Our economy is driven by conflict, as is our political process. We organize entertainment, sports, and recreation around conflict, and we learn through conflict. Conflict in this sense does not necessarily mean violence, animosity, or destructive behavior (although that, of course, is often part of the picture). Rather, it refers to the interplay of opposing forces and competing interests. The central role of conflict in our individual, familial, communal, and societal lives is why it is such a powerful phenomenon to wrap our professional identity around, and why our work brings us so close to the heart of the human experience and in so many different arenas—from international conflicts to family disputes, from grievances to large-scale environmental struggles. It is why the lessons learned in one area or level of conflict can shed light on the dynamics in very different arenas. It is why it makes sense for us to think of our field of practice as extending beyond the specific substantive types of conflicts we may be involved with and beyond our particular approach to conflict.

There is something about the nature of conflict itself that informs our understanding and our intervention no matter what our practice, which lends a depth to our frameworks and a significant collective meaning to our work. This does not imply that if we are experienced in one arena of practice, we are automatically qualified to work in others. A divorce mediator is not necessarily skilled at addressing complex environmental conflicts; an organizational conflict specialist is not automatically qualified to work on issues of elder care. But there is a common thread to all these approaches, and we are more powerful practitioners if we are open to learning and applying lessons gained from widely different areas of practice. As important as it is to develop the specific skills and obtain the particular knowledge that any one area of conflict intervention requires, it is also imperative that we continue to delve into the nature of the underlying unifying concept that ties the different strands of conflict work together. One of the universal thrusts of all approaches to conflict and of work in all arenas of our practice is the need for interveners to deal with the conflict paradox in some way. Although they can appear in broadly different forms, the seven key polarities are almost always present when we deal with conflict.

In fact, paradoxes and dualities are part of every element of our lives—and they provide the foundation for some of our most powerful intellectual traditions. Virtually the entire course of philosophical investigation into the nature or our existence is organized around the interplay of ostensibly conflicting or contradictory ideas, forces, or concepts. For example, Plato and Aristotle differed on whether the world of appearance (the realm of senses) or the world of forms (the realm of essence) should be the primary focus of philosophical investigation (Copleston 1985). The creative tension between these two philosophical approaches can be viewed as the foundational tension for the entire course of Western philosophy. We can see it in the contending theologies of St. Thomas Aquinas and St. Augustine (Kenny 1994; Burnell 2005) in the centuries-long debate about the distinction between the soul and the physical self (Crane and Patterson 2000), and in the argument between Descartes and Spinoza over whether there is a genuine distinction between the immaterial mind and the material body (Spinoza 1985; Descartes 2008). Current research in neuroscience has revisited and reframed the debate between Descartes and Spinoza about the interconnection between feelings and thinking (Damasio 2003). The central role of contradictions and their resolution into higher order of contradictions is at the foundation of both the Hegelian and Marxist concept of dialectics, where one historical reality breeds a contradictory reality, in turn leading to a higher-order reality that combines elements of each (Hegel 2004; Marx and Engels 1972).

Paradoxes and contradictions are central to modern science as well. The bulk of twentieth-century theoretical physics was dominated by the struggle between relativity and quantum mechanics. Both theories have addressed a seemingly paradoxical phenomenon—the behavior of light in particular as both a particle and a wave and of the duality of matter and energy more generally. The tensions among these apparently contradictory insights continue to be an essential creative driving force of modern physics (Lindley 2007). (For a discussion about how the wave particle dichotomy in physics parallels challenges faced by negotiators, read Ran Kuttner's "The Wave/Particle Tension in Negotiation" (2011). The theory of evolution deals extensively with the interplay between competition and cooperation in the struggle for species survival. We will return to this in the next chapter when we consider that particular paradox.

A Developmental Perspective

Developmental psychology provides important insights into how we respond to conflict. Most developmental psychologists argue that we proceed through developmental stages by resolving, in ever more sophisticated ways, basic conflicts between our individual needs and the demands of our environment. For example, Jean Piaget (2001) describes two fundamental mechanisms by which infants and children develop an awareness and the capacity to make sense of the world around them: assimilation and accommodation. He describes assimilation as involving the incorporation of new information within our existing way of thinking; in accommodation, we change our thinking to account for new information. Throughout life, there is ongoing interaction and struggle between these two approaches that is essential to our cognitive development. As we mature, we develop more complex and therefore adaptive methods of making sense of the world, but these two approaches are continually in play.

Piaget's work has been modified and adapted by others, most notably by Lawrence Kohlberg (1981), who focuses on the child's moral development; Carol Gilligan (1982), who has brought in the perspective of feminist theory; and Robert Kegan (1994), who has incorporated a cultural and environmental perspective. Kegan suggests that as we reach more advanced developmental levels, we increase our ability to handle complexity, and he makes particular reference to our capacity to deal with paradox, contradiction, and dialectical processes.

Conflict provides us with both an opportunity to grow and a vehicle to regress. As disputes escalate, we are more likely to resort to ways of thinking and behaving that are characteristic of earlier stages of development. Our challenge in working on conflict is therefore to help promote more complex thinking that accepts ambiguity, the truth in seemingly contradictory realities, and the truth in the contradiction or paradoxes themselves.

There is a well-known fable about two Jews in conflict who consult their rabbi, who in traditional village culture was not only a religious leader but an arbiter of conflicts as well. One version of this parable relates the tale of a married couple who have been fighting furiously and are considering a divorce. The woman goes to the rabbi and complains about her husband's poor record as a provider, father, and partner. After listening carefully, the rabbi replies that he understands her point of view and that, indeed, she is right. Then he speaks to the man, who says that no matter how hard he tries, how much he contributes, and how patient he is, all he gets from his wife is criticism, rejection, complaints, and anger. The rabbi again listens carefully, appreciates his point of view, and tells him that he is, indeed, right. After the man leaves, the rabbi's wife, who has heard all of this from the next room, confronts her husband, saying that they presented conflicting stories and can't both be right. After due consideration, the rabbi turns to her and says, "I understand what you are saying. You are right."

In a sense, this is what all effective conflict intervention is about—developing a greater capacity to accept the truth in seemingly contradictory realities, needs, and points of view. There is not only truth in each side of a polarity, but the polarity itself conveys a truth. A key intervention challenge, therefore, is to help people approach situations that are likely to induce more primitive ways of thinking with instead a more complex and sophisticated mindset.

How Conflict Promotes Less Complex
Thinking—and Simpler Thinking Promotes Conflict

As clashes escalate, disputants are more likely to see their choices in simpler and starker terms, and they are more likely to cast the conflict as a matter of right or wrong. As a result, they tend to latch on to one side of a polarity and to assume that their adversaries are doing the same (although not necessarily the same side). Rubin, Pruitt, and Kim (1994) suggest that escalated conflict is character-ized by a switch to more aggressive tactics; a tendency to see the conflict as more all-encompassing in terms of issues, people, and consequences; and an increase in zero sum thinking (i.e., a win for one equals a loss for the other). They also suggest that as people become more embroiled in a conflict, they are likely to change their desired outcome from "doing well," to "doing better than others," to "wanting to hurt" those with whom they are in conflict. In other words, our thinking becomes more dualistic as conflict escalates.

All of us tend to look for explanations of what is happening in conflict that reinforce the positions we have taken or the actions we have engaged in. One of our reactions to feeling affronted or mistreated is to create a narrative that justifies our behavior and emotions—and one way we do this is to use what I have described elsewhere (Mayer 2012a) as explanatory "crutches." We ascribe others' actions to their being "stupid, crazy, or evil." Though there may well be stupidity, irrationality, or maliciousness involved in conflict, these "crutches" are very simplistic ways of understanding what has gone on, and they tend to justify our own behavior, even if it, too, could be viewed as "stupid, crazy or evil."

Another approach is to consider how we explain behavior that we experience as injurious. Are we likely to blame an action that we do not like on someone's character or on circumstances ("dis-positional" versus "situational" attributions, to use the language of attribution theory [Allred 2000])? For example, if you have promised to meet me at a restaurant and you do not show up—do

I ascribe that to your being irresponsible, flaky, self-centered, or unreliable or to your being held up in traffic, under a different assumption as to where or when we were to meet, in an accident, or unwell? In reality, all behavior is a combination of personal and situational factors; but the more serious the impact an event has or the greater our emotional reaction to it, the more likely we are to narrow our thinking about the causes of it—and the more likely we are to ascribe dispositional attributions. Consider an example from a significant international dispute: When Russia annexed the Crimea in 2014, popular explanations of this centered around the devious and authoritarian personality of Russian President Vladimir Putin, and criticisms of the American response focused on the personal failings of President Obama. While it is perfectly legitimate to criticize leaders for their approach to conflict, international disputes are rooted in a much broader set of factors, and it is important to understand these if we are to craft an intelligent response.

Conflict also narrows our view of the choices we have. We are more likely, for example, to believe we must either stand firm or capitulate (to "blink first" or not), to accede to someone else's needs or to protect our own, to behave in a principled way or to compromise, to exert power or to be passive. In fact, we can look at each of the polarities discussed in this book with this lens. The more serious the conflict, the more likely we are to believe we have to choose one side of a polarity, to view the other as coming entirely from one side, or to believe that one element of a polarity is a better way to be in conflict. For example, we may view ourselves as cooperative, principled, rational, objective, and out for the greater good of the community (or family, or country, or organization). We therefore see those we are in conflict with as competitive, irrational, emotional, unrealistic, and out for themselves alone. And the more a conflict escalates, the more we are likely to see things this way. So the more we see things in these polarized terms, the more we *contribute* to conflict escalation—even when we don't want to. We tend to assume that the side of the polarity we have chosen is the wiser or more moral element and that the approach of those we are in conflict with is not as good as ours (we are realistic, they are naive; we are principled, they are not; we are committed to the greater good, they are out for themselves). The value we put on our approach to a polarity, coupled with our tendency to dismiss the approach of others, deepens the conflict.

How We Promote More Complex Thinking

Our first challenge as conflict professionals is to make sure we are not swept into a more primitive and polarized way of thinking ourselves. We can start by simply identifying the polarities and the framing of these polarities that is occurring. For example, Pauline—from the case described earlier in the chapter—may be defining her situation as a "matter of principle." Perhaps the company defines it similarly, and therefore suggests that compromise would be "unprincipled." As discussed in chapter 5, this is a very potent but unhelpful duality. Our first step is simply to recognize this dualistic approach to the conflict paradoxes. A dualistic approach to one paradox reinforces a similar approach to others, and it is helpful to recognize this as well. For example, the more the disputants believe that they have to choose between principle and compromise, the more they are apt to feel they also have to choose between cooperation and competition. They may also believe that they can't be both impartial (objective) and effective in advocating for their convictions.

But we may find in any conflict that some polarities are less cogent or operative than others, and this may offer an opportunity to promote a more sophisticated approach. For example, Pauline may not be naive about her chances of prevailing; by embracing the reality of her alternatives, she finds cause for being optimistic about the ultimate impact of standing up for herself. She may also be able to embrace the roles of emotions and logic in reinforcing each other in this situation. That provides the intervener, or those negotiating with her, with some purchase in changing the overall way in which this conflict is understood.

If we can identify which polarities parties are buying into—and be aware of our own tendency to fall into some of these—we take an important first step in working toward a more complex under-standing of a dispute. But simply achieving awareness isn't enough. We must then seek ways to challenge disputants (and ourselves) to move beyond a polarized or dualistic view of the choices we have in conflict—and, in particular, to take a more integrative approach to each of the seven dilemmas discussed in the following chapters.

There is no cookbook formula for how we do this. We get at it by posing new questions, framing the conflict differently, discussing the choices people face in a less dichotomized way, and helping people change the narratives with which they explain conflict. But the most important way we do this is by adopting a more integrative view ourselves. Interveners continually struggle to counter the pull of a more primitive, dualistic view of conflict and to promote a more complex, mature view. New incidents, re-stimulated emotions, the need to maintain in-group cohesion, and painful histories of conflict often reinforce simplification. Virtually every intervention conflict interveners undertake is in some way intended to make disputants' thinking (but not necessarily the issues themselves) more complex. As interveners or participants, we are torn by these forces as much as anyone else. The paradox here is that the more we engage in a conflict, the stronger the pull to polarize our understanding. The more we want to move in a constructive direction, the more important it is to see beyond the polarities.

Though this is the biggest challenge, paradoxically this also offers the biggest opportunity we have to make a significant impact. We can choose to take a more sophisticated view of conflict, and by so doing, we can make a difference in how others view it as well. And we don't have to ask anyone to give up his or her passion, commitment, power, or goals to do so. Instead, by reinforcing a complex view of conflict, we offer disputants a more effective way of understanding how to pursue their own interests. The chapters that follow present numerous examples of how this challenge arises in conflict and the ways both interveners and disputants have met it. Some of these efforts have been intentional; most have been natural responses to unproductive polarities. Not all have been successful.

Reflections from Practice

The most moving moments I have experienced as a conflict intervener have occurred when the parties involved begin to view each other differently—when they are finally able to move beyond their own stereotypes of each other and understand their choices differently. To employ a term that is overused in our field, these have been "transformative" moments on occasion; however, they have not always been large or dramatic transformations. Almost always, such transformations result from small changes in perception or understanding. Over time, the cumulative impact of these changes enables people to alter their view of a conflict and therefore to approach it differently. Sometimes, this has been very dramatic; at other times, these changes have been hardly noticeable. Seldom have these occurred because I have intentionally pushed for them; but by consistently working to create a more differentiated and complex view of conflict, I have inevitably had a part to play in these developments.

One of the most interesting changes occurred in a labor management conflict—when through a fairly amusing set of developments, the head of a bargaining team had to confront his own attribution biases.

> Alex was a long-term union activist, a skilled negotiator, and the chair of the negotiating team for a very large industrial union. Negotiations had broken down during the previous round of collective bargaining and

a strike ensued—hurting not only the company and its workers, but also the economy of the region in which the industry was located. As a result, the union and management leadership, including each of their negotiating teams, agreed to attend a weeklong training on conflict and negotiation for which I was one of three trainers.

We decided to do an exercise based on the "Prisoner's Dilemma" (which I discuss further in chapter 2), in which participants were divided into teams that engaged with each other in a series of interchanges. In each exchange, the teams had to choose whether to deliver a competitive or cooperative message. If both cooperated, they would each receive a good score for that round; if both competed, they would each receive a poor score. However, if one cooperated and one competed, the competing team would score extremely well and the cooperating team extremely poorly.

The exercise involved ten rounds of exchanges. Before the final round (which was worth ten times the score of previous rounds), each team could select a representative to negotiate a deal with the other team. This team member would then have to take the deal back to their entire team before making the actual exchange. By coincidence, one team's representative— Tyrone—was the actual head of the negotiating team for management. Alex represented the other team. They agreed to exchange cooperative messages during their negotiation, and Alex's team did exactly that. But Tyrone's team reneged on the agreement and submitted a competitive message, thereby scoring a great point gain at the other team's expense. Alex was furious—even though this was just a game. He insisted that this was exactly how management always behaved, that it demonstrated why they could not be trusted, and that it was clear evidence for why the union had to take a hard line.

However, it turned out not to be that straightforward. The teams in the training were intentionally mixed, so that each had members from both management and the union. Alex's closest associate in the union was the union's second lead negotiator, Robert. During this exercise, Robert was on Tyrone's team. When Tyrone returned from the negotiation before the tenth round, he advocated for his group to abide by the deal he had reached. Robert, however, urged him to renege, saying it would be "fun" and that Alex would appreciate the move and have a sense of humor about it. Tyrone reluctantly agreed to go along with this.

When this came out in the post-exercise debrief, the whole mood in the room changed. Robert owned up to his role somewhat sheepishly, and Alex experienced some very distinct cognitive dissonance. His friend and ally had been the cause of the behavior that he had ascribed to management—and had condemned. Fortunately, Alex was also able to see the humor of the situation by this point—and he accepted that he was acting on stereotypes and had overreacted. Throughout the rest of the training (which was part dialogue, part negotiation, and all conflict intervention), this experience—which occurred at the very beginning of the workshop—served to mitigate the otherwise strong tendency of all sides to see any conflict in polarized terms.

This was a dramatic, powerful, and amusing interchange that exhibited both the strength of the polarization and some very interesting ways in which polarization can be broken down.

For example, the venue for interaction was changed, diverse players were involved, the embers of empathy and insight were fanned, and we made shameless use of cognitive dissonance. But in very small ways, conflict interveners take similar action all the time. Consider this much more modest example—where *I* was the one who was engaging in dualistic thinking.

> A while back, I was riding my bicycle along a road that follows the north shore of Lake Erie near my home in Ontario. Though not a major roadway, there is a fair amount of local traffic as well as many bicyclists. I was cycling at about 29 kph (19 mph—I checked), when a car with Michigan license plates slowed down next to me, and the driver shouted something at me that sounded like, "Do you know that you are going 30 on this road?" and then drove off (the speed limit in that location is 60 kph, or about 37 mph). Actually, all I was sure that I had heard was the driver saying "you are going 30." The rest is what I thought I heard.
>
> I was riding about two feet from the side of the road, so the driver had to slow down to wait for traffic to pass before he could safely get past me, but this took only a few seconds. I assumed the driver was complaining about my biking on the road, and I shouted after him, "I have a right to be on this road. We share the road—sorry if I was not going fast enough for you!" I was annoyed and feeling righteously indignant. The driver shortly turned into a driveway and parked. I thought about stopping and asking him what his problem was—but decided to go on with my ride instead. The good news is that my adrenalin kicked in and my pace picked up for the rest of my ride.
>
> Clearly, I saw myself as a virtuous bicyclist and the driver as a bullying motorist who probably spent his

time drinking beer in front of his large, wall-mounted, high-definition TV (my stereotypes were running rampant). I chose briefly to engage in a competitive (albeit in my mind principled) way, and then to avoid any further interaction. I thought my emotional reaction was fully justified.

And I might just have left it at that. But as it happened, I was also teaching a course on conflict at the time of this incident—and we were discussing the topic of "attribution theory" (Allred 2000). So I posted this description on our course web page and asked for students to comment on how this illustrated the concepts of attribution theory. The discussion opened my eyes to how many alternative ways I could have looked at the situation, to how reactive I was, and to how my behavior might have contributed to ongoing stereotyping between motorists and bicyclists. To be sure, I was aware of some of this or I would not have used this as an example; but even with all my work in this area, I was amazed to realize just how polarized my thinking was at that moment. Turning my experience into an exercise forced me to take a few steps back, hear diverse points of view, and generally submit to a significantly more complex analysis of the interaction than I was prone to engage in on my own. It turned out to be a rich discussion and a great learning experience for me.

We all experience everyday interactions of this nature, which can be both irritating and energizing. Whether these are trivial or momentous, we are challenged in each of them to create a narrative of what has occurred, our part in the interchange, and what our response choices are. Sometimes these narratives help move a conflict in a constructive direction; at other times, they limit our flexibility, polarize our thinking, and contribute to destructive interactions.

We are more likely to resort to dualistic thinking when we are upset, angry, or scared; when we have a long history of negative interactions with those we are in conflict with (or impute such a history by stereotyping); when important values are at stake; when we feel very vulnerable; when we are protecting our sense of who we are; when we believe we are defending others we care about very deeply; and when our ability to communicate with others is limited.

Mostly, we create these narratives instinctively. And we are not apt to change them, once created, very readily. However, we can and do change them, and in the process, we can become more conscious of our cognitive process. Equally, we can help other people become more conscious of theirs.

How we do this is the essence of the conflict intervener's art. The heart of our challenge is to recognize the conflict paradox and to work on the key polarities that are discussed in this book.

chapter two

competition and cooperation

The biology of selfishness and altruism ... touches every aspect of our social lives: our loving and hating, fighting and cooperating, giving and stealing, our greed and our generosity.

Richard Dawkins, The Selfish Gene

The interaction between competition and cooperation may be the most analyzed dynamic in conflict. From conflict styles inventories (Thomas and Kilmann 1974), to leadership assessment frameworks (Blake and Mouton 1968; Follett 1942), to analytical tools for understanding negotiation (Deutsch 2006; Fisher, Ury, and Patton 1991; Lax and Sebenius 2006), conflict scholars focus on this dynamic as the foundation of much of what occurs in conflict. Competition and cooperation are often viewed as opposite, if interactive, strategies, and the general implication is that constructive work on conflict is about moving people from a competitive orientation to a cooperative stance. Unfortunately, for people who are in the middle of an intense dispute, this is a goal that often fails to resonate.

However, once we understand that competition and cooperation are intertwined approaches to conflict and recognize that we can't cleanly separate them, a new way of thinking emerges. If we understand that effective cooperation is motivated by competition, and that competition requires some form of cooperation, we can speak more clearly to one of the most important challenges that disputants face: how to offer nuanced and realistic responses to the complex messages that are exchanged in conflictual interactions.

The choices we face in conflict are much more complex than merely deciding whether to compete or cooperate. We have to recognize that we are always competing and always cooperating in a conflict. To proceed as if our choice is to do one or the other can easily lead us astray.

For example, if a contractor claims to have finished a construction project at my home, but I don't believe the work has been finished, I can respond with a range of communications—from very gentle to very demanding and threatening. None of these will be very effective, however, if I ignore the situation's competitive nature or the cooperative requirement to get through it. Let's consider this further, from gentle to harsh responses.

Before we close the books on this project, why don't we take a walk through together, just to make sure that we can talk about any questions I might have?
One tip-off that this statement, which appears to be mild and collaborative in spirit, has a competitive element is that it's hard to tell whether it's a question or not. The tone is friendly, implying that *if* there are problems, we can surely work these out; but there is also a clear sense that this is something we need to do before I make a payment—an implication that is unlikely to be lost on the contractor. In a sense, this is a compelling invitation to begin a negotiation.
I am concerned about some uncompleted work that I thought was included in our contract. I would like to clarify this with you before I submit final payment.
This is a more assertive statement, but one that still uses "I-messages" and indicates a desire to discuss the situation and a

belief that it can be "clarified," and it suggests that this might be an issue with communication rather than poor performance. However, the threat of withholding payment is explicit.

You promised to winterize the basement and you have not done this. That was clearly included in the price of your bid. So we need to talk about when you are going to do that (and an appropriate reimbursement schedule) or we will have to modify the price.

Although the language is harsher, the demand more explicit, and the consequences of not fulfilling that demand more direct, this is still about opening a negotiation. I am clearly stating blame in this one, but the purpose continues to be to arrive at a cooperative solution. The language of cooperation, interestingly, becomes more explicit just as the language of competition does. This is not unusual.

You have failed to complete the work that we explicitly agreed to. Unless you do so within the next ten days, I am going to withhold final payment.

Here the language of competition, demands, and consequences dominates, and a considerable level of emotion is suggested. But we can still see an offer of a deal that clearly is intended to motivate the contractor to cooperate in finishing the project or modifying the charges.

Which of these statements is likely to be the most effective—and how the mix of competition and cooperation plays out—depends on the circumstances, the nonverbal cues, the interactional dynamics, the history of our interaction, and the agreement governing the work. Regardless of these contextual elements, each of these statements not only includes both competitive and cooperative aspects, but they are inextricably linked and dependent on each other.

We can conduct a similar analysis of most comments that are made in conflict. We can consider the person's tone, the degree to which competition or cooperation is explicit or implied, the severity of consequences discussed, the specific nature of a request or demand, and the kind of interaction that is sought. When we unpack these elements, we see that each contains the intertwined elements of cooperation and competition as well. Competition and cooperation are two sides of the same coin—or, perhaps a more apt metaphor, the two strands that form the DNA of all conflict.

Influential Approaches to Cooperation and Competition

Because we are constantly dealing with the tension between cooperation and competition, there have been many efforts to analyze the relationship between them. Let's consider two particularly influential approaches referred to earlier in the chapter: the work of Kenneth Thomas and Ralph Kilmann and that of David Lax and James Sebenius.

The Thomas-Kilmann Model

The most popular framework for analyzing different approaches to conflict has been the Thomas-Kilmann conflict styles inventory, which posits a range of approaches based on the relative strength of our commitment to addressing others' needs, which they label as cooperativeness, versus our focus on meeting our own needs, which they label as assertiveness (Thomas 1992; Thomas and Kilmann 1974). Thomas and Kilmann (1974) describe competition as a style characterized by a high level of assertiveness and a low level of cooperation:

> Competing is assertive and uncooperative, a power-oriented mode. When competing, an individual pursues his or her concerns at the other person's expense, using whatever power seems appropriate to win his or her position. Competing might mean standing up for your rights, defending a position you believe is correct, or simply trying to win. (p. 8)

In this model, competition is defined by the absence of cooperative behavior. One of the five styles they identify in addition to competition is collaboration, which is characterized by a high degree of assertiveness and of cooperativeness:

> Collaborating is both assertive and cooperative. When collaborating, an individual attempts to work with the other person to find a solution that fully satisfies the concerns of both. It involves digging into an issue to identify the underlying concerns of the two individuals and finding an alternative that meets both sets of concerns. Collaborating between two individuals might take the form of exploring a disagreement to learn from each other's insights, resolving some condition that would otherwise have them competing for resources, or confronting and trying to find a creative solution to an interpersonal problem. (p.8)

Thomas and Kilmann's definition of collaborating comes fairly close to how many conflict authors have defined cooperation—working together to address each person's concerns or to achieve a common goal. (In fact, in most dictionary definitions of "cooperation," "collaboration" is a synonym, and it is used as such in this book.) The authors have carefully explained their definitions and concepts: within their framework, collaboration does not require participants to find a way to work with the interwoven threads of cooperation and competition. Rather, it's about advocating for our own concerns and those of others with whom we may find ourselves in conflict. For Thomas and Kilmann, collaborating and competing are fundamentally different styles. They do not address the challenge, possibility, or necessity of both competing and collaborating at the same time. What they do offer is a compelling model of different approaches to the tension between pursuing our own concerns and addressing those of others when we are in conflict.

Lax, Sebenius, and the Negotiator's Dilemma

One of the most incisive and influential books about negotiation, *The Manager as Negotiator* (1987), was written by two professors at the Harvard Business School who have been associated with the Program on Negotiation at Harvard: David Lax and James Sebenius. Lax and Sebenius discuss what they term the "negotiator's dilemma," the tension between pursuing the *value creating* element of negotiation (the integrative dimension) and the *value claiming* element (the distributive dimension). Value creating, which we can think of as "expanding the pie," involves an effort to identify outcomes that provide more overall benefits to the negotiators, leaving more of the "pie" to divide up. We can think of value claiming as trying to obtain a larger share of the existing benefits for ourselves—we want the largest possible "slice of the pie."

The tactics or approaches we use to *create* value may make us less able to *claim* value, and the approaches we take to *claim* value can inhibit our ability to *create* value. In the earlier contractor example, if I make high initial demands, threaten legal action, and try to intimidate the contractor, I diminish the chance of identifying "win-win" outcomes, because our communication will narrow and impair our ability to problem solve. The possibility of getting the necessary and additional work done at a price that seems reasonable to both of us may never occur to us, or we may no longer be willing to put it on the table. But I might be able to intimidate the contractor into finishing the job in order to get paid. On the other hand, if I immediately acknowledge that there could have been a misunderstanding about the expectation of work—that I am substantially satisfied with what he has done and I want to consider a fair settlement—I might encourage a more open communication that could lead to a creative solution. However, that might also encourage the contractor to hold firm.

Put more generally, creating value requires a free flow of communication, whereas claiming value tends to shut down communication. The two ways in which Lax and Sebenius believe we can most readily create value are to identify mutual interests (we both want this job completed) or different interests that are not in conflict with one another and that allow for trade-offs (I want additional work done; the contractor wants money), sometimes referred to as "logrolling." Using either of these approaches requires communicating our genuine interests, their relative importance, and information that will help clarify them. However, the more we discuss these matters, the more likely we are to make ourselves vulnerable to claiming tactics. If we are always preparing for the eventuality that we might end up in a legal action, we may be more prepared for court; but by the same token, such an approach is more likely to lead us there.

Lax and Sebenius suggest two broad strategies for finding our way through this dilemma. The first is to strengthen our alternatives by identifying our "BATNA"—the best alternative to a negotiated agreement—to use the language of Fisher and Ury (1991). They argue that this is the best way to protect against claiming tactics. For example, my best alternative in the contractor dispute might be to withhold part of the payment, but I might first want to investigate how to do this to minimize my legal exposure. The second alternative is to be as creative as possible in identifying mutual interests and different interests, thereby opening up the likelihood of identifying integrative (win-win) outcomes.

Though nuanced, this approach to competition and cooperation still implies that promoting cooperation and preparing for competition are very distinct activities. I have made this argument in discussing the negotiator's dilemma in *The Dynamics of Conflict* (2012a, 217–218), where I suggest that the negotiator's dilemma is a genuine dilemma—one that can't be easily solved in serious conflict, no matter how effective our negotiation tactics. But how distinct are they?

All of our actions in conflict move along both the cooperative and competitive dimensions. The metaphor of dimensions is useful, because in a two-dimensional space, we always exist in both dimensions or are defined along both dimensions. For example, we don't choose whether to have width or height; we have both. Similarly, virtually every value-claiming tactic involves a value-creating component, and vice versa. There is, of course, tension between these, and one may be more dominant, but every move we make (or choose not to make) has value-creating and value-claiming implications.

Evolution and the Prisoner's Dilemma

Perhaps the most sophisticated analysis of the interplay between cooperation and competition comes from the very different but increasingly overlapping worlds of evolutionary biology and game theory. Game theory attempts to analyze human interaction and social phenomena through the interaction of different players in a series of structured and scored interactions. The most famous of these games is called the "Prisoner's Dilemma," and the most influential discussion of this is in the work of Robert Axelrod. Axelrod's extensive experimentation with the Prisoner's Dilemma is presented in *The Evolution of Cooperation* (1984). We can use the insights this game provides to consider the broader issues of cooperation and competition in conflict—in particular, how we can integrate these two approaches.

The basic concept of the Prisoner's Dilemma is quite simple. Two players are asked to exchange messages that are either cooperative (let's call this a "y" message) or competitive (an "x" message). Each must submit a message without knowing what the other has submitted, which results in four possible message combinations: yy, or both cooperative; xx, or both competitive; xy, or mixed; and yx, or mixed. A yy message will yield a good outcome for both players, an xx a poor one for both, and a mixed message is a very good score for the x message (better than would be received in the yy situation) and a very bad score for the y message (worse than with xx). Figure 2.1 shows one particular version of this.

Player A

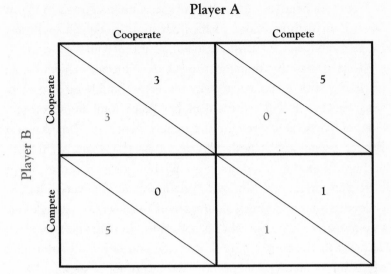

Figure 2.1 Prisoner's Dilemma

Of course, the numbers are arbitrary—they could be 20, 20; 40, −40; −40, 40; 0, 0; or any other set of numbers that fit the criteria. Furthermore, they could represent any unit—dollars, years in prison (the name Prisoner's Dilemma comes from the concept of prisoners "ratting" on each other—competing—or remaining silent—cooperating—when accused of a crime), shares in a company, or pieces of candy.

The Prisoner's Dilemma is meant to model any interaction in which there is more to be gained overall by cooperating, but where in any single round of interaction, either player will score better by competing. This is a variation of the "tragedy of the commons" (Hardin 1968), or of the advantage and danger of striking first in war, or of keeping a promise to support one another in a difficult political vote—and, in fact, of almost all complex human interactions. When an interaction involves the negotiator's dilemma, the mixed pull of cooperating and competing, of asserting our interests and accommodating others, we can use the Prisoner's Dilemma to model this. An argument can be made that the tension between cooperation and competition is characteristic not just of all human interactions such as negotiation, but all biological interactions—indeed, this is a defining feature of all evolution.

To return to this simple version of the Prisoner's Dilemma, an obvious question arises as to why player A should *ever* cooperate since he or she will receive a higher point total by adopting a competitive strategy. But by the same token, why should player B ever cooperate? If both players follow this logic, then both end up competing and doing considerably worse than they might have done by cooperating with one another. This very dilemma bedeviled nuclear strategists during the Cold War. Why should one side not strike first? But what if both sides thought the same way? This led to the very bizarre, but in the end effective, strategy of Mutually Assured Destruction (with the very apt acronym, MAD), whereby each side developed the capacity to survive a first strike, at least to the extent of being able to destroy the other side with a second strike (via hardened silos and nuclear submarines). As in nuclear strategy, in which deterrence of first strikes was accomplished by developing a second-strike capacity, the basic solution to the conundrum is to consider multiple rounds of interaction. Standalone interactions are rare in life; some would argue they are nonexistent. We almost always have multiple interactions or their functional equivalent (e.g., I may destroy you, but not all your relatives, or friends, or associates). We may perceive an interaction to be a one-time event, such as when we negotiate the end of a construction contract, but the potential for future consequences is almost always present. And, of course, there is always *karma*.

When we think of a conflictual interaction as a standalone event, we often find ourselves acting more aggressively than we would if we were fully conscious of the ongoing implications. If I see an empty parking space in a crowded lot that another driver may or may not be approaching, I might scoot my car in and take it. It's not very nice, but it's not very likely to have long-term consequences— unless the other driver ends up sitting next to me at the meeting

I have come to attend. As negotiators and mediators, we know that invoking the "shadow of the future" (i.e., the reality of an ongoing interaction), whether between divorcing parents, partners in a business, or labor and management, is often critical to successful negotiations.

Therefore, the real challenge is not how I score on this one "round," but how well I can score *over time*, which begs this question: how can I best induce you to cooperate with me over time? There have been some very interesting experiments exploring just that. In fact, more than thirty years ago, Robert Axelrod conducted the most famous of these using a computer program and the Prisoner's Dilemma.

The Evolution of Cooperation

In the early 1980s, Axelrod, a political scientist at the University of Michigan, conducted an experiment in which he invited game theorists, mathematicians, political scientists, and conflict scholars to submit a strategy in the form of a computer program for how to play the Prisoner's Dilemma. These individuals then played each other in a computerized version of the game with a scoring system similar to that described earlier. Each strategy played other strategies, including itself, in an interaction that went on for about two hundred rounds (the exact number of rounds was variable). The strategy that won the tournament was a deceptively simple one named "Tit for Tat" (t4t). Tit for Tat always opened with a cooperative move, and then on each successive move, t4t did what the other player had done in the previous round. So if player B had offered a cooperative move on the previous round, t4t offered one on the next round. If player B then switched to a competitive move, on the next round t4t delivered a competitive message. Axelrod published the results and ran a second tournament with a much larger pool of strategies. Again, t4t won. Why and what can we learn from this?

Axelrod (1984) suggested four characteristics of t4t that explained its success:

- **t4t is nice.** It starts out with a cooperative move and is never the first strategy to defect to competition. And it will always remain cooperative as long as it is met with a cooperative response. Cooperative responses are rewarded with more cooperation, and any two cooperative strategies attain the mutual benefit of a cooperative interchange.

- **t4t is provocable.** It offers consequences to others for competing, thereby insuring that it is not in their interest to continue to compete. Without this, there would be no disincentive to others for competing.

- **t4t is forgiving.** Even if another player has taken advantage of t4t in the past, once that player starts to cooperate, t4t will start cooperating, thereby offering an incentive to switch from competition to cooperation. An element of this is that t4t is not greedy. t4t will never do better in any single match than to tie the score of the other player, and it will often score lower, but by successfully motivating others to offer cooperative strategies, over the entire tournament it ended up with the highest cumulative score.

- **t4t is transparent—clear rather than clever.** There is no subterfuge or deception in this strategy. Simplicity breeds trust.

Axelrod argues that this strategy of reciprocity works even with untrustworthy players, and even when there is no central authority to set the rules. To illustrate this point, he discussed the practice that emerged during World War I in which soldiers on opposite sides would refuse to shoot at one another or to attack the wagons bringing enemy supplies or the roads on which they were delivered, knowing that this would elicit a similar attack from the enemy.

Let's consider each of these strategic concepts in terms of the challenges they suggest for conflict interveners.

Niceness. Effective negotiations often start with conciliatory opening moves. Intermediaries often try to orchestrate such moves to promote a constructive interchange. Consider some examples of niceness: Egyptian President Anwar Sadat travelled to Israel in 1977 to show his seriousness about negotiating a peace treaty. Hassan Rouhani, shortly after he was elected president of Iran, offered greater transparency about his country's nuclear program. And on the home front, frequently, an important early step in divorce negotiations for a couple with children is for both parties to assure each other that they understand the importance of maintaining each of their roles as active and involved parents. Each of these strategies is an initially cooperative move that will hopefully elicit a response in kind. However, they by no means ensure a cooperative response or a successful negotiation; indeed, Israeli Prime Minister Benjamin Netanyahu responded to Rouhani's transparency offers by insisting the Iranian president should not be trusted. But we know how much easier it is to make progress after a cooperative opening than after a hostile or aggressive one.

Of course, we face significant challenges in applying this principle to actual conflicts. Disputants are often so angry, upset, or mistrusting of each other that genuine cooperative moves are not possible until they have expressed their feelings or justified their actions. What one party may think is a significant cooperative gesture on their part (as with Rouhani) may appear to another to be too little, too late, or disingenuous (as with Netanyahu). This is sometimes a matter of perception and negotiating tactics, but at other times, this may reflect genuine differences in the parties' views about the significance of the cooperative move itself.

The challenge that disputants face is to identify genuine, unambiguous, and meaningful cooperative moves, and to ensure that these moves do not make the party offering them dangerously vulnerable to competitive responses from the other side. For instance, I may want to show my good faith in a salary negotiation with employees by indicating exactly how much total money is available for pay raises, hoping that we can now work on an equitable distribution system. But instead, they challenge me on the accuracy of this information, my personal level of compensation, and my priorities. It may prove wise to have shared this information, but I may also have put myself at a significant disadvantage.

This is a version of the negotiator's dilemma that Lax and Sebenius and others have discussed. For a conciliatory move to be meaningful, it has to involve some risk, and the amount of risk necessary for it to appear meaningful to others may be quite considerable. A significant part of our responsibility as conflict interveners is to help people think through these and other complexities of the "niceness principle" and to help parties recognize the genuine cooperative elements in each other's communication.

Provocability. Provocability may be the most counterintuitive principle for conflict specialists, because we so often see our role as encouraging cooperative moves. In essence, being *provocable* means that disputants have to be willing to develop effective ways to pressure others to be cooperative or to develop alternatives if a cooperative relationship is unlikely. For example, although worker strikes are almost always destructive for both unions and the organizations their members work for, a union's bargaining power is severely diminished without a credible threat of strike. Business partners must devote considerable energy to developing an effective collaborative relationship, but if one of them repeatedly exploits the other, there is a point at which the exploited partner has to push back to motivate a change.

Conflict interveners must often help disputants figure out just how to respond to others' aggressive moves in a way that helps set some limits on behavior but does not escalate a conflict unnecessarily or preclude the possibility of returning to a more cooperative interaction. We often see that parties cannot make the switch from "nice" moves to appropriately powerful responses to others' competitive moves without becoming overly aggressive themselves. Frequently, after having offered a series of cooperative moves that aren't reciprocated, parties feel angry or upset. As a result, their competitive moves—intended, perhaps, to encourage a change in behavior—are often harsh, overdone, and therefore unproductively escalatory. The dilemma here is that for a move to have the potential to motivate a change in strategy, it has to be powerful enough to suggest meaningful consequences for maintaining a competitive stance. If, however, it is strong enough to have a genuine impact, it is also likely to evoke a negative emotional reaction, which can easily reinforce the other party's determination to maintain the competitive stance the move was meant to alter.

Many conflicts escalate because someone is convinced that the time to be provocable has arrived, thereby setting in motion a chain of "provoked" interactions. That is why it is so important to develop the capacity to include a cooperative opportunity within a provoked response. Consider the following neighbor conflict.

> Alex and Jamie had been next-door neighbors for more than twenty years when Alex married Marianna, a forty-year-old recent immigrant from El Salvador with two teenage sons. Jamie was a widow who lived by herself. In Jamie's backyard was a large maple tree that hung over Alex and Marianna's yard and dropped branches into the couple's yard every time a significant wind blew. Over the years, Alex periodically had

the parts of the tree that extended over his property trimmed, but he had recently been advised that the tree needed to be cut down, because of its age and the degree of fungus that had damaged it. Alex had casually mentioned this to Jamie, but she had not taken any action, and Alex had not pursued the issue.

Marianna was less inclined to ignore the problem, however. After a particularly strong storm caused a substantial limb to drop on their yard, damaging some shrubs and a flowerbed, Marianna again asked Jamie to do something about the tree. Jamie said that she was sorry for the problem but that she planned on selling the house in the next couple of years and was not inclined to spend the money to take the tree down. Marianna suggested that Alex and she would be willing to share this cost, but Jamie suggested, politely, that they should instead trim back that part of the tree that overhung their yard.

Several weeks later, another storm blew a medium-sized limb down, which destroyed several flower pots and a chair in Alex and Marianna's yard. Marianna, now quite angry, had her teenage children put the remains of the limb, the branches, the leaves, the chair, and the flower pot on Jamie's door step with a note demanding that Jamie do something. Jamie then called Alex and told him to "Get your green-card-seeking wife to leave me alone, or I will call the cops."

Both Jamie and Marianna could well feel that their initial responses were reasonable, polite, and essentially cooperative but that their neighbor's responses were hostile, aggressive, manipulative, and insensitive. We can see from either point of view why they may have felt the time to be provocable had come, yet each of their resultant responses was overly aggressive. Once they abandoned the cooperative approach, both took an extremely competitive stance. Their anger compromised their ability to deliver a more nuanced message, and the conflict escalated. It continued to escalate until the police were involved, formal complaints were made, and the case was referred to mediation, which facilitated a more balanced exchange of messages and resolved the immediate conflict.

The challenge here was not to induce the parties to forgo delivering competitive messages to each other, but to help them do so in a more strategic, complex way so that the message carried the competitive element but also the promise of a return to a more cooperative interchange. This reflects Axelrod's principle of forgiveness.

Forgiveness. Effective interaction strategies require that we be willing to move away from a primarily competitive stance when others show a willingness to offer more cooperative moves. One of the challenges negotiators face is to recognize an implied or hidden cooperative message and to respond in kind. As a mediator, I have often interpreted a message from one disputant as containing a considerable conciliatory element, while the other party heard only continued competition or manipulation. Once, for example, in an effort to deal with a backlog of grievances, the labor relations officer for a company offered to submit to arbitration those cases that both management and union agreed were unlikely to settle and to mediate the rest as a class. To me, this seemed like a significant concession, because management had previously been very reticent to take anything to arbitration or to aggregate cases. The union, however, perceived this as a manipulative threat from management to stonewall on grievances that the union believed should be settled. Of course, the union knew the other party better than I did, and I do not assume that this was just perverse stubbornness or reflexive "dispositional attribution" (Allred 2000). Often, however, a disputant's inability to recognize and reinforce their opposition's initial cooperative move prevents a negotiation from moving in a more constructive direction. We see this in negotiations from the simplest interpersonal interaction to extremely complex international disputes.

At the time of writing, the United States and several other nations have concluded an initial agreement with Iran about its nuclear development program, with the intention of negotiating a more permanent treaty over the next six months. As noted earlier, several US allies, notably Israel and Saudi Arabia, have been adamant in labeling Iran's willingness to enter into such an effort as manipulative, insincere, and intended solely to lull the Western powers into allowing the Iranian nuclear weapons program to proceed.

In this case, the immediate issue is whether sanctions against Iran should be relaxed to reward the nation's cooperative moves or whether sanctions should be maintained (or even increased) to keep pressure on Iran to end its nuclear program. A failure at for-giveness can ensure ongoing conflict and could lead to significant escalation, including possible military action, when a negotiated solution might otherwise be possible. But being naively forgiving could reinforce manipulation and insincerity. Of course, at the same time, Iran has been making similar calculations in terms of how it responds to apparently cooperative moves from the United States and its negotiation partners. By the time this book goes to press, there will have been many more moves in this extremely important dance of cooperation and competition.

Axelrod suggests two elements to forgiveness. One element is *not having too long a memory*—or at least not basing our conflict moves on too long a history. If the neighbors in the maple tree example exchanged a series of increasingly competitive moves— such as threatening letters from lawyers, calls to the police, or minor acts of vandalism—it might be very difficult for either party to respond constructively to a potentially cooperative or concil-iatory move, or even to recognize one. Although forgetting may not be possible, decisions about forgiving—at least in the sense of arriving at an appropriate response to a cooperative gesture—should be made with a focus on recent interactions. While easier said than done, all important breakthroughs in intense conflict have been characterized by this to some extent.

The other aspect of forgiveness is *modesty of goals*; in other words, it is important not to be jealous of the other's gains. The success of t4t, which could do no better than tie in any given matchup, suggests that our focus in negotiations should not be on winning but on achieving good results for ourselves, which we measure by how well we have satisfied our essential interests. This should make intuitive sense to anyone who has tried to forge durable business relationships. If we try to come out "on top" in every negotiation, we are likely to sour the possibility for a long-term mutually beneficial relationship. The same is true in any relationship or interaction that goes beyond a single or very short-term relationship. Disputants often substitute a focus on winning, that is, achieving an outcome that is better than what the other side achieves, for clarity about what their own needs and goals should be. Assisting disputants to stay focused on what is really important to them is one of the most important tasks of conflict interveners. But even if the relationship is short term, this principle suggests that their focus ought to be on meeting their essential goals rather than besting the other side. And the cumulative costs of trying to outdo the other side over many time-limited interactions can interfere with the capacity to achieve their essential goals.

Simplicity. Axelrod's final principle is simplicity, which we might also think of as transparency. The most effective strategies are clear, and to some extent, obvious. Being too clever or inscrutable generally encourages others to be mistrustful, which in turn leads them to resort to protective—which tend to be competitive—strategies. We often equate taking the competitive approach to being more courageous, risky, or daring, but, at least in game theory, being *cooperative* is the riskier strategy, because it exposes us to exploitation. What most affects a strategy's success is its ability to induce other players to choose a cooperative approach, and transparency, rather than cleverness, is most effective in this regard.

The simplest, most straightforward approach to a conflict is usually the most effective. We often try to find convoluted paths through conflict that allow us to deal with difficult issues or unpleasant emotions without actually confronting them or sharing our feelings. But this can easily build suspicion, distrust, and defensiveness. Sometimes, simply naming the issue, the feelings, and our intended response opens up productive new lines of communication. As a mediator, I have often found that openly acknowledging the level of distrust, antagonism, and suspicion that exists between parties actually promotes conversation. Similarly, disputants are often willing to respond constructively when the alternative to negotiation is clearly stated—especially if this is done in the sense of providing information rather than exerting pressure. This approach helped deescalate the tension that Carlos and Kay were experiencing in their divorce negotiations:

> Kay and Carlos were going through a very conflictual and convoluted divorce process, which had seriously bogged down when I was asked to mediate. Each had committed to a collaborative process, but it was pretty obvious that they were "at the end of their collaborative rope," and each party was covertly planning to take the matter to court. Each was trying to gain as many concessions from the other as possible and to obtain as much information as possible, maintaining an appearance of collaboration while also preparing for litigation. After observing several of these exchanges, I said that I expected they were both feeling unsure about whether they could reach a voluntary agreement with each other and that I completely understood this. It would be wise for them both to consider how they might proceed if

they could not come to agreement, even as we continued to do all we could to try to arrive at one. I said that
this probably meant preparing to go to court if necessary. In reality, this was totally obvious, but their elaborate dance around this issue was exacerbating their
distrust of one another. By naming the reality of the
alternative that both were obviously considering, the
level of mistrust actually diminished, as did the overall
tension in the room.

Of course, the applicability of the Prisoner's Dilemma to real-
life challenges can be overstated, but the game does provide useful
insights into the complexity and subtlety of the interaction of competition and cooperation. These insights can help us understand
not just conflict interactions but the very basis of life itself.

Evolutionary Lessons from the Prisoner's Dilemma

Axelrod called his book *The Evolution of Cooperation* because he
suggests how cooperative strategies can prevail over competitive
ones in a manner analogous to the process of evolution as described
by Darwin. He ran a simulation in which he eliminated the lowest
scoring strategies after each round-robin tournament. After a number of successive rounds, the only remaining strategies were those
that he defined as cooperative, meaning they were never the first
to initiate a competitive move. He discovered, with some experimentation, that even in a field of primarily competitive strategies, if
there were enough (somewhere around 25 percent) players using a
cooperative strategy so that they could find and reinforce each other
in a competitive field, the cooperators would eventually prevail.

In *The Selfish Gene* (2006), Richard Dawkins (who consulted
Axelrod on the development of his experiment and the interpretation of his results) discusses how Axelrod's results explain
fundamental evolutionary processes. Dawkins suggests that if the
payoffs are viewed not in terms of points or of money but in terms of

offspring—i.e., the number of new players replicating the strategy of the successful players of earlier rounds—then the "survival of the fittest" in evolutionary biology is in essence replicated.

Martin Nowak, a professor of mathematics and biology at Harvard, has developed an innovative and extensive application of the Prisoner's Dilemma to evolution. Nowak conducted an elaborate model of evolution using game theory and produced remarkable results that shed light on the nature of cancer, the development of human speech, the spread of HIV, and the very origins of life (Nowak and Highfield 2011, Nowak, 2012). He argues that to understand evolution, we have to look at the impact of not only natural selection and mutation but also cooperation. Novak concludes that without cooperation as a major force, evolution would not be possible. Cells would not form, and neither would proteins, bacteria, multicell organisms, or more complex forms of life. Human speech can be understood as allowing enhanced cooperation, and cancer can be seen as a failure of cooperative mechanisms at the cellular level.

The results of Nowak's experiments are compelling. He created a computerized method of testing many different strategies for the Prisoner's Dilemma against one another, eliminating those that performed very poorly and allowing those that performed very well to proliferate. As with Axelrod's studies, in Nowak's experiments, cooperative strategies prevailed as long as they met a fairly low threshold of prevalence in any one environmental field. However, Nowak also introduced mutations. He allowed new strategies to emerge gradually, which could be competitive, cooperative, or some combination. Over many iterations of Nowak's experiment, cooperative strategies continued to prevail but became less robust in the face of the lack of competitive strategies (less provocable in response to competition, for example). This allowed a few mutant competitive strategies to take hold that would eventually overcome the cooperative strategies.

Eventually, however, in the absence of challenging strategies, the now prevailing competitive strategies became less robust, and mutant cooperative strategies would take over once again. The cycle continued, with cooperative strategies predominating most but not all of the time. Nowak and Highfield (2011) summarize these results and their application to the "real world" of businesses and governments as follows:

> The good news is that a reasonably nice strategy dominates the tournament. . . The bad news is that, in the real world, these cycles could sweep out over years, decades, even centuries. Plenty of anecdotal evidence suggests that these cycles turn in human history too. Kingdoms come and go. Empires spread, decline, and crumble into a dark age. Companies rise up to dominate a market and then fragment and splinter away again in the face of thrusting, innovative competitors.
>
> Just as these tournaments never see one strategy emerge with total victory, so it seems that a mix of cooperators (law-abiding citizens) and defectors (criminals) will always persist in human societies. The same goes for beliefs. (p. 37)

Or from Jewish (and other) lore, we hear, "This too shall pass." No one strategy *always* works. Cooperation without competition is more often ineffective than effective, as is competition without cooperation. But sometimes purely competitive strategies prevail, and sometimes purely cooperative ones do. In the sweep of human history (and of evolution), however, this is the exception. Strategies that offer cooperation but are provocable are most likely to prevail most of the time.

Limits of the Prisoner's Dilemma

I have engaged in this extensive discussion of the lessons we can learn from the Prisoner's Dilemma because of the important insights it offers about the interplay between cooperation and competition and the way in which it demonstrates that effective approaches to conflict require the wise use of both strategies. But there are some significant limits to this approach—specifically, five shortcomings are especially important to recognize.

The Prisoner's Dilemma is a game; real conflict is far more complex. This is the fundamental problem of all laboratory replications of human behavior. No matter how many computer simulations are run or complex algorithms are developed, reality is and always will be more complex. Our real conflicts occur in much more involved environments than game theory can ever mimic. Human beings are not simply strategy calculating entities; we react emotionally, bring seemingly unrelated considerations to bear (such as saving face or impressing friends), continually change our valuation of different outcomes, and are sometimes optimistic and at other times pessimistic—for no apparent reason. Communication is never perfect, and sometimes it's wildly dysfunctional, so we often don't understand the messages we are sending or receiving. Different cultures may interpret the same message in different ways, and so may any one of us at different times in our lives or our day. So while the interplay of cooperation and competition is always present in our interactions, how we engage in this process and the strategies we use to respond to them are more complex, varied, and inconsistent than simply choosing a cooperative or competitive response.

Messages are never purely cooperative or competitive. Whereas each individual message is clearly cooperative or competitive in the versions of the Prisoner's Dilemma Axelrod and Nowak analyzed, almost all exchanges in human interactions contain both cooperative and competitive elements. Additionally, the amount of each element that is present in any given interchange depends on the relational system among those involved. When Carlos, from the divorce negotiation example, claimed that he was trying hard to come up with a reasonable agreement, but Kay was not making it easy, the cooperative and competitive elements were completely intertwined; everyone involved heard the message differently. Carlos may have intended to be delivering a hopeful and positive message, with a little zinger meant to pressure Kay to come around. Kay may have heard this as an almost entirely hostile message that laid all the blame for the difficulties in their negotiation at her feet. And a third party may have seen it as a complicated message that called for a constructive reframe. How disputants interpret each element depends as well on subtle nonverbal cues, the parties' history of communication, their level of fatigue, their ability to see ambiguities at times of emotional stress, and many other factors.

What is clear is that the competitive and cooperative elements of such communications are inextricably interwoven. Therefore, the challenge of delivering unambiguously "nice" or "provocable" or "forgiving" communications in real conflict is at best daunting—and complete transparency is almost impossible. Deborah Tannen (1986), a sociolinguist who has written extensively on conversational style, says that being direct and transparent in communication is not only impossible but undesirable:

> But even if we wanted to be direct, we couldn't, for the following reasons: First, deciding to tell the truth leaves open the question, which of the infinite aspects of the truth to tell. Second, being direct isn't enough because countless assumptions underlie anything we say or hear . . . Third, stating just what we mean would often be hurtful to others. And finally, different styles make honesty opaque. Saying what we mean in our natural style conveys something different to those whose styles differ. (pp. 71–72)

The great challenge *and* opportunity for conflict interveners is to help parties decode and respond to these messages in a productive way. One way we do this is by helping disputants grasp that no message or move in a conflictual interaction is simply good or bad, cooperative or competitive, nice or aggressive. Instead, almost every message contains the potential to reinforce the cooperative element and the challenge of responding to the competitive element.

Disputants do not deliver messages in a clearly sequenced way. The Prisoner's Dilemma experiment can be run as a series of simultaneous exchanges (as in Axelrod's experiment) or as sequential interchanges: Party A delivers a message, Party B responds, and then Party A does, and so on. In experiments comparing these, each approach benefitted different strategies, but this did not alter the essential conclusions (Nowak and Highfield 2011). But we are not just responding to a clear set of messages, either sequentially or simultaneously, in real-life interactions. We are responding to past messages, extraneous messages, contemporaneous messages, and the anticipation of future messages. Also, we are not just responding to the message from the party delivering it but to related messages and similar communication styles of others as well. I know that if someone points a finger at me, no matter how constructive they mean to be, part of me will respond like a child who is being criticized by a parent. When I am aware of that, I can, to some extent, counteract that element of the message, but more often I am not aware of it in the moment, so the competitive element of the message becomes more prominent, and I don't even realize that this is happening or why it is happening.

Although almost all human interactions are iterative, some involve a more extensive series of exchanges than others. The results of the Prisoner's Dilemma experiments I have discussed are premised on a set of interactions with many rounds. The more rounds, the longer the "shadow of the future" looms—and the more likely it is that a cooperative strategy with a provocative component will prevail most of the time. But many conflicts either do not involve multiple rounds of interaction (e.g., a landlord-tenant dispute over the return of a rental deposit, an unpleasant interaction with a taxi driver, a disagreement over the terms of termination of employment) or participants do not perceive there to be a "shadow of the future" (e.g., "after the divorce is finalized, we won't have to have anything to do with each other").

What is primarily a cooperative message toward one player is often seen as a competitive message to another. When the United States and others reach out to Iran, both Israel and Saudi Arabia interpret this as a threat to their interests. If a child of divorced parents tries to reconcile with a parent he or she has been in conflict with, the other parent may feel rejected. Students of family systems argue that triangles are the building block of families (Bowen and Kerr 1988; Minuchin 1974). Our understanding of the cooperative and competitive elements of messages flows from the constellation of all these relationships.

The beauty of the Prisoner's Dilemma experiments is their ability to draw insights by isolating interactions from these complexities. However, this is also their greatest limitation. We can learn a great deal from these insights, but only if we do not overstate them.

A New Approach to Cooperation and Competition

When we understand that cooperation and competition are not opposites but essential aspects of every communication, then our responses can be more nuanced, creative, realistic, and effective. In general, we can respond to messages that involve both cooperative and competitive elements (i.e., virtually all messages in conflict) in one of six ways:

- We can ignore the message.

- We can try to clarify the message.

- We can focus on one element of the message.

- We can respond to both the cooperative and the competitive elements.

- We can respond to both elements as an integrated message.

- We can respond to the message that was not delivered but that is either implied or that has the potential to address the underlying concerns in a more constructive way.

Most responses are an amalgam of all of these, because our responses are just as complex as the original message. Let's consider how each response might look in the Carlos and Kay conflict.

Carlos: I am really trying to come up with an arrangement that works for both of us, Kay, but you are not making it easy.

Kay's potential responses could include the following:

Ignoring: Right, so let's talk about how much your business is really worth.

Clarifying: What do we have to accomplish for the arrangement to work for both of us? Or what can I do to make this easier?

Focusing on the cooperative element: I am glad you want this to work for both of us. I do, too. Let's see how we can make that happen.

Focusing on the competitive element: You seem to think that all the problems we are having in reaching an agreement are my fault.

Responding to both separately: I want this to work for both of us, too. My advocacy for my legitimate needs is not about making this difficult.

Responding to the integrated message: I appreciate that it is important yet difficult to work this out so that both of us have our needs met. We have to try to honor each other's needs and to stand up for our own.

Responding to the message that was not delivered: I think maybe I should try to come up with a proposal that might work for you as well as for me.

As we craft our own response to complex messages, or help others to craft theirs, we are constantly making subliminal choices about which of these six archetypical responses might be most appropriate and effective. We mostly gravitate to one of the first four types of responses; but the more we are able to work on the final two, the more flexible and adaptive our range of responses will be. If we can recognize the complexity of the message or the nuances contained within a seemingly straightforward competitive or cooperative message, then we can begin to make our own thinking about conflict more complex and strategic and help those we are working with do the same. This is a critical step in promoting a more sophisticated and constructive approach to conflict.

Our chances of being able to deploy the last two strategies increase if we work on enhancing our understanding the codependent relationship between cooperation and competition. We are only as effective in promoting a cooperative approach to conflict as we are in helping people contend with the genuinely competitive challenges that conflict presents. But if it is naive to think that a purely cooperative approach to conflict will succeed, it is equally naive to believe that a purely competitive one is effective. None of this suggests that the cooperative and competitive elements are always equally prevalent or powerful in any single communication. We are hardly likely, for example, to react to being sued by focusing on the cooperative element in a claim for damages. But whether we focus on it or not, whether we perceive it or not, or whether it is intended or not, almost every suit contains some indication of the potential to settle, almost every act of war contains an implication for what peace would require, and almost every aggressive negotiating tactic suggests a potential bargaining range.

Reflections for Practice

I realized fairly early in my mediation practice that the cases that initially seemed to be especially difficult were not necessarily the most intractable, and those that seemed ripe for settlement were often much more challenging than they first appeared. In part, this is because disputants often show one face at the beginning and another when they begin to feel comfortable with the mediator and the process. When facing seemingly impossible cases, I started reminding myself that the mediation process really does have power; it is important to "trust the process" and make no assumptions about where it could or should lead. But I also kept in mind that there was a reason why people ended up in mediation, even in those cases that appeared at first glance to be straightforward and easy to resolve.

Eventually, I came to recognize a critical factor at play in virtually all conflict: the complex relationship between cooperation and competition. When a predominantly competitive set of messages dominated an interaction, it was easy to overlook the cooperative dimension, and vice versa. I began to realize that I could easily fall into the very same bifurcated thinking I was attempting to help disputants overcome. So I began to discipline myself to recognize the complex interaction of competition and cooperation even in the most unambiguous sounding statements. Let me offer a few examples from my practice as a conflict intervener.

Large public dialogues often provide a stage for overt displays of cooperative and competitive behavior. Competitive behavior often makes for better drama and is frequently more obvious than the cooperative dimension of interchanges, but both elements are always present.

> At a public meeting to discuss wolf control in Alaska, an elderly Alaska Native made an argument that culling wolf cubs was a traditional practice, and as he put it, "Aren't we part of nature?" A young animal rights activist from New York responded with an impassioned statement about our duty to treat all living creatures with respect. The Alaska Native then turned to the activist and said, "Don't you respect your elders?"
>
> The activist responded with stunned silence, followed up by a somewhat defensive response questioning

how that was relevant. Other animal rights and environmental activists complained about what they thought was a manipulative effort to silence them, and they were bolstered in this view by several Alaskan residents who said they thought this was a ploy used frequently by Alaska Natives. I was mostly impressed (and I have to confess, amused) by how effective it was. The nature of the conversation completely changed in a way that was favorable to that elder's point of view, namely to a discussion of how the wisdom of Alaska Natives should be brought to bear on this issue.

At the time, this seemed like a very competitive play, which is how others perceived it. But this interchange also opened the door to an important and constructive conversation that might not have occurred otherwise.

One justification I often hear from divorcing parents for their competitive behavior is the important message they believe this behavior will deliver to their children. In the following example, a competitive approach to the other parent was equated with an effort to establish a more cooperative relationship with a child.

During a custody mediation one parent made it clear that agreeing to anything other than receiving full custody seemed like an act of betrayal toward a child. The parent put it this way: "I might lose in court, but I have to try as hard as I can to get custody to show my daughter that I am not abandoning her." To this parent, losing in court seemed a more acceptable outcome than negotiating a workable agreement outside of court.

Of course, this could simply be rationalization of the kind of competitive behavior that would have occurred in any case. In other circumstances, this stance may be a way to avoid genuine involvement in parenting, without taking responsibility for making this choice. I chose to respond to the "message that was not delivered." I opened a discussion about what messages they wanted their daughter to hear from them individually, and what messages would be good to give her jointly. This did not magically end the hostile interaction, but it moved the discussion in a more productive direction—which honored both the competitive realities and cooperative potential of their circumstances.

Some of the most egregiously racist statements I have heard in my professional life have been directed toward the Roma (Gypsies). On one occasion, I decided to make what I considered to be a very risky and competitive response to some racist comments, only to find that I was also making an ultimately cooperative move.

During a project on multicultural cooperation, I participated in a meeting at a city hall in a midsized city in Bulgaria. At this meeting were people who worked in schools, social welfare organizations, health care, and city government.

Several participants in our project were also present, including two who were Roma. I participated with the assistance of a translator. Somehow, the conversation got around to the plight of the Roma, many of whom lived in extremely destitute conditions. When I expressed an interest in trying to find a way to work with this community, one of the leaders of the social welfare organizations said (this is a translation), "You can't work with those people. They are thieves. They teach their children to be thieves—that is why they have so many of them. They are liars and drunks. They are dirty. They don't deserve our help." I was stunned. When I checked to make sure I heard the translation correctly, I decided that I had to say something, even though I had been generally careful not to assert values that were rooted in my culture and not theirs. So I said (something like) this: "That is racist. I am not claiming there aren't challenges, but to label a whole group that way is racist. We are here to try to overcome those attitudes and to work on real problems. Labeling people in that way will not help."

I felt like a pushy American, frankly, but I also did not feel OK about passively listening to this. I thought I had been given a very competitive message and that I had to deliver a "provoked" response. I expected that this was going to be the end of our ability to work with this group, but in fact, I had it backward. We all went out to dinner afterward, and the conversation continued more informally. My directness seemed to earn me respect, and people really wanted to talk about the issue. I heard more racist statements, and I responded, but they were less drastic, less harsh, and gradually, more self-aware. We ended up creating a very productive program in this community. What I thought was a very competitive response to a competitive statement was understood as an honest effort to engage.

Sometimes, what sounds to an outsider like a very cooperative statement is much more competitive when viewed from the inside.

"I know that you have been gravely affected by the misconduct of the previous director, and the board recognizes we have the responsibility to do what we can to make amends to you. We will do all we are capable of doing to address your concerns." On one level, I could not have crafted a better statement from this representative of the board of a nonprofit

> organization that recently fired its longtime director
> for his abusive conduct toward clients and staff. But it
> did little to ease the tension in the room. All the staff
> heard were the words "what we can" and "what we are
> capable of." These they interpreted to mean that they
> were not going to get much by way of compensation
> for their ill treatment.

As it turned out, the staff was right. Behind this very cooperative-seeming and well-meaning statement lay a lurking reality that staff members were well aware of—the board believed that the resources available to address their needs were much more limited than the staff believed them to be. This proved to be a very protracted, difficult (but ultimately successful) negotiation. Cooperative and empathic language that covers up a fundamentally rigid negotiation stance or that hides bad news is seldom credible to people who have lived with a problem and who hear the competitive reality underlying the friendly sounding words.

I was asked to mediate a dispute between two partners who were in business together and arguing about a range of issues, including decision-making, compensation, and workload.

> After a couple of mostly unproductive sessions, one of
> the partners turned to me and said, "It comes down to
> this: either he goes or I go. And I think it is going to
> have to be him." As you might imagine, he delivered
> his message in a harsh, overbearing, and arrogant way.
> His associate replied that this attitude was exactly why
> the business was not working.

What was interesting about this, however, is that the statement was true. It really was *not* possible for the two of them to work together in the business, and their inability to make any decisions together was driving the business (which had some potential) to ruin. Furthermore, the first partner was also right in that he was really the only one who had the potential (and resources) to make it work on his own. Harsh as this was, it clarified what had to be discussed—the terms of ending the partnership. It wasn't easy, but it was much more productive. The key indication that there was in fact a cooperative element to the communication was the words "I think." He was softening his statement just enough to indicate that it could be discussed.

Conflict professionals understand the dilemma that disputants face in addressing the cooperative and competitive elements of all conflictual interactions, although we conceptualize this in many different ways. We have talked about the integrative and distributive dimension of conflict, about "power with and power over," about positional and interest-based bargaining, and about how to protect our interests and preserve our relations. I have suggested that, on an emotional level, we often experience this as a choice between being a "jerk" or a "sucker" (Mayer 2012a). The answer to all of these polarities, which are all versions of the compete/cooperate challenge, is that we have to do both. In fact, we are always doing both.

chapter three
optimism
and realism

I always like to look on the optimistic side of life, but I am realistic
enough to know that life is a complex matter. With the laugh comes
the tears and in developing motion pictures or television shows, you
must combine all the facts of life—drama, pathos and humor.

Walt Disney, How to Be Like Walt: Capturing the Disney Magic
Every Day in Your Life

Optimism and realism require each other. We cannot be genuinely optimistic in conflict without also being realistic, and
realism without optimism is not truly realistic. How we integrate
these two attitudes is emblematic of the emotional, intellectual,
and ethical challenge we face in conflict.

Conflict is emotionally demanding. The emotional resources
we bring to it are critical to finding a constructive way forward.
Our emotional resilience and outlook in conflict are formed and
expressed by our capacity to embrace both optimism and realism.
For us to sustain the energy and commitment that serious conflict
work requires, we must have at least some degree of optimism. To
be prepared for the challenges, setbacks, limits, and frustrations
that such work inevitably presents and to take a strategic approach
to conflict, we must be realistic as well. Realism puts boundaries

around optimism. Optimism suggests that we can have a powerful effect on the reality we face. All of us get tangled into this web of emotionally contradictory forces as we approach conflict, and we constantly calibrate how to adopt elements of each. We may declare ourselves to be an optimist, a pessimist, a realist, or even a cynic, but all of us operate with internalized hopes and skepticisms.

The intellectual dimension of this paradox is manifested in our level of clarity about what is occurring in a conflict, what needs to occur, and both the desirable and possible outcomes. We can think of this as a continuum between complete certainty and utter confusion. It's natural to move along this continuum as we deal with conflict. Sometimes we experience both ends of the contin-uum at the same time—a mixture of utter confusion and complete certainty, strange in concept but familiar in experience to most of us. More concerning is when people are solidly locked into either end of this polarity. An overly optimistic (or pessimistic) stance can breed unwarranted certainty, whereas realism that is not tempered by optimism often leads to high levels of confusion. Utter confusion is immobilizing. Complete certainty breeds rigidity and closes down communication. The realistic element of our approach to conflict recognizes its unpredictable nature, while the optimistic element suggests that we have some capacity to guide its course.

We have an obligation to bring the energy that optimism gen-erates and that effective conflict work requires—particularly when we act as interveners—as well as the recognition that the efforts and risks people take by engaging in a conflict process must be jus-tified by the potential to make progress. If we don't believe progress is possible, then we have to question what we are doing. We also have an obligation not to lead clients down a path toward uncertain ends that they are unaware of and unprepared for.

This means that we have an ethical obligation to be both opti-mistic and realistic. Our optimism is related to our caring for others and our willingness to offer them kindness and an open mind, even as we are locked in a bitter conflict. Realism suggests that we need to be aware of the role of power in conflict as well—something that Dr. Martin Luther King Jr. addressed in a 1967 presidential address at the Southern Christian Leadership Conference:

> Power without love is reckless and abusive, and love without power is sentimental and anemic. Power at its best is love implementing the demands of justice, and justice at its best is power correcting everything that stands against love.

We often think of pessimism as the opposite of optimism. Certainly pessimism can be a drag on productive engagement in conflict interactions, the cure for which often seems to be a healthy dose of genuine optimism. But the real antidote to destructive levels of pessimism or cynicism is not simply optimism, but also realism, or more precisely, an integration of optimism and realism. While there is some evidence that pessimists may be more realistic than optimists (Seligman 2005), pessimism and realism are not the same. A pessimistic attitude itself is no more realistic than an optimistic one, and cynicism is a crutch that all of us sometimes use when the emotional and practical demands of dealing with difficult problems and difficult people are too great. Pessimism may be the opposite of optimism, and as we seek to integrate optimism and realism, we inevitably deal with pessimism as well. But pessimism and optimism do not really express a paradox in conflict, nor do they define the most important polarity in conflict work. We don't make progress by adding optimism and pessimism together, dividing by two, and ending up with realism. Constructive engagement in conflict requires that we act with conviction that our actions matter and with the courage to act in the face of limits on our power and uncertainties about the future.

We often view optimism and pessimism as *personality traits*. No doubt some of us are by nature more likely to be optimists and others pessimists, some idealists and others realists. But regardless of our natural inclinations, our challenge is still the same: we have to deal with the demands of integrating optimism and realism and contend with the frequent pulls that we all experience toward pessimism.

This chapter takes a look at the emotional, intellectual, and ethical dimensions of optimism and realism and discusses what these suggest for how we approach conflict, both as participants and as interveners. First, however, let's take a closer look at what we mean by the terms themselves.

The Faces of Optimism and Realism

We understand "optimism" in several not entirely consistent ways. We may define it as the belief or expectation that things are going to get better and that the vast majority of people are basically well intentioned. We see optimists as looking at the positive or hopeful elements in a situation ("the glass is half full") and in general as having a positive, happy disposition. Many of our images of the optimist suggest someone who is lighthearted, happy-go-lucky, perhaps a bit goofy, and who does not succumb to the rampant cynicism around (or within) him or her.

For our purposes, the most important element of optimism is the belief that our actions can make a difference and that we can make intentional efforts to improve our own situation or those of the people with whom we are working. More generally, optimism is related to the belief that we can play a positive role in making the world a better place. In this sense, optimists believe—at least metaphorically—in the power of love, as did Dr. King. This does not necessarily require a cheerful disposition or a belief that most stories have a happy ending. Instead, it suggests a general faith in our capacity to make a difference in the world.

We understand "realism" in a variety of ways as well. Realism has been the name given to schools of philosophy, literature, and art. Philosophical schools of realism argue that the properties of the material world exist independently of human perceptions and beliefs (Miller 2010). Realism in art and literature are movements that aim to portray in a genuine way how people experience the world, rather than presenting a more romanticized or idealized version. For some, realism suggests a willingness to face the presence of evil or at least maliciousness in the world and to recognize that not all people are motivated by good intentions. Realism is equated with pragmatism, and in this sense suggests a focus on "getting things done" rather than "tilting at windmills"—on achieving the achievable rather than the ideal. In this sense, Voltaire's comment, "the perfect is the enemy of the good" (1780), is a tenet of realism.

For our purposes, the most important expression of realism is our willingness to face hard truths with courage and fortitude and to accept the limits on our capacity to achieve our goals. Realism does not imply fatalism about making progress in achieving our goals in conflict or more generally about improving our world, but it does suggest a willingness to face what we are up against and to be aware that we cannot always get what we want, when we want it, in the way we want it. If optimism relates to a classic definition of comedy, there is a tragic element to realism in the sense of understanding that we are not totally in control of our destinies and that justice does not always prevail. Good guys do not always win. But on the other hand, they don't *always* finish last.

Optimism and Realism: The Emotional Dimension

Andrew was a highly regarded toxicologist and expert on substance abuse, considered one of the "elders" of the field. Andrew was also a staunch advocate for continuing to classify marijuana as a highly dangerous drug associated with higher rates of suicide and significant developmental delays in youth. Other experts in his field felt that Andrew's position was extreme, based on a few very questionable studies, and more driven by a political agenda than by science. The battle (and it seemed like a battle—full of professional and at times personal insults) among these scientists had been going on for at least ten years at conferences, in professional publications, and in policy-making forums.

A professional organization to which many of these scientists belonged and at whose conferences many of their battles had been conducted received a grant to organize a dialogue among scientists and representatives of policy-making organizations about the impact of marijuana use and the implications of this for policy. The purpose was to identify areas of agreement, to frame the disagreements in constructive ways, to make policy recommendations, and to suggest a research agenda. I was asked to co-facilitate this process, which took place over a period of three days at a retreat center.

At first, Andrew expressed considerable doubt that much could be accomplished. "People are set in their opinions, not open to data, and are just here to put on a show for each other." Then later, as some common points of agreement were identified, he said, "I think we can do this. We can come out with an agreement that recognizes the significant psychological dangers that cannabis presents." When several others said they thought this was a bridge too far, Andrew responded by saying, "If we can't agree on this, then this whole process is a waste of time. Nothing we say here will make any difference."

Andrew's emotional swings had a powerful impact on the group's overall energy. The organizers and most of the participants felt that considerable progress was possible. However, they worried that if we tried to achieve the agreement Andrew was pushing for, we would lose the potential for tangible progress. The organizers tried to reinforce the desire to look for significant areas of agreement and to promote an atmosphere of frank and respectful discourse, but we also recognized the depths of some of the disagreements and the limits about what we could achieve in this setting. In other words, we tried to encourage a realistic approach to what could be done and to appreciate the importance of this opportunity within those limits.

In the end, as in most complex policy dialogues, participants arrived at some surprising areas of agreement, experienced frustrating areas of ongoing dispute, had some excellent discussions, worked through some personal animosities, and agreed on some potentially significant next steps. But there was no overall agreement about the dangers or benefits of marijuana. Andrew viewed this outcome as not exactly useless, but not enough to justify the effort that went into it.

This dance, in which the organizers tried to balance Andrew's high expectations and all-or-nothing approach with their own combination of optimism and realism, is a common pattern when people with a long and contentious history and profound differences get together. As Andrew expressed great optimism, the organizers and facilitators tried to provide some emotional ballast by appreciating his commitment to making significant progress but also recognizing the challenges involved. As Andrew became frustrated and discounted the value of the effort, the organizers attempted to reinforce people's desire to make progress where they could and to appreciate the spirit in which people who had often fought bitterly with one another were entering into these discussions. This approach is one strategy that interveners use in dealing with the optimism–realism dynamic, but it is not always the most effective strategy.

As in this dialogue, we often see not only a changing assessment of what a conflict engagement process can accomplish, but also very intense emotional swings about the process. It was not simply Andrew's view of what could or should be attempted that had such an impact on the group, but his *emotional response* to that assessment. While we may speak the language of logic, rational discourse, and conflict analysis, the emotional space that optimism and realism occupy is often the most critical determinant for how a conflict engagement effort unfolds.

Consider this in relation to family conflict. When divorced spouses try to agree on a plan for dealing with a difficult child, their hopefulness or hopelessness about whether this is possible is often as determinative of where the interaction is going as their assessment of what the child might need or the level of animosity between them (of course, these are all interrelated). Similarly, if we are working with business partners in a dispute, the optimism they feel or the doubts that are nagging them can become self-fulfilling prophesies.

The kinds of emotional vacillations that Andrew expressed are common, although often not as clearly articulated. Conflict provides us with many reasons to be wary and cautious, and it is natural to want to guard against being disappointed, but conflict also presents opportunities for change, and this is cause for optimism. If we are genuinely engaged in a conflict, we will be continually exposed to both of these pulls. And unless we are cut off from our own emotional reactions, we are likely to experience feelings similar to Andrew's as we undergo a conflict process. We may handle these feelings differently, temper the degree to which we let any emotional reaction predominate, and be reluctant to acknowledge or express them. But if we are genuinely engaged, we will experience a mixture of hope and caution throughout the life of the conflict.

Let's consider some of the ways disputants handle the emotional dimension of this polarity.

- *Safety through hopelessness.* We are less likely to be disappointed if we are hopeless, pessimistic, cynical, or withdrawn. We may present this as realism, but in fact this is about protecting ourselves. If conflict interveners try to counteract this by pointing to the potential for progress, we are in fact asking people to make themselves vulnerable. That is why it takes courage to be optimistic (just as it takes courage to offer a cooperative move).

- *Optimism is the nice road.* Embedded in our culture is a belief that optimists are nicer, more fun, happier, and even more ethical. A commitment to presenting an optimistic face is not the same as being optimistic and is therefore not always either genuine or realistic. Sometimes people embrace an optimistic stance without being genuinely optimistic, because they believe it to be the higher road.

- *Realism is cooler.* If optimists embody a nice approach to life, then realism, or even cynicism, can seem "cooler," wiser, worldlier, or more powerful. This is embedded in our cultural symbols as well. One of our classic heroes is the person who bravely (but not optimistically) does whatever he or she can to try to right a wrong while believing the situation is basically hopeless (like Frodo in *The Lord of the Rings*, Mel Gibson's William Wallace in *Braveheart*, Gary Cooper as the marshal in *High Noon*, or Katniss Everdeen in *The Hunger Games*).

- *Anything you can do I can do better.* Sometimes disputants try to outdo each other in expressing whichever side of the polarity they detect being put forward by the other. In other words, if you are optimistic, I am going to be more optimistic, and if you are going to play the role of the doubter, I will outdo you in that, too.

- *The cheerful pessimist.* This is a substitute for a genuine integration of optimism and realism. It allows us to take on the positive emotional attributes of optimism without taking the risks that genuine optimism imposes. I may doubt that much good can come out of our attempts to deal with our conflict, but I can act as if I am optimistic by adopting a cheerful outlook, almost reveling in my negativity.

• *The closet optimist.* Somewhat akin to the cheerful pessimist, the closet optimist is actually optimistic by nature or conviction but does not express this because of a concern that this will make him or her vulnerable or that expressing optimism might actually interfere with potentially positive developments. However, underneath this is a belief that things can and most likely will get better. I have often experienced this as a mediator when I have believed that disputants were on the verge of making significant progress but have felt that it would be unwise to express this.

• *Stuff happens.* In other words, I am not going to get emotionally involved with this issue at all. But without emotional involvement, genuine engagement in conflict is not possible.

• *There is a time for every emotion.* As with Andrew, some people can switch abruptly between being excited about the potential or depressed about the limitations of what can be accomplished by engaging in conflict. This may seem like a more flexible emotional response, but it is rigid in its own way, because whenever one side of the polarity is experienced, the other side is denied. There is a pathological version of this approach when mood swings are rooted in personality disorders, but we do not have to be bipolar to go through a wide range of emotional reactions throughout the course of a conflict.

None of these approaches is entirely authentic. Each involves an effort to handle the emotional demands of optimism and realism by accessing only part of the polarity. Even if we are optimistic by nature, that optimism can be truly genuine only if it makes room for the fear, doubts, and even grief that realism imposes on us at times. And genuine realism does not shut out our hopes and aspirations, because they are part of the reality that determines how conflict will unfold. We grow in conflict when we open ourselves to the emotional demands conflict makes on us, and one of the most significant of these is the conflicting emotions elicited by optimism and realism. Shutting out either limits our ability to adapt to circumstances as they unfold.

Embracing Uncertainty: Realistic Thoughts, Optimistic Attitudes

> I'm a pessimist because of intelligence, but an optimist because of will.
>
> *Antonio Gramsci,* Letters from Prison
>
> Don't believe everything you think.
>
> *Anonymous bumper sticker*

When I work with disputants who adopt what seems to me a rigid position or act as if they know for sure what "really" happened, what was motivating other's behavior, what is likely to happen in the future, or what is likely to happen if a dispute is taken to court, I sometimes want to shout, "Be less certain!" I have a similar inclination when people adopt a moralistic approach to a complex conflict, assuming that there is only one righteous way to think or act. This may come from years as a mediator, and I know that certainty can motivate people to act forcefully and courageously. But if I were to adapt Gramsci's statement to conflict, I would say that we should embrace uncertainty in our thinking but act with conviction.

We are more effective in communicating during conflict if we believe that what others say might have a significant impact on our own thinking and behavior. Of course, it may not be the impact that others want, but if we are open to escalating a conflict based on our counterpart's statements, we ought to be open to de-escalating it as well. If nothing another person does or says can make any difference in our own thinking, then genuine communication is very difficult. Of course, this is a two-way street. It is also hard to communicate with someone who is either totally uninterested or totally defended against whatever we might have to say. But the surest way to encourage someone else to be open to what we say is for us to be open to what they have to say.

The tension among certainty, flexibility, rigidity, and confusion is an intellectual manifestation of the emotional dimension of optimism and realism. Optimism requires some confidence in our capacity to know what to expect in the future. So does pessimism. But realism requires that we face uncertainty. The more certain that optimists (or pessimists) are, the less likely their optimism is grounded in realism. The more certain realists are, the less likely they are to be truly realistic. People announce certainties in the name of realism all the time ("let's get real"), but in a complex conflict, we are seldom able to be completely certain about what is happening, what will happen, or why.

Realism requires that disputants understand the limits on anyone's ability to predict the outcome of events that take place in chaotic systems—which is to say, all human interactions. Realism also requires that we face the difficulties inherent in dealing with deeply divisive issues; the complexities of power, culture, and personality; and the imperfections of communication. But too much uncertainty is immobilizing as well as unrealistic. We may not know or be able to control what is going to happen in a conflict, but we can see options and probabilities, and we can rule out certain outcomes as extremely unlikely. Finding the sweet spot where we can accept a certain amount of uncertainty without being immobilized by it is a continual challenge in conflict. We often try to force ourselves to be certain or abandon ourselves to confusion, but we find ourselves more often somewhere in between.

Consider a range of approaches, from total certainty to utter confusion. Let's think of this in terms of some of the things people actually say in conflict:

Total certainty: We think we completely understand what is going on, what will happen, and what we should do.

- "The only reason they are saying this is because . . ."

- "We have a slam-dunk case."

- "You will never get a better offer."

- "Anyone in their right mind can see . . ."

High certainty: We are very confident in our understanding of the conflict and our best course of action.

- "They must be saying this because . . ."

- "We have an extremely strong case in court."

- "There is no doubt in my mind that this is a very good offer."

- "If we say . . ., then I bet . . . will happen."

Confidence: We have confidence in our analysis of the situation and our ability to respond to what is occurring.

- "I understand them to be saying . . ."

- "I believe we can make a clear case to the court that . . ."

- "We can present our ideas in a way that will be very persuasive to them."

- "The most likely response to this is . . ."

Clarity: We feel clear about the situation we are in and the choices we face.

- "The message they seem to be delivering is . . ."

- "I think the court is likely to decide the case on the basis of . . ."

- "What they will get out of this offer is . . . , and what might worry them is . . ."

- "I believe this is where their key concerns lie, and some of the ways we can try to address these are . . ."

Questioning: We want to find out more and are pretty clear about the questions we need to ask.

- "I would like to find out more about what they are trying to say."

- "I wonder what the judge will find most persuasive about each of our arguments."

- "How can we shape our offer so that it is most appealing to them?"

- "This is how the situation appears to me, but I am not sure if that is how they would see it."

Doubt: We are not clear about how well we understand the conflict or about what the impact of our actions might be.

- "I am not sure of what they really want and need."

- "I think these are our best arguments, but I am not sure how the judge will react to them."

- "I don't know what we can really offer them."

- "I think they are telling a very different story than we are, and I am not sure what to do about that."

High uncertainty: We do not understand why others are acting the way they are, what they are thinking, or how to have an impact on the conflict.

- "I have no idea what they are talking about."

- "Going to court will be a complete crapshoot."

- "There must be something they want, but maybe they just want to keep fighting—who knows?"

- "I have no clue how they will react to anything we say."

Utter confusion: We don't know what the conflict is about, who it involves, what choices we have, or what people are saying.

- "I don't even know what this conflict is about."

- "I have no idea if we can go to court."

- "Nothing I say or do seems to make any difference at all."

- "I don't know who these people are, and I don't understand what they are talking about."

Disputants might experience all of these levels of certainty or confusion at different times during a conflict, sometimes in quick succession. They even might feel confusion about their certainty. Sometimes we want to feel more certain than we actually do, so we convince ourselves that we are clear; we act as if we are clear, and we make statements imbued with the language and energy of certainty. But this may cover a great deal of uncertainty. People frequently take clear positions, draw "lines in the sand," and present overly decisive narratives because they do not want to deal with their own confusion. In this way, the fear of uncertainty breeds rigidity, often in the name of "being decisive."

Conversely, sometimes people resort to utter confusion as a means of avoiding conflict, avoiding making any decisions, or avoiding taking responsibility for their actions. If I am utterly confused, how can I be effective or clear about what I am thinking or feeling? Furthermore, disputants do not adopt their level of certainty in a vacuum. If those we are having a conflict with are completely clear about their position, that might drive us to act with greater clarity than we really feel, it may undercut whatever degree of confidence we feel, or both.

Neither end of this spectrum is constructive in conflict, because each makes the integration of optimism and realism, certainty and doubt difficult. We have to consider how to nurture and travel along the more flexible middle range of the spectrum. As interveners, we need to try to help disputants understand that doubt and uncertainty are often not only justified, but useful, and to help them grasp that uncertainty and confidence are not contradictions but may reinforce one other. This was critical in helping two therapists learn how not to work together.

> Jeanne and Felix were senior therapists at a community mental health center. Jeanne had recently been appointed director of the adult outpatient team on which Felix also served. At one point they had been friends, and Felix had served as Jeanne's clinical supervisor early in her career. But their relationship soured after Jeanne became Felix's team leader. A couple of events precipitated this rupture, but the underlying problem seemed to be that neither Jeanne's management style nor Felix's approach to team participation worked for the other. Jeanne made decisions quickly and did not always seek out others' input. Felix could be very confrontational and was often critical of

Jeanne's leadership and decision making, but he was thin-skinned and easily offended if others questioned his actions.

This tension came to a head at a meeting to discuss a grant proposal they were both working on. When Jeanne asked Felix why he had not completed a section of the proposal by the time she had requested it, he said her deadlines were unrealistic and the way they were approaching the project made no sense. Jeanne became very angry and said that Felix always blamed others for his own lapses and that she was tired of being his scapegoat. Felix told Jeanne, in rather colorful language, that he did not think she knew what she was doing and to get off his back. The meeting ended in turmoil; Felix stormed out of the building and filed a complaint against Jeanne. The situation was referred to the director of human resources, who investigated and dismissed the complaint, but said they needed to do something about their working relationship. Felix and Jeanne were referred to mediation, which is how I became involved.

Both said they were committed to keeping the team insulated from their conflict, but they were very hurt and angry at each other. Jeanne was certain that Felix's concerns were entirely based on resenting her promotion to team leader; she felt he needed to be disciplined for "insubordination." Felix was equally certain that the real problem was that Jeanne was a terrible manager with an anger management problem. Each thought the only solution was for the other to change and that the only way that would happen would be for management to step in and take decisive action. They were convinced nothing else would help.

After a number of go-rounds about this, I suggested that maybe they were *both* right. Maybe the only solution was for the clinical director of the center to step in, decide who was at fault, and insist that that person change or face disciplinary action. What would likely happen then, I asked? They readily agreed that would probably not accomplish much in the long run; but each remained convinced that the problem resided entirely in the other. The more they talked, the more it seemed to me that no matter what they agreed to do or not do, they would remain very unhappy if they had to work in a setting where one had power over the other.

I wondered if there was more to their history than they were letting on, but they did not indicate this in any way. I pushed them to play out how things might work if management did exactly what they were asking, and the more they considered this, the more confused they seemed to get. In the end, they decided that for now, at least, it would probably be best if they did not try to make their relationship work as members of the same team. Felix decided to accept an offer to work at a branch office. They pulled this off in a constructive way, and the team was able to move on without getting caught in their conflict.

This was not a very satisfactory solution to me; it seemed the conflict could easily erupt again, and they had not dealt with any of the underlying issues between them. But when I checked in several months later, both Felix and Jeanne seemed happy with their current working situation and very pleased not to have to deal with each other.

Their initial certainty about what needed to happen—namely, that action had to be taken against the other—was not helpful and covered up their genuine confusion about what to do. They were each very confident in their own capacity to be constructive team members and equally certain of the other's dysfunctional approach. But in order to move forward, I had to challenge their clarity about what should be done. I accomplished this not by trying to urge flexibility but by asking them, several times, to go with their ideas and see where they took them.

This interaction clearly showed the interplay of certainty, confidence, and confusion. But where in it can we discern optimism or realism? I had the sense that they both were trying to occupy the "realist space." Although there were flashes of optimism in that they thought they knew how to make things better—punitive though that may have been ("all will be OK if Jeanne is removed as team leader," or "if Felix is disciplined, he will understand that he can't just defy me all the time")—this optimism was very fragile and unrealistic. I thought I would not get anywhere by trying to model a more positive sort of optimism, and I also thought their efforts to play the realist were actually not very realistic. Often, when the realism that people are putting forward lacks any element of constructive optimism, it is not very realistic. By aligning with each of their tendencies, I was able to get them to accept a certain amount of doubt, and in that way, they could become more realistic. Naturally, there were many other things going on, but by indirectly challenging their certainty about what needed to happen, I was able to help them to be more realistic, and in the end they were more genuinely optimistic about their work at the mental health center.

Martin Seligman, a prominent psychologist and the author of numerous works on optimism and pessimism, argues that we can learn to be optimistic, and that doing so will lead us to be more successful, happier, and healthier. Seligman, who is associated with positive psychology, uses the tools of cognitive therapy to help people become optimistic by changing their way of thinking and thereby developing more constructive explanations for events that might otherwise challenge their sense of themselves. But he also warns about optimism that is not tempered by realism. Optimism provides the energy and courage to innovate, take chances, delay gratification, and work for the common good; but pessimists, he argues, are more realistic, better able to read warning signs and to characterize complexities more accurately. He therefore equates pessimism with realism (2005):

> Depressed people—most of whom turn out to be pessimists—accurately judge how much control they have. Nondepressed people—optimists, for the most part—believe they have much more control over things than they actually do, particularly when they are helpless and have no control at all. (p. 109)

So while his essential message and mission is to help people learn to be more optimistic and thereby to increase their well-being, Seligman thinks we need a mix of pessimists with optimists, but with optimists predominating, to promote healthy organizations and communities. As he explains, we need the pessimists to promote realism:

> Pessimism serves the purpose of pulling us back a bit from the risky exaggerations of our optimism, making us think twice, keeping us from making rash, foolhardy gestures. The optimistic moments of our lives contain the great plans, the dreams, and the hopes. Reality is benignly distorted to give the dreams room to flourish. Without these we would never accomplish anything difficult and intimidating, we would never even attempt the just barely possible. (p. 114)

The challenge that Seligman sees in leading a fulfilling life is much the same as the challenge I have described about bridging the gap between optimism and realism as we deal with conflict:

By understanding the single virtue of pessimism [its ability to discern reality], along with its pervasive, crippling consequences, we can learn to resist pessimism's constant callings as deep seated in brain or in habit as they may be. We can learn to choose optimism for the most part, but also to heed pessimism when it is warranted. (p. 115)

Although Seligman expresses this in terms of the need to "heed pessimism," we can also think about this as a call to nurture optimism without the loss of realism. It's a useful way of thinking about the part these twin forces play in conflict and how we as interveners need to work with both elements of this paradox.

Seligman's work primarily addresses the affective dimension of optimism and pessimism, but he also suggests that we can change our affect by thinking differently. Conflict provides a wonderfully rich field for challenging people to think differently about the problems they face. By challenging people's certainty, whether pessimistic or optimistic, and encouraging them to be open to reasonable doubt but to proceed with confidence, we help people find that magic connection between the energy and courage that optimism provides, and the wisdom and balance realism offers. We do this as interveners; but if provided an effective process and arena for interaction, disputants can do this for each other as well. Jeanne and Felix were each certain that any objective observer would see things their way. They were also certain that nothing short of decisive action against the other would accomplish anything. Although my intervention played an important role in encouraging them each to think carefully about the certainties they were espousing, the most important challenge to their certainties was the equally strongly held, but opposite, certainty expressed by the other party.

The Ethics of Optimism and Realism

In the 2008 US presidential election between John McCain and Barack Obama, the issue of negotiating with adversaries was repeatedly raised. McCain tried to paint Obama as dangerously naive and unrealistic, and Obama argued that approaching enemies with an open mind was the right and wise thing to do. For example, Obama's foreign policy website (http://change.gov/agenda/foreign_policy_agenda/) says the following:

> If America is willing to come to the table, the world will be more willing to rally behind American leadership to deal with challenges like terrorism, and Iran and North Korea's nuclear programs.

He continues to take this line. In a speech to the United Nations General Assembly in 2009, Obama said,

> We have sought—in word and deed—a new era of engagement with the world. And now is the time for all of us to take our share of responsibility for a global response to global challenges.

McCain took a very different view. For example, he stated the following during his campaign:

> I don't fear to negotiate. Instead, I have the knowledge and experience to understand the dangerous consequences of a naive approach to presidential summits based entirely on emotion. ("McCain Fires Back on Foreign Policy" as reported by Mark Murray at NBCnews.com, May 21, 2008)

Obama said, in essence, that it is a leader's ethical responsibility to reach out to adversaries with an optimistic spirit. McCain said that optimism alone won't accomplish much and that it is the president's ethical responsibility to be realistic. This issue became a central theme in the election. And because political campaigns emphasize differences, it is not surprising that the candidates gravitated to very different elements of this polarity. However, they raised a fundamental dilemma that all leaders face—the need for a proactive and optimistic approach to complex problems coupled with a strategic awareness of risks.

As I write this, similar arguments are being made about the wisdom of negotiating with Iran over their weapons production, of pushing for negotiations between Israel and Palestine, and of entering into an agreement with Syria about its chemical weapons. As any leader must, Obama has had to develop his own capacity to deal with this paradox. In the fall of 2013, at the same time he refused to negotiate with House Republicans about the government shutdown, he pushed for negotiations with Iran about their nuclear program but promised that he would not agree to anything that was not meaningful, verifiable, and enforceable. Whether or not we agree with any of the specifics here, we can easily recognize this familiar political dance—one that reflects the need to be both hopeful and wary.

But this is not just a political challenge; it is an ethical one as well. When the stakes are high, leaders have an ethical responsibility to take risks to achieve important ends, but they also must pay heed to the significant dangers involved.

For conflict interveners, the ethical dimension is pervasive. We have to approach our work with optimism; otherwise, why would we bother doing it? We must believe that some good can come out of our intervention, even if it does not result in a comprehensive agreement, or we will inevitably approach our job with cynicism, and the disputants will sense that. On the other hand, we also have an obligation to be aware of the limitations on what we can accomplish and the genuine difficulties all parties have to face. The ethical challenge for interveners, therefore, is to find that integration of optimism and realism that propels an engagement process forward while maintaining and conveying a clear-eyed view of the challenges and dangers involved.

This is not an abstract issue. Conflict interveners face this challenge in almost every statement they make. Consider these examples:

- A divorcing spouse questions whether to go to mediation at all. She believes her former partner is manipulative and rigid and wonders if she should not just go to court.

- An employer is not sure whether to give a difficult employee another chance at a job.

- An environmental activist is reluctant to join in discussions about how to mitigate the impact of a proposed highway project because she thinks it would be best if the project did not occur at all.

It's not necessarily our job as interveners in any of these situations to make a suggestion or offer advice, but the manner in which we respond, the questions we ask, and the way in which we frame disputants' concerns all convey our own sense of optimism and realism—and clients are very sensitive to this. How we approach this tension between optimism and realism, clarity and doubt, may be as critical to maintaining a coherent ethical stance and maintaining our credibility as are the more widely recognized and prominent standards of confidentiality and impartiality. Our capacity to be positive and hopeful about the potential for making progress on a conflict, while we convey our awareness of the difficulty involved in doing so, plays a major role in how clients perceive us. It also has a significant impact on how receptive they are to our interventions, even though they are often not aware of this.

Integrating Optimism and Realism, Clarity and Doubt

As conflict interveners (and those who train them), we are usually focused on specific techniques, tactics, or actions that we can take to help people through conflict. As important as reframing, affirming, searching for underlying interests, identifying areas of agreement, and other specific approaches to conflict intervention may be, our most powerful tools are always the attitudes and beliefs that we bring. So how we experience and understand the polarity of optimism and realism ourselves is critical to how we help others. As with so much that we do, therefore, effective practice is reflective practice. We can refine our own beliefs and understanding by reflecting on what actually happens when we intervene in conflict.

To explore some of our choices in how we approach optimism and realism, let's consider further my reflective process in the policy dialogue about cannabis discussed earlier in the chapter. Often, the richest reflections about our thinking and actions in conflict come from looking at specific moments or interactions and asking ourselves the following questions:

- What was challenging or poignant about that moment?

- What did I specifically do or say?

- Why? (This may be retrospectively providing an explanation for actions that were driven by instincts and unconscious processes, but still helps us uncover our beliefs and guiding concepts.)

- What was the impact?

- What can I learn from this?

As I think back on the policy dialogue—specifically, my interaction with Andrew—one moment jumps out at me, a critical point where I did almost nothing. This occurred when Andrew said that "we can do this"—i.e., the group could reach an agreement about the dangers of cannabis. This was a challenging moment for me, because I was pretty sure that the kind of agreement that Andrew wanted was not possible in this forum, and I was concerned that spending too much energy pursuing it would get in the way of accomplishing what I (and others) believed really *was* possible. But I did not respond to this statement when Andrew said it. I said nothing at all, and instead allowed time for the group to respond. There was some minimal discussion of Andrew's comments, and the participants decided to designate a small group to try to formulate some potential points of agreement about the dangers of cannabis (as part of the design, participants were going to divide into small groups to discuss specific topics). Some interesting proposals emerged that acknowledged general agreement about certain dangers, several areas where there was no agreement, and additional research that was needed. This was less than Andrew hoped for (and he left the forum feeling the process had failed), but it took considerable time to get even that far.

I have asked myself why I acted as passively as I did in that moment, and what else I might have done. In retrospect, I believe I was concerned about not wanting to squelch Andrew's newfound enthusiasm, and I did not want to alienate him. But I also truly did *not* feel optimistic about the approach he was advocating. I had not yet arrived at an effective integration of optimism and real-ism for myself, and I therefore did not think I could successfully formulate one for the group. It therefore felt better to me for the group to express their own views about this rather than for me to do so. Instead, by soliciting from the group a process to explore this question further, I encouraged them to work through their own integration of optimism and realism.

I would not change much in retrospect, but I wish I could have articulated the dilemma more effectively for the group, perhaps something along these lines: "Andrew is encouraging us to go for an agreement on a particularly contentious issue. If we can get there, that would be great, but on the other hand, I know many of you are doubtful that we can and are eager to work on issues that you feel more hopeful about. There may be real value to be gained by trying to get an agreement about this issue, knowing that there are very different opinions about this in the room, because by doing so, we may be able to identify more agreement than we thought possible, we can clarify areas of disagreement, and we may be able to agree on next steps. But we have to do this in a way that does not preclude or limit other discussions that people want to have." I don't know if a statement of this nature would have made a great deal of difference in terms of the end result, but it might have helped the group take a more integrated look at the potential and limits on what we might accomplish.

My effort here to engage in a reflective process using the lens of optimism and realism (or any of the polarities discussed in this book) shows how doubt and certainty are largely a parallel challenge. The earlier discussion about my work with Jeanne and Felix was a similar effort at reflection. Engaging in a reflective process using the lens of optimism and realism is often the most powerful way to enhance our ability to help disputants (and ourselves in disputes) to handle this dilemma. Doing so increases our capacity to understand the nature of this paradox, to work with it, and to convey an integrated approach to others. Engaging with others in a reflective process—in peer consultation groups, clinical supervision, or with co-interveners—also enhances our ability to do this.

In addition to reflection, interveners often employ several specific approaches to help disputants contend with the pulls of optimism and realism.

Countering the group's predominant mood. As we tried with Andrew and the policy group, interveners can express hope when people despair and caution when people seem excessively confident. We can seek to clarify in the face of confusion and raise questions in response to certainty. We need to remember, however, that there is a limit to how much we can do this and still maintain our effectiveness—and we seldom have special knowledge that makes our pronouncements especially credible or persuasive. The most effective approach is to hold our own emotional center and to maintain a demeanor of hopefulness and a discourse of realism. The more a disputant occupies the optimist space, the more we might engage them in a conversation about realistic alternatives, and the more they take on the realist role, the more we might attend to the maintenance of an optimistic spirit. This approach may have had less impact on the Andrews than on the energy and approach of the group as a whole. By giving legitimacy to all elements of this polarity, we can make room for others to find their own natural response.

Mirroring. Interveners can mirror the dominant mood in the room or that of the dominant player. If someone is very negative in the name of being realistic, we can align with this. I am naturally suspicious when everyone involved in a conflict is sure that it can be readily dealt with. (I always wonder, if it is so easy, why am I here?) Nonetheless, I seldom find it problematic to reinforce that optimism, perhaps with a slight note of caution, by saying for example something like, "I am glad there is so much hopeful and positive commitment to work on this, and that should make our task a lot easier. However, I am sure there is still a lot of hard work ahead of us." Similarly, in the face of a predominantly "realist" stance, it is often helpful to reinforce everyone's desire to go into the process with their "eyes wide open," aware of the challenges, uncertainties, and complexities. By doing this, we make any sign of optimism that we do show more credible.

Naming. Rather than mirroring, it is often more effective simply to name where people are on this polarity. For example, sometimes we may point out that people seem cautiously optimistic, others very doubtful, and a few very hopeful. We can also name the level of certainty or confusion people are exhibiting. By naming this, people become aware that they are coping with the need to be both hopeful and realistic.

Going with it. As I did with Felix and Jeanne, sometimes the best thing we can do is to take whatever people are expressing and run with it. If they are optimistic, we can reinforce this to lay out just how they think progress can be made; if people are focused on the obstacles they face, we can emphasize these and discuss them further. I tried to challenge Felix and Jeanne's certainty by accepting it, and then asking them to discuss in detail how the administration might intervene and how that might work.

Challenging. Because our goal is to help people be both optimistic and realistic and to see these as necessary to each other, I do not think it is useful to challenge either of these. Yet it is often valuable to challenge the certainty or doubt that makes it hard to take an integrated approach. Obviously, we have to be very careful in how we do this, but it's sometimes helpful to question *why* people are so certain or so confused, especially if we can do so by suggesting unknowns at the same time as we look for areas of clarity.

Deferring. Often, we simply ask people to hold on to their doubts, their hopes, their misgivings, and even their cynicism, but nonetheless to engage in the process and try to make it work. I have often said something like, "I am not asking that you be optimistic or hopeful, simply that you *try*. If this process has a chance to work, it will require that you help it do so. That does not mean that it will work, just that we will have tried our best."

Referring. Referring the paradox itself to the disputants puts the question of integrating optimism and realism where it belongs. For example, I could have said to the policy group, "How confident are the rest of you that we can deal with this issue, and how central is it to our goals for this discussion?" The danger would have been to divert the group into a conversation about a conversation, but on the other hand, this might have provided an opportunity to grapple directly with an important dilemma.

Ignoring. Probably the most frequent intervention strategy is none—that is, to let things play out as they will and not to address the issue directly at all. There is always so much happening in a conflict that we can never take on everything. We are always, mostly unconsciously, deciding what to address and what not to—and sometimes the best move is to remain as inactive as possible.

Integrative reframing. The ultimate goal here is to encourage people to bridge the gap between being optimistic and realistic, hopeful and cautious, confident and uncertain. As with all of the polarities we discuss, our whole process of engagement and intervention in conflict has the goal of encouraging this integration. Sometimes the very best way to do this is to propose an integrative framework for addressing a particular expression of this dilemma. Winston Churchill's exhortations rousing Britain during some of the most difficult moments of World War II were effective in part because of his ability to achieve this integration. Perhaps the most famous example of this comes from a speech Churchill delivered in November 1942 shortly after the Allies' decisive victory over German forces at El Alamein:

> Now this is not the end. It is not even the beginning of the end. But it is, perhaps, the end of the beginning. (Churchill, 1943)

Families, communities, organizations, and societies work because they are able to approach difficult issues with an optimistic spirit—but one that allows them to look at hard realities. Finding a way to give voice to this can be a very powerful contribution to constructive conflict engagement.

Further Reflections from Practice

Looking back on my practice as a conflict specialist, and particularly as a mediator, it seems now that dealing with the dynamic between optimism and realism was almost always essential to establishing rapport and credibility with clients. Often, the positive attitude and energy that I conveyed helped clients to accept me initially.

My belief that something constructive could happen in a dialogue or consensus-building process was essential to convincing disputants to give a collaborative effort a try. However, my credibility would diminish if I conveyed this optimism without also conveying a realistic appraisal of the situation, as if I were a cheerleader or salesman. Sometimes disputants would even try to prove to me that their situation was truly impossible. And, of course, if disputants really want to prove this, they almost always can. Looking at it from their point of view, this makes perfect sense. Why should they let me in on a very difficult, painful, or high-stakes conflict if I seem to believe that all you need is a positive attitude and a willingness to make things work and all will be well? But if I failed to have that attitude and willingness, why should they trust me? Disputants are constantly deciding how much faith to put in a process or an intervener. So as I look backward, handling this paradox effectively seems essential, and it is one of the very first things disputants experience as they interact with conflict specialists.

I was not very focused on or even aware of this challenge for most of my career, however. Perhaps this was because I have always believed, if not that any conflict could be solved, that at least something good could come out of almost every interaction. Several things happened to bring home the central role the optimism–realism polarity plays in developing rapport with clients. In many instances, disputants have put the question very bluntly to me. Here are some examples:

- "Do you believe you can resolve any dispute?" (in a high-stakes environmental dialogue)

- "He will never agree to anything; can you really help?" (in a divorce mediation)

- "OK, I am here for this meeting. Are you going to 'facilitate' me?" (The person then takes a classic meditation position, with upturned palms, thumb and forefinger forming an o-shape on either knee—the implication being that this was all a "touchy-feely" fantasy.)

- "I am afraid of getting my hopes up and then getting hurt again." (child protection mediation)

- "Someone is going to get killed before this is over." (organizational conflict)

These and many other clients' statements challenged me to recognize just how difficult their conflicts really were. Often these have been implied criticisms; no one who really understood how bad the situation was could possibly want to get involved. On the other hand, each seemed to carry an implied plea for hope, indirectly stated but nonetheless powerful. Finding the right way to bring both the reality and the hope together was critical to moving the situation forward. Of course, sometimes the conflict was really beyond what a collaborative process could handle, yet there was almost always a constructive next step to take—even if that meant not going forward with a collaborative effort at all. So I began to say just that—that I could not promise or predict that we would reach an agreement or even make a great deal of progress, but that there was almost always a constructive next step, and our job was to try to find it.

As I got older, people were less likely to assume that I was naive and more likely to want to know whether I had worked with similar conflicts that had been resolved. My basic answer has not changed much, but it is received differently, and with practice and experience, I have found it easier to provide a response that effectively integrates realism and optimism. So I could answer with the conviction of experience and not just faith that I thought progress could usually be made, even on very difficult disputes. However, I also came to appreciate the enduring nature of conflict, and I now frequently work with disputants to identify the long-term elements of their disputes and ask them to consider the challenge of engaging with these over time, rather than to expect them to be resolved imme-diately. This is the subject of a previous book, *Staying with Conflict: A Strategic Approach to Ongoing Disputes* (2009). My discussions with disputants about the enduring aspects of conflict have become nat-ural and productive, and have also alerted me to the underlying benefit of taking on the challenge of the optimism–realism paradox.

Another factor has been the maturation of our field. We are no longer the salespersons for a new process or concept that we were thirty years ago. We are specialists delivering proven, if underuti-lized, services, and yet we remain aware of the limits on what we offer. We have matured as a field in the more integrated way we bring optimism and realism to our work.

Finally, several substantive arenas have forced us to contend with the optimism–realism paradox on a policy level. For example, the long and productive conflict about the appropriateness of medi-ation in domestic violence has revolved around this dilemma. Can we hold out hope to domestic violence victims that we may be able to help them extricate themselves safely from dangerous relation-ships, as we simultaneously face squarely the enormous obstacles and dangers that they face and the real limits on what we can offer? I believe that the progress we have made on discussing the issue of mediation where there has been domestic violence—and we *have* made considerable progress (Ver Steegh and Dalton 2008)—has come about because we have taken a more nuanced view of the nature of the problem. As a result, we've been able to offer more sophisticated ways of approaching it.

We have also faced this challenge in dealing with environmen-tal disputes, ethnic conflicts, and international conflicts. In each of these arenas we have been forced to look into ourselves and ask, What can we really do? Can we help? Might we make it worse? How can we respect the reality people involved in these conflicts face? It is tempting to come down entirely on the side of being realistic in order to avoid leading people into potentially dangerous situ-ations or coming across (particularly in international settings) as "naive Americans" (or Canadians or Australians or . . .). However, I have come to realize that people also *want* us to be optimistic. Many years ago, when I was working in Eastern Europe not long after the fall of Communism, I found that while people often teased us about being naive or not understanding just how bad things really were, they were truly seeking a bit of optimism and a "can-do" spirit. And while this might have had a tinge of naiveté to it, it also carried with it the hope, commitment, and belief that are essential to trying to make things better (Mayer, Wildau, and Valchev 1995).

The complexity of this paradox is the fundamental challenge we face in presenting ourselves in an honest and effective way to disputants. It is also essential to our own professional identity. Finding our way through this is what builds and maintains our balance, our energy, and our self-respect in conflict. When we share with disputants an integrated approach to being optimistic and realistic as we approach conflict, then we are truly working as a team.

This paradox operates on a much more universal level as well. It is easy to become discouraged, cynical, and hopeless as our world faces seemingly insurmountable challenges—climate change, nuclear proliferation, population explosion, income inequality, the depletion of our natural resources, and the spread of terrorism, to name a few. Yet hopelessness in the face of such apparently intractable problems is a self-fulfilling prophecy. Unless we approach the problems of our world with a degree of optimism about our capacity to make a difference, we won't have the will or the energy to make the effort necessary to have any chance of success. On the other hand, naive optimism will also lead us astray. These are very difficult problems, and the path ahead is uncertain. Our challenge is to try to address them with the hope that we can find a way forward that will make a difference and with the full knowledge that there is no guarantee that we will succeed.

chapter four

avoidance and engagement

Peace is not the absence of conflict but the presence of creative alternatives for responding to conflict—alternatives to passive or aggressive responses, alternatives to violence.

Dorothy Thompson, journalist

Life constantly presents us with choices about whether to engage or avoid conflict. Consider the following scenarios:

- The office manager of a university department believes that one member of the faculty in her unit is having inappropriate contact with students.

- Your teenager seems to be spending more time on social media than on his homework.

- Your spouse is involved in an extended custody battle with his ex and you think he is fixated on this rather than moving on with his life.

- A co-worker comes back from lunch increasingly late each day with alcohol on her breath.

Sometimes these issues involve moral dilemmas. (What does the office manager do to protect students when she has no proof of the faculty member's misconduct?) Sometimes they may be annoying more than essential. (Yet again, I have to clean up the kitchen or live with the mess my roommate created.) And sometimes they may be trivial. (My spouse left the toilet seat up again.) We are constantly having to decide which conflicts to take up, which to avoid, and how best to do so. The way we approach these dilemmas says a lot about the power dynamics of our relationships. It also gives expression to our values and our commitment to others.

Avoidance and engagement are the third of the major dilemmas we face in conflict. Although we may see this as a straightforward choice—I will either raise a conflict or ignore it—it is far more complicated than that. As with other paradoxes, we have to understand that avoidance and engagement are essential to each other. When we avoid one conflict, we may be setting up another. When we choose to engage in one conflict, we are likely avoiding another. We all pick our battles in both our personal and professional relationships. We need to do this in order to initiate a serious conflict engagement process. If we raise every possible issue we might have with someone, we risk obscuring our most important concerns and making genuine communication impossible. So to engage effectively, we also have to avoid. How we approach conflict always involves an element of both avoidance and engagement.

For example, consider this typical interchange between two longtime friends:

Norman: Nice to see you, Randy. It's been a while.
Randy: That's true. You seem to have been too busy for us to meet.
Norman: I have been busy, but it's great to see you. How have you been?
Randy: Perhaps if we had been more in touch, you'd know that I had surgery on my knee and then I had pneumonia last spring.
Norman: I'm sorry to hear that. No, I didn't know about that.
Randy: So I gather.

Though he hasn't come right out and said so, Randy has made three comments indicating that he is upset with Norman for being out of touch. He is expressing his feelings indirectly and passive-aggressively. Norman is trying to sidestep the issue, but if this relationship is at all meaningful to him—perhaps even if it is not—he could well be feeling annoyed or tense about the interchange. If he continues to avoid this issue, he is, in essence, opting for a shallower friendship. By making a series of such choices in his interactions with Randy, he is contributing to a more distant relationship. On the other hand, addressing this issue directly will not necessarily improve things. Let's speculate about what each might be thinking and what they might say next.

Norman: (*Ugh—Randy is guilt-tripping me yet again about not being in closer touch. But what does he expect if every time we get together I have to put up with this crap? I see him as often as I can, and I try to stay in touch through other means as well. And why is it always up to me to take the initiative? Maybe if I can redirect this away from being in contact, we can have a better conversation and that will make things OK.*) So, Randy, are you OK now? How's your knee? Are you still able to ski?

Randy: (*He really doesn't care about me. Since I let him know I was not so pleased that he's been out of touch, he is faking interest in my health. I don't know what I am getting out of this friendship. He won't even own up to the fact that he has been unavailable. Every time we get together, he wants to have these superficial conversations and to end them as soon as possible. I'm not sure there is a point in trying to change things. Maybe we should just go on with our lives.*) I'm fine now, and the knee is pretty much OK. Not ready for skiing yet.

Norman: (*This doesn't feel very good. I'm going to have to say something.*) Randy, you seem annoyed with me. Are you upset that I couldn't make it to your daughter's wedding last year? I really wanted to come, but I had a long-standing commitment that I couldn't get out of.

Randy: (*He doesn't get it. It's not the wedding, but the whole
pattern—I am just not very important to him. I will give this just one
more try.*) No, I understood that, but it always seems like you're
too busy to find time to get together.

This kind of interchange is probably familiar to all of us. Maintaining relationships is always a balancing act between what we
bring up, what we let slide, and how we deal with the issues that
others raise. Each segment of this interaction (likely mirrored in
their nonverbal communication and the tone of their comments)
requires that Randy and Norman deal with the twin pulls of avoiding and engaging in a potentially conflictual interaction. None of
these are straightforward, clear-cut decisions, and we process much
of this in an unconscious way. As we are making our choices, those
we are communicating with are making theirs, and we send each
other subtle signals all the while that affect our decisions.

We see this happening on an intergroup and societal level
as well. Diplomacy is full of conventions that seem to be about
"making nice" and raising conflict at the same time. Labor and
management frequently engage in an elaborate dance that
expresses both flexibility and rigidity about what will or won't be
discussed. In just about every significant policy dialogue I have
witnessed, participants engage in an ongoing exchange characterized by complicated combinations of avoiding and engaging
statements. Here are actual statements from policy roundtables:

> *You are murderers.* Said by an animal rights activist to
> a trapper, this is highly challenging and escalatory, but
> the effect and perhaps the intention was to stop an
> interaction.
>
> *I respect your research, but I don't agree with your
> results.* This raises a real issue, but the speaker does not
> own the fact that she really does not respect the
> research or the researcher.

If you don't like our proposal, why don't you picket us?
This was said as if a joke by a developer to a community activist—acknowledging past conflicts but putting down the community's concern and using humor both to connect and place barriers.

The dance of avoidance and engagement defines all communication in conflict—all statements made during conflict contain both elements. Furthermore, our actions, emotions, and thinking are seldom completely in sync. Avoidance and engagement are not the opposites we often believe them to be. Without effective choices about what and how to avoid, we cannot effectively engage with others; similarly, avoidance is a rigid and brittle approach without some engagement. Maintaining meaningful relationships requires that we deal with essential conflicts, but we must be wise about how, which, and when. In this chapter, we will look at the nature of avoidance and engagement, both from an individual and interactive perspective, and we'll consider how conflict specialists work with this paradox.

The Dimensions of Avoidance and Engagement

As with conflict as a more general concept (Mayer 2012a), avoidance and engagement do not simply refer to what we do or say, but to how we feel and think as well. We can see the disconnect between some of what Norman and Randy are thinking and saying in the preceding example. Although their actions may be intended one way—perhaps to avoid talking about a conflict—they have the opposite effect on their thinking or feelings. The more Norman avoids speaking to Randy directly about Randy's "guilt-tripping" him, the more Norman's feelings may intensify, and, therefore, the more emotionally engaged in the conflict he becomes. By acknowledging Randy's feelings and inviting a conversation about them, he might at least diminish some of the emotional intensity he is experiencing. Sometimes we can avoid the emotional demands of engagement by simply refusing to acknowledge or deal with a con-flict. Perhaps if Norman had continued to ignore Randy's barbs, Randy would have eventually let them go and the emotions would have subsided as well. But the more significant the issue or the rela-tionship, the less likely that will happen. The interaction among how we feel, how we think, and how we act in conflict is complex, and each of these dimensions defines an important aspect of our approach to avoidance and engagement.

Behavioral Elements of Avoidance and Engagement

Avoidance behavior consists of actions intended to prevent or insulate disputants from having to deal with a conflict. Similarly, engagement behavior entails actions intended to increase or intensify interaction about a conflict. These behavioral aspects of avoidance and engagement are their most tangible elements, and we often equate these with the conflicts themselves.

Behavior to avoid conflict can range from passive approaches (such as not bringing up a conflict, ignoring provocative comments from others, or avoiding interacting with someone at all), to very active steps (such as solving a problem before the underlying conflict is raised, escalating behavior in a way that discourages interaction, cutting off contact with someone). The common thread is that all this behavior is about preventing or ending interaction about the actual conflict.

Avoidant behavior can be intentional and conscious or uncal-culated and unconscious. It can also be effective or ineffective in actually forestalling involvement in conflict. And what starts out as avoidant behavior can turn into something very different, depend-ing on the response it evokes both internally and externally. If I try to avoid a sensitive issue with my spouse by changing the subject whenever it comes up, it may in fact mean we do *not* deal with it, it may provoke her to intensify her efforts to raise the issue with me, or I may find myself feeling increasingly uncomfortable with the issue and therefore focused on it. Avoidant behavior always involves a conscious or unconscious acknowledgement that a conflict exists. The mere act of seeking to deflect attention from a conflict serves to point out its existence. And we have all gone to extraordinary lengths to avoid dealing with very simple conflicts. Often we do this out of kind intentions and a desire to preserve relationships, but we also do it because we are afraid of the consequences (often for good reasons). Frequently, we employ avoidance behavior because we do not have confidence in our ability to engage constructively or successfully.

Although our desire to preserve a relationship is often what motivates us to avoid conflict, there is almost always a distancing component as well. That is, to the extent we do not deal with someone about the issues or conflicts we have with them, we put boundaries around how close or genuine our connections with them can be. However, all relationships involve some conflict avoidance. No relationship can thrive if people bring up every issue they have, every time, in a completely open way. It wouldn't be possible to do that even if we tried, because so much of the interaction that breeds conflict is nonverbal or indirect (Tannen 1986). So we have to make choices about what to raise and what to dance away from in all our interactions—and we do this continually.

Perhaps family relationships offer the most intense challenge in this regard, and one we face from our earliest days. As discussed in chapter 1, progressing through developmental stages involves a process of *differentiation*. Both overly rigid and inadequate boundaries inhibit human development (Bowen 1985; Bowen and Kerr 1988; Minuchin 1974). The establishment of boundaries through the way we both engage in and avoid conflictual issues is an important part of our developmental progression into adulthood. Families are the arena in which our most intense work on this occurs, and although they can be the safest place for us to engage in this work, they can also be the most dangerous. Families are the context for our most intimate and lifelong connections, which make boundaries essential. I will return to this dynamic in chapter 8.

Our efforts to preserve relationships through avoidance some-times work, but often the limits this approach imposes ultimately undercut the relationship itself—a lesson I learned playing poker many years ago.

> John was a colleague at a youth center in New York City. When several of us who worked there began playing poker together, John was eager to be part of the group. We started what became a regular (monthly) poker night. The stakes were low, and we thought that we had to be either incredibly lucky or unlucky to win or lose more than $25 in an evening. Somehow, John managed to lose considerably more every time we played. He was not particularly unlucky, just inept. He seemed to think that folding was an act of cowardice, and as a result, the game soon became an exercise in taking money away from John. The rest of us kidded him about this and tried to coach him as well, but he would become defensive and play more erratically when we did this. Making matters more complicated, John was the lowest paid staff member, the only one with a wife and child, and the only one without a college education (not that college teaches better poker skills, but it did reflect a difference in class background). The amount John was losing on a regular basis was problematic for him and for his family.
>
> The situation became painful. We did not want to exclude John, but something had to change. After some covert communication among the rest of us, we decided our relationship with John would be hurt if we tried to deal with the problem directly. So we simply did not tell him about the next game. After we had done this a couple of times, he began asking about when we would play again. We avoided the question,

saying something like, "Not sure, lots going on." This felt awful, too, and soon the poker nights just stopped happening. We never openly discussed this with John, and the rest of us didn't talk about this much either.

I never felt as connected to John after this. Nothing bad happened, but I felt a barrier had been erected that I did not have the courage, commitment, or wisdom to break down. Several months later, he took another job and we gradually lost contact. Sadly, I think this event also put a damper on the other connections in the group. What had started out as a nice bonding experience became a symbol and cause of the limits to our closeness. The most interesting thing to me in looking back at this experience is that I still remember it so well. This occurred more than forty years ago, and yet I can still recall the feelings, the conversations—even some of the poker hands. It did not feel right to me at the time to avoid this issue the way we did, but none of us had a clue how to handle it better, even though half of the group were trained therapists. All the "I-messages" and active listening in the world would not have solved this dilemma. If the relationship with John had been important enough, we would have found a way to bring it up, perhaps, but who knows how that would have gone.

I would like to think that after forty years of practice and training as a therapist and conflict specialist, I now have better skills and more courage that would enable me to take this on more effectively. But, to be honest, I am not sure. This kind of situation is emblematic of the core of the avoidance–engagement dilemma. To be sure, there are far more significant conflicts and relationships, and the stakes are often higher, but being able to find that right combination of engaging and avoiding that both respects and preserves a relationship while dealing with important concerns is always difficult.

Engagement behavior can also range from active to passive. Sometimes, the most important thing we do to engage a conflict is not avoid it. When someone is upset with me and lets me know it, I often feel the urge to avoid, and I can use a wide range of methods to do so. For example, I may want to minimize the issue, deny responsibility or intentionality, solve the problem, get angry, or focus on one small element rather than the overall concern. Being aware of this tendency is helpful to me, and I often find that the best way to deal with this impulse is the simplest: ask for more information and try very hard to understand what I am being told. It's almost as if the less I do, the more engaged I become. Of course, I have to say something eventually, but overcoming that first impulse to avoid is sometimes the most significant step we can take to promote constructive engagement. This is why encouraging disputants to stay with a difficult interaction is often the single most important contribution conflict specialists make.

Even when we are the ones with an issue to raise, sometimes doing less is actually doing more. This is in part about waiting for an opportune time to raise our concerns, but it is also a matter of waiting for an issue to "mature," so that it becomes clear that a discussion of the problem is necessary and so that the exact nature of the issue comes into focus. Perhaps if, instead of kidding John about his playing, we had waited a bit longer to allude to our concerns, the nature of the problem would have been more obvious to everyone, including John. Sometimes, if we wait before we try to fix a problem, we are more likely to end up engaging with its most significant element.

Perhaps the most difficult element of engaging is simply naming the conflict both to ourselves and to others. In their classic discussion about how an "injurious experience" becomes a full-fledged dispute, Felstiner, Abel, and Sarat (1980–81) introduced the catchy phrase, "naming, blaming, and claiming." The critical first step, they suggest, is naming an event as injurious to oneself or others. The next is to assign blame for causing that experience. The third step, claiming, is the assertion of what should be done to compensate for the experience (such as monetary compensation, an apology, or punishment). Their model requires that all three steps take place for an injurious experience to turn into a dispute.

Naming, blaming, and claiming are always about both engaging and avoiding, because each involves drawing a boundary around a conflict and defining some aspects of the conflict as fitting within that boundary, and some without. For example, by naming the conflict with John as being about his irresponsible and inept poker playing, we defined the conflict in terms of his personal characteristics and excluded class dynamics from the definition. So although naming, blaming, and claiming are intended to promote engagement, there is often a significant avoidant component to the process as well. For example, I may say in a clear and straightforward way that I do not believe I have been compensated adequately for work that I have done, and this may be an important first step to engagement. But if I say this in an angry and provocative way and aggressively insist on immediate payment with interest, this may have the effect, and perhaps the intention, of shutting down interaction and forestalling genuine engagement.

It is not behavior alone that determines the level of avoidance and engagement, but rather how the other person responds to that behavior, and how it influences the emotional and cognitive aspects of this dilemma. That is why some of our best-intended efforts to enter into a constructive conflict engagement can backfire, and why efforts to avoid engagement can sometimes actually promote it. Consider the following scenario:

> Beth and Maurice had been business partners and friends for many years. They worked well together but they often quibbled, almost like siblings. Maurice found Beth a bit controlling and pushy at times; Beth thought Maurice could be self-absorbed and a bit arrogant. But despite this, their friendship was important to both of them. Two things about Maurice drove Beth particularly crazy. One was that he often would relate

to a story Beth was telling by interrupting and telling of an experience he'd had that her story reminded him of. The other was that Beth felt Maurice ate in a way that was vulgar—slurping his soup, talking while eating, and hovering over his plate as he ate.

Feeling her irritation with Maurice growing, Beth decided to bring up his eating habits with him. She gave quite a bit of thought to how and even consulted some mutual friends about it. On a trip to a project that they were jointly conducting, Beth raised this issue. The conversation went something like this:

"Maurice, I have something I want to discuss with you that is a bit hard for me to bring up—and I want you to promise not to get defensive."

Maurice, now feeling quite defensive and guarded responded, "OK, shoot."

"It's about your eating. You know you often slurp, talk while you are eating, and sort of shovel food into your mouth rather than finishing one bite before taking another. I adore you, Maurice, but this is a real problem for me, and I would like you to work on it, particularly when we are with clients."

"I'm sorry you feel that way about my manners, Beth. I will certainly try to do better, but you know we do come from very different cultural backgrounds, and where I grew up—well, that is how people ate."

"I know that, but it is still a problem. Would it be OK if I gave you some feedback about this from time to time?"

"OK."

But it wasn't OK. Despite what he said, Maurice was upset and hurt, and he communicated that indirectly. When Beth did give him some feedback, his words were appreciative, but his affect was not. And finally, he told Beth that he got the message; he would try, but she needed to back off. So she did. They never talked about this again, but both felt hurt by the interaction, and their relationship suffered as a result. Both of them tried to deal with this issue directly and constructively. Beth had tried her best to raise the issue in a kind way, and Maurice tried to respond in the same spirit. But he was too hurt to do so. His words and his affect gave contradictory messages, and he did not know how to deal with this. Although she was trying to open the subject for discussion, Beth also tried to close it down right away by suggesting her solutions (how Maurice should eat, how he should react to what she said, what should happen if she saw him continuing in the same manner). Her request that he respond without being defensive had the effect of making him feel that he could not respond at all except to say he would try to comply—which was itself a conflict-avoidant move because he hoped by agreeing to change he could end the conversation.

When Beth raised the issue of Maurice's interrupting and self-referencing at a different time, things went much better. In that case, Maurice acknowledged what Beth was saying, suggested that they may have different styles of communicating, and said that he would really try to do better. He also *invited* her ongoing feedback (which she gave).

Why did this second attempt at engagement turn out more constructively? Maurice may have been in a more receptive mood, and this issue may have been less toxic to him. In addition, however, it is likely that a more effective integration of avoidance and engagement occurred. Beth succeeded in raising the issue in a focused way that did not seem to invoke Maurice's character, personality, or culture.

It's not easy to find that "sweet spot" where we can bring up something important without provoking an avoidant response. Finding that spot inevitably requires avoiding some elements of the conflict and focusing on others. Hard though this may be, it is essential to constructive engagement. Much of this is accomplished through the nuances of what is said and through the affect and the nonverbal communication that accompanies direct messages. We can think this through, plan it, and be sensitive to the responses we are likely to receive, but because so much of what happens is inevitably spontaneous (and has to be if it is to be authentic), we can go only so far in intentionally working with this dynamic.

Emotional Elements of Avoidance and Engagement

Both the poker incident and the communication between Maurice and Beth involved significant interaction between the behavioral, emotional, and cognitive aspects of this duality. I believe the reason I still remember the poker incident so well is that I did not succeed in avoiding the conflict itself—only its behavioral manifestation. I ended up far more emotionally engaged than I might have been had we not resorted to such stark avoidant behaviors. And my emotional engagement with this issue had a significant impact on my relationship with John. Perhaps John sensed that something was off, which could have contributed to our changing interaction. Maurice and Beth engaged in behavior that, on the surface, was classic constructive engagement behavior, but despite his words, Maurice experienced a strong emotional pull toward avoidance. So behavior notwithstanding, his predominant approach was avoidant.

The distinction between avoidance and engagement breaks down when we look at the emotional dimension. The more Maurice felt an intense emotional pull toward avoidance, the more engaged he became. The less intense the pull toward avoidance, the less engaged disputants tend to be. The emotional elements are not independent of the behavioral ones. Our emotional take on a conflict influences our behavior, and vice versa—but not always in a straightforward way. Sometimes the very intensity of our emotional involvement is an inducement to avoid behaviors that might lead to more interaction about the conflict. At other times, our emotional involvement precipitates engagement behavior. Beth was so upset by Maurice's manners that she felt she had to do something. This had been a concern of hers for quite a while, and her emotional involvement with this issue was increasing as time went on. She felt impelled, perhaps even *obligated*, to raise the issue.

Frequently, our emotional involvement pushes us both to engage and disengage at the same time. People in divorce mediations are often so emotionally involved in a conflict that they want to run out of the room and end all contact, yet they are also driven to spend a great deal of time dealing with the conflict, to raise issues repeatedly, and to bring up a wide variety of related challenges. In other words, they want to avoid and engage simultaneously. When an emotional reaction is triggered, people's responses are often spontaneous and inconsistent. For example, consider this workplace interchange that was described to me in a mediation (I have reconstructed the dialogue):

Jennifer: (*the supervisor, on arriving at work in the morning and passing Amy, who is sitting at her desk*) Good morning, Amy.
Amy says nothing, does not look up.
Jennifer: I said, "Good morning!"
Amy grunts and still does not look up.
Jennifer: What gives, Amy?
Amy: OK, OK! Good morning. Are you happy? Now you can go into your office, shut your door, and ignore us for the rest of the day like you usually do.
Jennifer: That's unfair. Why are you always so grumpy with me? Will you get over it? I am now your supervisor not your enemy. Stop treating me like one.
Amy: Just leave me alone, and cut all the "let's pretend to be friendly" crap.
Jennifer: I am not going to be talked to like this.
Amy: Then stopped acting like you care when you don't.
Jennifer writes up a disciplinary note. Amy files a grievance. I mediate.

Amy was sitting on a lot of anger. In one respect, she engaged in a series of avoidant moves. At first, she did not respond to Jennifer—and when she did, she basically said, "Go away." But she could not help but give voice to what she was feeling, at least in part, which was a move toward engaging. However, she did it in a way that was also in part a further attempt to push Jennifer away. We deliver messages of this nature, which say, in fact, "We have a conflict and I am very angry; now leave me alone," all the time. It is sometimes the stock and trade of parent-adolescent interactions. Statements like this, which give expression to the underlying emotional pulls toward both avoidance and engagement, make it difficult to do *either* effectively. They raise the conflict, sometimes very clearly and dramatically, but they also imply that the conflict will only get worse if the interaction continues, and therefore it should end. They are in part a form of "avoidance by escalation" (Mayer 2009). But at the same time, this may also be a step toward engagement. Jennifer and Amy did eventually have a frank and productive discussion of their working relationship, but not until reprimands and grievances had been filed and an intermediary was brought in.

Jennifer's action also included components of both avoidance and engagement. She asked Amy what was going on, but she never suggested that they sit down and really try to communicate about it. In fact, Amy's issue was in large part about Jennifer's avoidant behavior. She saw the superficially nice greeting as an example of a phony engagement that masked an avoidance of meaningful interaction. Interchanges of this nature had been going on for a while, and it is not clear why this one led to the reprimand and grievance. Those were also both avoidant and engaging moves. They led to the next step and ultimately to a constructive interaction, but in and of themselves, they were taking the issue away from a direct communication, perhaps to an emotionally safer format.

Grievance procedures and other formal systems of interaction can be understood in part as efforts to promote certain types of conflict engagement while avoiding others. Sometimes they provide constructive forums for the integration of avoidance and engagement, but often they are institutionalized mechanisms for avoiding the more serious issues. In many of the workplace grievances I have mediated, the issue that has been grieved, such as overtime or job assignment, functions as a surrogate for concerns about performance, respect, communication, and fairness. But grievances are about rights and obligations under a contract or established rules and procedures; therefore, people often have to express more fundamental issues in terms of their symptoms.

Low levels of emotional involvement also have an important effect on how people approach conflict. To avoid engaging thoroughly, it would seem useful not to care much about a conflict, relationship, or issue. And often that is the case—but not always. Though low emotional engagement might make it easier to take up an issue, it can also push others to increase the intensity with which they present an issue to try to provoke an emotional response. Sometimes, the only way to maintain an emotionally disengaged stance is to engage in a conflictual interaction. We frequently see variations on this in family conflict. One party is extremely insistent on dealing with an issue; the other is not so eager to do this, but if the other wants to get the first party "off his back" and not get emotionally engaged, it may be easier to address the issue than to ignore it.

Each disputant's emotional stance is profoundly affected by the others and can change readily and often. People experience complicated patterns of emotional engagement and disengagement throughout the course of a conflict, which are intertwined with their behaviors in complex ways. Sometimes the behavioral and emotional dimensions are in sync with each other, but often they seem to be pulling people in opposite directions.

Attitudinal Aspects of Avoidance and Engagement

How we understand and think about avoidance and engagement constitutes the third dimension. Although the terminology of avoidance and engagement may not be familiar to most people, the concepts are. We all know expressions like "backing off," "turning the other cheek," "grabbing the bull by the horns," "letting sleeping dogs lie," and "rushing in where angels fear to tread." These metaphors indicate how we think about the pulls to avoid and engage. When we listen to the stories people tell about their disputes, we find that a significant element of their narratives is about engaging or avoiding conflict. For example, consider this story (my paraphrasing) told by a manager involved in a painful conflict with a contractor:

> Paul and I used to be very close. We have worked together on many projects, we've had dinner in each other's homes, and I have thrown a lot of work his way. Then, all of a sudden, something went wrong. The only thing that I am aware of happening is that I had to reject a couple of expenses he submitted because of company policy. I explained the policy to him, and I wish I could have approved them, but I really had no choice. He was obviously angry, and now he won't talk to me, answer my e-mails, or return my phone calls. I have asked to talk. I am not sure if I should apologize to him (and I don't know for what), wait for him to come around, offer to travel to his office (in another state), or tell him to go to hell. I don't deserve to be treated this way. And he is the one who submitted the inflated expenses.

The manager was clearly feeling hurt, angry, and powerless to make things better. Her narrative was in large part about Paul's conflict avoidance, but she wavered between options in considering how to respond: wanting to go out of her way to engage with Paul, wanting to give Paul time so that constructive engagement might become more likely, avoiding the conflict by not bringing it up, taking false responsibility, or escalating.

The manager's comments highlight the role of apology in avoidance and engagement. We often use apologies to avoid engaging in conflict. It's as if we are saying, "I apologized, all right? Now can we talk about something else?" Such apologies are frequently counterproductive and end up escalating a conflict. For an apology to be meaningful, it has to invite further engagement. The message needs to be, in part, "I am sorry, and if you are willing, I would like to talk with you about this further."

How we understand and think about the avoidance–engagement duality is present in virtually every conflict narrative or dramatization of conflict. Let's look at three archetypical narratives about avoidance and engagement:

- *I turned the other cheek.* Or as Thomas Jefferson (1905) said, "When angry count to ten before you speak. If very angry, count to one hundred."

  The narrative suggested here is, "I tried and tried and tried to avoid conflict. The more it escalated, the more I stayed calm." One common assumption is that if we have done all we can to avoid a conflict, then the conflict is neither our fault nor our responsibility. Another assumption is that avoiding conflict is a morally superior approach and that by avoiding we are "taking the high road."

- *I stepped up to the plate.* Or as Ronald Reagan (1982) said, "Peace is not absence of conflict; it is the ability to handle conflict by peaceful means."

  This is the engagement narrative. The assumption here is that constructive engagement is a morally superior approach and that conflict isn't the problem, but rather how we engage in it. This is the primary narrative of our field, put forth by numerous trainers, writers, and conflict specialists who suggest that conflict is an inevitable, essential, and even beneficial part of life. Our task is therefore to learn to deal with it effectively and constructively rather than to avoid it. For example, see the Dorothy Thompson quote that opens this chapter. Or consider this from John Paul Lederach (2003): "Conflict flows from life.... Rather than seeing conflict as a threat, we can understand it as providing opportunities to grow and to increase our understanding of ourselves, of others, of our social structures." (p. 18)

- *I avoided the problem until I had to let them have it.* Or as Mark Twain (1999) said, "When angry, count to four; when very angry, swear."

  We can think of this as the "realist" narrative. You can avoid only so long before you have to react, at which point you should react with "both six-guns blazing." A child psychiatrist I once worked with used to admonish parents to avoid power struggles with their adolescents at all costs, but if they found themselves in one, to win at all costs. This harkens back to the tit-for-tat strategy discussed in chapter 2. The assumption here is that the best approach is to prevent or avoid conflict as long as possible, but when that is no longer feasible, to engage in a very powerful way. The implication is that if we have tried to avoid a conflict, we are in a morally superior position when we engage in it. Perhaps this is the underlying cultural assumption behind the "Make My Day" and "Stand Your Ground" laws that have been enacted in many states and which seek to protect people who have used force to defend themselves.

There are, of course, numerous possible narratives to explain our approach to a conflict, and we are not necessarily consistent in which we choose—nor do we necessarily stick with one throughout the course of a conflict. No single narrative is "right" or morally correct. Each has different implications for how we understand and manage the pulls toward engaging in and avoiding conflict.

As with the emotional and behavioral dimension, the attitudinal dimension—reflected in the narratives we tell ourselves and others—is neither simple nor straightforward. And our understanding of our own choices and approach to conflict is not necessarily consistent with what we do or how we feel. Our story may follow along from our behavior or emotions (and we may seek to justify these). We may attempt to rewrite the history of how we behaved or felt. Our narratives may lead us to change our behavior and even to begin to feel differently about a conflict. We often recast our narratives, sometimes almost continuously, throughout the life of a conflict to account for our evolving feelings and actions.

I am not suggesting that we do not have a predominant tendency in how we approach a conflict. We may try with all of our might to avoid being part of a conflict or to put considerable efforts into engaging in the conflict. We may work very hard to direct the conflict toward an area where we think engagement will be productive and avoid other areas (e.g., focus on parenting schedules, avoid religion). But the idea that we have a simple, clear approach to engaging or avoiding complex conflict is misleading. Over the course of our involvement in a conflict, we continually recalibrate just how we engage, and we do this along all three dimensions—behavioral, emotional, and cognitive. This is one of the most difficult challenges people face in conflict. Therefore, one of the most important responsibilities we take on as conflict interveners is to help disputants navigate this dilemma effectively.

Avoiding and Preventing, Engaging and Escalating

As the examples and discussion in this chapter suggest, we often have inconsistent and even contradictory views about avoiding and engaging in conflict. Sometimes we see one approach as positive, sometimes the other. This becomes evident when we consider two related concepts: prevention and escalation. We tend to understand and value these concepts differently than we do avoidance and engagement—but how different are they?

Preventing conflict seems like a worthy goal, but avoiding it often seems less so. Whether prevention is a truly constructive effort depends on whether a conflict *has* genuinely been prevented, and whether it *should have* been. It is often easier to prevent a conflict than to resolve it, especially if the preventive framework deals with the essential issues. The establishment of the United Nations, prenuptial agreements, partnering processes between contractor and client in large construction disputes, community involvement efforts to discuss transportation or other infrastructure proposals, and labor management consultation groups are all examples of often successful preventive efforts.

One durable example of a successful preventative effort in international relations was the establishment of the Outer Space Treaty ("Treaty on Principles Governing the Activities of States in the Exploration and Use of Outer Space, Including the Moon and Other Celestial Bodies," 1967), which was initially ratified by the United States, the United Kingdom, and the Soviet Union in 1967 after about a decade of negotiations. The treaty prohibited the introduction of nuclear weapons or other weapons of mass destruction into space and prohibited attempts to colonize any celestial body. This treaty was ratified during one of the most difficult periods of the Cold War, and the countries involved have adhered to it for more than forty-five years.

If genuine, conflict prevention is usually a worthwhile goal. However, some conflicts ought *not* to be prevented, because they become the crucible for important changes. Preventable conflicts often represent more substantial conflicts that are not so easily prevented. Averting preventable conflicts may be a positive move, as long as it does not mean that more significant conflicts are allowed to fester. In other words, preventing one element of a conflict may contribute to the escalation of another. Assessing this is no simple matter, as I observed in a discussion of a proposal to build a dam in the Colorado Rockies.

> A number of years back, I was part of a team hired to facilitate a series of public discussions about how to mitigate the potential impacts of a dam that was being proposed in Colorado. The organizers felt that this was a unique opportunity to reach consensus about the issue of mitigation before the conflict became so intense and positions so polarized that discussing anything other than whether or not to build the dam would be impossible. Several of us raised questions about how a consideration of mitigation could possibly be separated from the question of whether or not to build the dam to begin with, or the broader issue of how to meet the water needs of the heavily populated Front Range of Colorado. The organizers felt these issues had to be separated if we were to make any progress—and they were clear about the focus of this meeting in the publicity for it.
>
> Not surprisingly, the public felt differently. Many, if not most, participants, particularly residents of the mountain communities where the proposed dam would be located and environmentalists, objected to the separation. They saw it as an effort to avoid the larger issue and perhaps an attempt to subvert the movement that was building in opposition to the dam.

Perhaps these meetings accomplished something useful. In retrospect, however, it seemed that the effort to engage in one issue while avoiding the larger conflict aroused suspicion of consensus-building efforts on the broader problem. In the end, permitting agencies scratched the proposal to build the dam and requested the development of alternative approaches to supplying the area's water needs.

In the Outer Space Treaty, even though the deeper issue was the arms race and the Cold War, putting parameters on militarizing space defined an important limit on the arms race. The challenge of preventing the weaponization of space continues, but this treaty has provided an important framework. As in this case, most effective prevention efforts are intended to avoid future conflict, but they are not simply an effort at conflict avoidance. Indeed, none of them would have occurred without some significant conflict engagement efforts. The Outer Space Treaty required that the United States and the USSR take on a potential conflict that could have been sidestepped at that time. Initial efforts foundered because of a desire by the USSR to include other issues, such as the deployment of short- and intermediate-range missiles in foreign countries. Eliminating this requirement—and thereby avoiding that particular conflict—allowed the parties to continue negotiating the treaty.

If prevention always involves an integration of avoidance and engagement, escalation does this as well. We seldom think of escalation as conflict avoidance, nor do we think of it as constructive conflict engagement, but it is often both. People often escalate an issue to avoid having to deal with it. Those opposing negotiations in the Middle East (or even those who ostensibly support them but are not really eager to participate) have often escalated disputes to forestall a conflict engagement process. When a business partner, spouse, or teenager storms out of a room after loudly and angrily protesting about something that has been said, we can see this as fight as a means of flight—an effort to avoid dealing with the conflict by becoming belligerent (Mayer 2012a). But this act also forces attention to an issue that the organization or family may have been carefully avoiding. In other words, escalation may be necessary to foment a genuine engagement effort.

Part of our responsibility as conflict interveners is to help people develop effective means of escalating an issue in a way that promotes a constructive engagement process, *without* providing a mechanism or an excuse for others to avoid the issue. Escalation is an important mechanism for *both* avoidance and engagement, often simultaneously.

The Ethical Challenge

Finding our way through the maze of avoidance and engagement is not just a strategic challenge but an ethical one as well. Some of the most difficult decisions we make in our lives are about whether to take on morally demanding conflicts. And some of our biggest moral failures occur when we don't address these courageously. An ethical approach to conflict sometimes requires us to turn away from a conflict, and sometimes it means we must dive into it.

This is the dilemma involved in using military power to interfere with the actions of abusive governments—such as Syria, Libya, Iraq, Rwanda, Kosovo, and Bosnia. We have an obligation as societies to take *some* action—but what? Avoiding is in some ways essential if we are not to bring warfare with all of its unintended consequences to the people we are trying to protect. Yet engaging is essential as well if we are to find a way to protect the vulnerable and counteract horrendous abuses of power. Finding the right combination of avoidance and engagement is the key to effective and ethical foreign policy and to finding a constructive way to use our power. There is no algorithm, checklist, or set of rules that can identify the optimum way to integrate avoidance and engagement. Sometimes what appears as inconsistencies in our decision making about the use of force is a reflection of the different calculations we make about avoidance and engagement under varying circumstances.

We frequently face this challenge on a personal and professional level. We encounter a moral challenge when trying to figure out how to deal with someone who is in denial about their use of alcohol or who is avoiding significant mental health issues. Perhaps the most serious challenge we face is deciding whether or how to intervene when people are being victimized. We are bound to encounter abusers and victims in our work as conflict specialists, but also in our communities, families, and friendships. Sexual assault and domestic violence, for example, have been tolerated and many perpetrators have acted with impunity, because so many of us have decided not to get involved in a conflict that we can avoid.

The moral dilemma is clear—we must not avoid, but we can't always engage effectively. So what do we do when we hear allegations of sexual abuse against a friend, a family member, a colleague, or someone we have admired? Do we stay out of what is "not our business"? Do we feel an obligation to support our friend or relative? Or do we recognize that sexual abuse is a systemic problem and that victims are often not believed, despite consistent and credible evidence that false accusations are extremely few and far between (FBI 1997; Starmer 2013; Lonsway, Archambault, and Lisak 2009)? As easy or tempting as it might be to hide behind uncertainty and loyalty, doing so revictimizes those who have suffered sexual assault.

When Woody Allen's adopted daughter Dylan Farrow wrote an open letter in the *New York Times*, detailing her accusations of sexual abuse perpetrated by her father (http://kristof.blogs.nytimes .com/2014/02/01/an-open-letter-from-dylan-farrow/?_php=true& _type=blogs&_r=0), she specifically asked some actors who had worked with him how they would have felt if she were their child. Alec Baldwin tweeted in response to a question about this: "You are mistaken if you think there is a place for me, or any outsider, in this family's issue" (Gibson 2014).

Is Baldwin's response the right one? Or are we collectively abandoning victims, in fact participating in continuing to victimize them, by avoiding the conflict in this way? Victims of child abuse, domestic violence, rape, and incest are often revictimized by others' avoidance—individuals as well as institutions. We have seen examples of this with the sexual abuse scandals in the Catholic Church, the BBC, and the military. In such circumstances, we have a moral obligation to confront the avoidance of those who are in a position to protect the vulnerable.

We must check our instincts simply to avoid when we encounter issues of this import in the course of our professional or personal lives. We should not reflexively hide behind our supposed neutrality or our stated desire not to intrude in other people's lives. This was the rationale of thirty years ago, when many chose to look the other way when there was any suspicion of domestic abuse. But here too, we have to decide what to engage and what to avoid. This is not simply a matter of facing the particular stories of Dylan Farrow and others like her, but of facing the pervasive culture of misogyny that we are all part of.

There is often no simple road to engagement, but we have a moral obligation to find a way to get past the choice of avoiding because we don't want to interfere on the one hand and rushing to judgment when we do not know the facts on the other. This is a challenge we all face. The road through these choices is not easy, but it's one that we must navigate with courage and integrity.

The Conflict Specialist's Challenge

Our essential goal in working with others on avoidance and engagement is to help them understand the nature of their own approach and how they might best align it with their goals in conflict. This requires that we help people look at how they are characterizing their approach to engaging and avoiding conflict, and how accurately this narrative reflects their actions and feelings. People are often unaware of their own as well as others' narratives, but we can help to raise their awareness by reflecting on what we are hearing, the behavior we are seeing, and the emotions being expressed.

An essential part of our role is to hold up a mirror to disputants so that they can better reflect on the approach that they are taking.

For this to be effective, it has to be nonjudgmental. We need to proceed with a deep respect for each disputant's right to avoid and engage in conflict as they deem appropriate. We may think that people are making self-destructive decisions about avoiding and engaging, and we may want to urge them to alter their approach, but we have to begin with respect for disputants' assessment of their own needs. We may think it is best to be transparent, to act earlier rather than later, to be direct, and to look for mutually beneficial outcomes, and we may be right—but not necessarily. Sometimes, people's best alternative is to avoid a conflict, and sometimes the best way for them to do so is by escalating it in what appears to be a nonconstructive manner. I have on occasion worked with people who needed to end a business or personal relationship in which they felt trapped, and they chose to do so by becoming angry and accusatory and then storming out. To me, this usually seemed a mistake. But their emotional engagement with the issue and their fears about the future have sometimes meant that this was the only way they could leave. It's not what I would have hoped for, but it may have been the only way they could find the resolve to end a relationship that was no longer working for them.

Of course, as discussed earlier, sometimes we face a responsibility more important than our commitment to client autonomy, especially if there is abuse or violence involved or if vulnerable third parties are affected. The need to respect the approach clients take, while simultaneously attending to our ethical responsibilities, is a manifestation of the dilemma of avoidance and engagement that is especially relevant to the conflict specialist.

Another challenge for interveners is to help disputants align their approach with their goals, hopes, and expectations. We do this as coaches by reflecting on the approach disputants seem prone to take, asking them to consider how well this is likely to achieve their goals, and helping disputants consider alternative approaches.

As advocates, we work to make sure that the voice we provide, which involves its own integration of avoidance and engagement, reflects the needs and desires of the people we are representing. We do this as third parties as well, but in that role, we also focus on helping disputants work out a mutual pattern of avoidance and engagement that helps them interact effectively. Sometimes this means facilitating a direct conversation about exactly this: which elements of the conflict we should raise and how to raise them, and which elements we should avoid. Sometimes it means supporting parties in avoiding a direct conversation until they are ready and the timing seems more appropriate.

We also try to help disputants learn from their own experiences. How has their approach worked? Were they able to engage with the issues they wanted to address and avoid others? What might they do differently next time? On this dilemma, as well as others, we want to help disputants reflect on their experiences so that they can adopt a more nuanced way of thinking about how to approach conflict.

Reflections from Practice

I believe that I am a conflict avoider, and I sometimes think that is part of what brought me to this field. I was a student in the sixties and an activist in the civil rights movement, the anti-war movement—and lots of other movements. I was often outspoken and not infrequently in trouble. Although age and the kind of work I have done have certainly mellowed me a bit, many of the values and personality characteristics that motivated me then still motivate me now. I continue to be an activist in spirit and an avoider by nature.

There seem to me to be two primary reasons to look at myself in this way. First, while I am *emotionally* an avoider of conflict, I have been less of an avoider on the behavioral dimension. I dislike interpersonal conflict, but I seem to have had no shortage of these conflicts over the course of my life. My behavioral and emotional approaches have often been out of sync. Second, I often ended up in the position of being the negotiator. This is a role that requires engagement but gives plenty of space to avoid as well. Despite the fervor and often unwarranted certainty I displayed as a young activist, I have often been able to speak to people with whom I had profound disagreements, and they to me. Not always, but often enough. I believe this trait thrust me into several leadership positions, because I was seen as someone who did not readily compromise but who could still talk with others. Two memories of incidents from that time illustrate this.

The first occurred in 1967 when students at Oberlin College conducted a sit-in to prevent military recruiters from operating on campus. I was an active organizer of the sit-in, as well as the president of the student government, so I ended up being one of two students to negotiate with the administration while the sit-in was taking place. From what I could see throughout this process, the president of the college was extremely irate and on the verge of completely losing his temper. So I communicated instead with his assistant and with the dean of students. We carried out these discussions under a threat of immediate expulsion of all students who were interfering with college operations—including me. Somehow, we were able to work out an agreement accepted by both those engaged in the sit-in and the leadership of the college. I maintained my position about the issue but ended up becoming a close friend of the dean of students. We continue to be friends to this day, almost fifty years later.

The second incident is about Fred, a student with whom I had previously had a very loud, angry interchange in which I behaved badly (yelled, put him down, attributed motives—in short, all the things I work with people on not doing). He had behaved much better and at the same time had adamantly maintained his point of view. One day, after a meeting in which he had gotten into a loud argument with several of my friends (but not with me) about the war, we found ourselves talking to each other. I was in a consid-erably better frame of mind this time, and I mainly listened to him as he talked about how hard it was for him to be treated the way he was. I tried to explain to him how others felt but was also empa-thetic to his situation. He turned to me and said, "I don't know why you are the person I am talking to about this, but you are." I didn't know why, either, but we did communicate, which helped calm down a volatile situation.

I do not point to these interchanges as examples of effective conflict engagement by any means. I view my actions in those days with mixed feelings. However, they do illustrate my experi-ence from early on with the complex interaction between being conflict-averse and conflict-prone, between avoiding and engaging, and between our behavioral, emotional, and cognitive approaches. They show how being both conflict-prone and conflict-averse sometimes has its advantages.

As a conflict specialist, I quickly realized how painful it can be to be buffeted by the twin pulls toward avoidance and engagement. During one of the first divorce mediations I ever did, one of the disputants turned to me after we had reached a tentative agreement and said, "I know I could do much better in court, but I am going to sign this anyway." I immediately called for a private meeting and questioned her about this. She gave me a tutorial in the wisdom of avoidance. She needed to leave town, end the relationship, and move on emotionally. Avoiding some of the remaining issues made a lot of sense to her. I privately did not think she was getting that bad a deal, but that really was not the point. She felt she had not done very well in some respects, but when she considered her entire situation, she felt she had achieved the very best outcome she could hope for.

Over the years, I have worked with many disputants who have agreed about only one thing—that they never want to be in the same room with each other again—and they have often chosen to work on agreements that were primarily intended to accomplish just that. Every other issue was secondary and often left unresolved. One of the most dramatic experiences I have had with this, which I have described elsewhere (Mayer 2012a), occurred when I was asked by two adult siblings to facilitate a meeting in which they said goodbye to each other forever. The issues were complicated and so were the emotions—but this is what they both wanted to do. Rather than deal with the negativity of trying to work on their relationship, they wanted closure. It seemed to me similar in some ways to a last meeting between a parent and child before the child is given up for adoption. I challenged each of them during preliminary conversations as to whether this was *really* what they wanted, but they were adamant. So we had a very intense meeting in which they expressed to each other some appreciation for better times but also said why they wanted to end their relationship. It was a difficult but very moving meeting.

Often the most difficult decision people have to make about mediation, negotiation, or other dialogue processes is whether to enter into them at all. This is in large part a decision about the degree to which disputants want to engage in or avoid conflict. Sometimes the choice to mediate represents a clear-cut desire to enter into a constructive engagement effort, but it is usually more complicated than that. The alternative to mediation is seldom simply avoidance. Often the alternatives that disputants might be considering are direct negotiations, lawyer-conducted settlement efforts, litigation, or public protests. Sometimes disputants see mediation as a means of avoiding conflict, dancing around the real issue, and "making nice" instead of taking decisive action. My conversations with people about whether to participate in mediation (or any similar effort at direct dialogue) are therefore inevitably discussions of both avoidance and engagement. I came to realize early in my mediation practice that my job was not to sell mediation but to help people think through what element of the conflict they wanted to engage in, what they wanted to avoid, and how the alternative processes available to them matched up with what they wanted in this regard.

The more I conducted these conversations with an open mind as to whether mediation or dialogue were optimal approaches, the more we were able to focus on how to make the process work. This consideration of "how," would then help them decide whether it made sense to undertake such an effort, but only if I did not use the "how" discussion as a means of selling a process. If I did not have a position on "whether to mediate," I could focus much more effectively with parties on how, with whom, when, where, and with what focus. This process of mutual education increased my credibility as a third party and allowed disputants to own the "whether" question. As a result, if they chose to enter into whichever process we were considering, they were more likely to do so with a constructive attitude and less likely to expect me to "prove" to them that this was a good idea. This was a critical element in the work I did with Joaquin and Norbert:

> Joaquin was the director of a small social agency, and Norbert was a long-term agency employee. Joaquin had suspended Norbert for two weeks because of reports that he had come to work inebriated, a charge that Norbert denied—but he decided not to contest the action. The president of the board of directors suggested mediation, because she felt the tension was so high between the two that the whole situation was likely to erupt again.
>
> I called each of them to discuss the possibility of mediation. Joaquin did not feel he could refuse because the board president had recommended it, but he felt not much good would come of this as long as Norbert denied his substance abuse problems. Norbert was reluctant as well. He felt that Joaquin had made his mind up about him and nothing he could say, short of falsely admitting to a problem he did not believe he had, would make any difference. On the other hand, he did not know how he could continue to work at the

agency, where he had been employed for three years, under the circumstances.

I told each of them that I had no idea if mediation was the right choice. I suggested that it depended on whether they wanted my assistance in saying something directly to each other and hearing what the other had to say, and I did not know if that would be effective or wise. I then asked each of them to tell me what they were hoping for about their working relationship with each other. Each of their initial responses was in essence that the other person should change. I suggested that I did not think that was a likely outcome of mediation per se. More likely was the possibility that they would each better understand where the other was coming from and perhaps reach some agreement on communications, job expectations, and next steps. They each knew this, without my having to say it, but nonetheless it helped them to hear it from me.

In the end, Norbert agreed to try to mediate because he did not believe he had a good alternative. Joaquin agreed to mediate because he felt he had to honor the request of the board president. I expressed some misgivings about them going into this without a clear sense from both of them that it might be useful, but I agreed to work with them anyway.

Perhaps the most useful aspect of the meeting was a discussion of the concerns about alcohol. Norbert said he actually appreciated Joaquin's concern, and that if he were the director and had a similar concern he would want to deal with it directly. However, he maintained that he did not have an issue with alcohol and that the suspension was unfair. Joaquin said that he thought that Norbert was in denial, and that he did not realize how much his work was affected. Something had to change, Joaquin said, but he also agreed to give Norbert another chance. They also agreed to meet frequently to discuss how things were going. They engaged in a direct discussion of alcohol, up to a point. But they avoided quite a bit as well. For example, Joaquin did not talk about the numerous complaints he had received from other staff and some clients, and Norbert did not go into any detail about his actual use of alcohol or other substances. I opened the door for such a discussion, but they both chose to stay away from these areas. I do not know how things went after that, and to this day I am not entirely sure whether the mediation was helpful. My sense at the time was that they had started a good conversation, but they had also pulled their punches.

Many of the experiences I have had as an intervener have made clear the point that a healthy amount of avoidance is necessary to make most conflict engagement efforts work, and that sometimes our job is to help people avoid dealing with a conflict as best they can. However, I have made some of the worst errors of my conflict intervention practice when I have tried to prevent what I believed to be a destructive effort at taking on a conflict. Often my intervention was intended to disrupt a personal attack or hostile interchange, but the effect was to interfere with someone's effort to tell others exactly what they thought. One example that I often think about occurred when an environmentalist started loudly lambasting a developer for not caring about nature, the planet, people's health, or community, and instead caring only about money. I intervened—and I think I needed to—but instead of inviting the environmentalist to take a moment to collect his thoughts and express his opinion (and inviting the developer to do the same), I summarized a couple of his key points and moved the discussion forward. Rather than helping him say what he really wanted to say, I lost a potentially valuable opportunity for a frank interchange.

In general, when I have been more focused on making sure that people said things in a calm and rational manner than on helping them to express the intensity of their feelings, I have lost an opportunity that sometimes does not come again very quickly.

Of course, it is not always wise to let people vent or attack each other. Instead, our task is to help them say the most difficult things they have to say, with the intensity with which they feel them, and as much as possible in the manner they want to say them, but to do so in a way that opens up communication rather than shutting it down. Encouraging direct and open exchange about important issues and intense feelings in a way that maintains the personal dignity and emotional safety of all involved is the fundamental challenge that peace builders and conflict interveners face. This is why the interaction between avoidance and engagement is so central to our work.

chapter five

principle and compromise

Principle without compromise is empty. Compromise without principle is blind.

Stephen B. Smith, "A Lincoln for Our Time"

If you're a man of principle, compromise is a bit of a dirty word.

Former Vice President Dick Cheney, "In the Darkness of Dick Cheney"

One of the most misleading lines we hear in conflict is, "I can't compromise on a matter of principle." Or as Thomas Jefferson is reputed to have said, "In matters of style, swim with the current. In matters of principle, stand like a rock." Although a nice sentiment, this is an unrealistic and often self-defeating guide to action. One cannot be truly principled without sometimes compromising in very significant ways. Moreover, the value of principles in our lives is to guide us in making the essential compromises that life requires.

Compromise is necessary in all parts of our lives—as parents, spouses, leaders, advocates, teachers, writers, scholars, and, of course, as conflict specialists. But without the guiding filter that our values and principles offer, the compromises that we make are neither effective nor wise. The complex interplay among principles, values, compromise, and pragmatism is a familiar concept to students of history, political science, and ethics. It is also at the heart of what conflict specialists face as we help people navigate their way through conflicts. As interveners, we are constantly working with disputants to consider the compromises that working through conflict demands, while helping them articulate and adhere to their underlying values at the same time. Sometimes those values suggest that no immediate compromise is advisable, or even that no current communication with an adversary is likely to be fruitful, but values are seldom promoted by a steadfast refusal to compromise, even on matters that are very close to the core of a person's beliefs. On the other hand, as important as compromise is to advancing values and satisfying interests, the most important sources of power any of us have in conflict are the clarity and conviction we have about the principles that govern our lives. Unless we appreciate, respect, and embrace these principles, we sacrifice something essential about our identity and therefore our capacity to achieve our most important life goals.

Compromising on principles is widely seen as a sign of moral and personal weakness, while being unwilling to compromise is frequently viewed as a sign of personal rigidity, arrogance, and immaturity. Depending on our views on a particular issue and the nature of the compromise being promoted, we may see compromise as a sign of wisdom or weakness, progress or regression, practicality or naiveté, leadership or abdication. In most protracted conflicts, disputants at some point have to learn to find their way between the seemingly contradictory calls to stand by principles or to compromise in the name of practicality. How we as conflict interveners help disputants navigate the complicated terrain of compromise, values, principle, and practicality is a fourth major paradox that we face.

Principle Without Compromise Is Seldom Principled

Like lawyers and conflict specialists, social workers often function at the crux of unresolved societal value conflicts. For example, they have to contend with the competing beliefs that the state should generally not interfere in family life, but that protecting children from abuse and maltreatment is a fundamental responsibility of society. They also have to deal with expectations that they support parents as they struggle to overcome deficiencies, but they must also move quickly to find stable and suitable homes for children whose parents do not seem able to provide appropriate care for them. These are important principles, embedded in state and federal laws, but there is an inescapable tension between them. When we add the consideration of cultural norms about parenting, the intervention challenge becomes even more complex. A number of conflict intervention strategies, such as child protection mediation and family group conferencing, have been developed to help deal with these challenges. They inevitably contend with the demands of principle and the need for compromise, as they did when working with Maria and Ruth Ann in rural Alaska.

Sometimes it not only takes a village to raise a child; it takes a village to *protect* the child. Villages, however, are not recognized as caregivers in child welfare regulations.

Maria was a young single mother, an Alaska Native with a serious drinking problem, living in a small village in rural Alaska. When she was sober, she was an effective and loving parent, but she struggled with staying sober. Sometimes Ruth Ann, her eight-year-old daughter, would return from school to find her mother passed out. At other times, her mother was not at home at all and did not return for hours. Although this was not an everyday occurrence, it probably happened about once a month. When her mother was passed out or failed to return, Ruth Ann would go to her next-door neighbor who would take care of her until Maria sobered up and was able to attend to Ruth Ann.

Eventually, this situation came to the attention of the local health clinic, who reported it to the child welfare agency as required by law. A dependency petition was filed and Maria was given a treatment plan that required she receive substance abuse treatment, regular testing, and parenting counseling. At first, Ruth Ann remained in the home with Maria, but after Maria twice failed to show up for counseling and drug tests, Ruth Ann was placed in the nearest available foster home. Efforts to find a placement in her village did not succeed because there were no licensed foster homes. Finding her a place with others in her family was also not possible, because Maria's family was scattered, not available, or not appropriate.

The nearest available home was near only by Alaskan standards, which made it very hard for Maria and Ruth Ann to maintain regular contact. Though she made some progress, Maria still had occasional relapses and felt overwhelmed by the demands of meeting the expectations set out in the treatment plan. Eventually, the strict timelines in child protection laws (enacted to make sure that children did not drift from one placement to the next without a stable, long-term living arrangement) required that a permanent placement be made, and Maria's parental rights were terminated. Ruth Ann was placed with a foster family who planned to adopt her, but by then she was twelve years old. She lost contact with her mother, her family, her village, and, to a large extent, her cultural roots.

This story, which is an amalgam of several cases about which I consulted, is a fairly typical one in child protection. Every principle that was applied here was reasonable. Steps were taken to make sure Ruth Ann was safe. The social agency was understandably concerned that Ruth Ann was returning home to a drunk or absent parent. Efforts were made to insure that the family's rights were respected. The treatment plan included elements intended to support Maria in her parenting role. Efforts were also made to keep Ruth Ann with her own family, or at least in a familiar cultural setting. Attention was given to the time it would take for Maria to complete her treatment plan and to include provisions to allow her the opportunity to show that she was able to resume functioning as an effective parent. However, limits were put on how long this effort would go on to ensure that Ruth Ann was not exposed to numerous placements and extended periods of instability.

A variety of conflict intervention strategies were used to try to resolve the dilemmas posed by this case—for example, family group conferencing and child protection mediation. But those involved faced the inexorable problem of the rigidity with which these principles are applied (and which, to a large extent, the law requires). The village's capacity to work as a support system, with the next-door neighbor's active involvement, was not a viable solution, because it violated too many important principles and the legal frameworks that are intended to enforce them. Perhaps Ruth Ann fared well with her foster-adoptive family, but the history of children of her age moving into an entirely new situation is not encouraging (Strijker, Knorth, and Knot-Dickscheit 2008; Stinehart, Scott, and Barfield 2012).

In working with situations like this, child protection mediators and other conflict interveners constantly face the challenge
of looking for flexibility in the midst of important, thoughtfully
crafted, yet often inflexible standards. The system's failure to build
in flexibility to compromise is one of the reasons that child protection interventions often protect the child's *physical* safety, but not
his or her *emotional* well-being.

In conflict practice, we face variations on this theme—when
the overly rigid application of important principles leads to undesirable and less than optimal outcomes. Consider the following, for
example:

- The need to offer victims of workplace harassment a safe
  and confidential mechanism for reporting their experience
  and the need to be able to marshal evidence to take decisive
  action against the perpetrators. The all-too-frequent result
  of this dilemma is that no decisive action is taken, so that
  the victim is forced to choose either to leave the workplace
  or to continue to work with the aggressor.

- The legitimate concerns about subjecting victims of
  domestic violence to mediation that have led many
  jurisdictions to adopt policies precluding mediation where
  there has been a history of abuse. This sometimes protects
  victims, but it can also prevent them from getting
  potentially helpful assistance in ending their relationships
  when the alternatives of litigation or lawyer-led negotiation
  are not necessarily any safer.

- The principle that we should neither bargain with terrorists
  nor allow them to pressure us into negotiations—and the
  reality that "terrorism" is a political and ideological framing,
  and the alternative to negotiations can be years of violence.

- The standard that mediators and other third parties should
  not be beholden to one party—and the frequent reality that

only one party can afford to pay for their services (e.g., a corporation or the government in a community dispute or the administration in a university conflict).

- Almost all significant legislative achievement (e.g., the Affordable Care Act, the annual budgets passed—or not passed—by Congress, the Farm Bill) involves significant compromises. Some of these have cut close to the bone of the essential values behind the legislation.

Whether we are disputants or conflict interveners, we encounter the tension between principle and practicality all the time. We want to stick with our principles and be consistent, but we also want to make a difference. Our ethical standards are important to us, but sometimes they lock us into destructive conflict that does not further our values. At times, the principles that guide us as conflict interveners, such as neutrality, independence, and confidentiality, prevent us from providing the genuine assistance that people need. Unless we find a way through this dilemma, we may find that our principles point us in exactly the wrong direction. Or as a teacher of mine used to say, "Never let your values get in the way of doing what is right." The dilemma that these and countless other examples present is that principle without compromise is not really principled. Principles that are not grounded in the reality of the world we live in and the context in which we work, or that are not flexible enough to adapt to change, are ineffectual guides to decision making.

We tend to understand our principles, or values (terms I am using interchangeably), as *absolute* commitments that must either be upheld or sacrificed. In conflict, this often translates into an unwillingness to consider partial solutions, a resistance to negotiate with those we dislike and distrust, or a reluctance to question our own actions or narratives. To approach conflict with creativity and openness, disputants have to take a more flexible view about the nature of our principles. This means that we need to help people look at principles as existing in a context, often in complex inter-action with other principles and within an evolving reality.

I am not advocating that principles should be creatures of circumstance, with no core meaning or universal implications. Instead, I am suggesting that principles can be effective as guides only if we understand them in context and in relation to the principles of those with whom we are in conflict. The context is what requires people to compromise, but the compromise should always honor the essential intention and foundation of our most important principles. If disputants are to make even halting progress toward principled ends, they often have to compromise, sometimes on essential interests, while at the same time remaining steadfast in their commitment to their core principles.

To work with disputants as they struggle to find their way through this dilemma, we need to help them broaden their thinking in a way that allows their values to continue to guide them, but without preventing the creativity and flexibility that is essential for constructive engagement. To do this, we may think of principles in several ways:

- *A spectrum from foundational values to behavioral norms.* The more intense a conflict, the more likely people are to see every principle as essential to their identity and purpose in life and as a clear-cut issue of right or wrong. But often, our beliefs may be more accurately understood as *guidelines* for behavior that may not be universally applicable or foundational. In other words, underneath each principle is another principle, and the deeper we go, the less likely we are to be willing to compromise—but also the less likely we are to have to compromise to remain true to our values. While I might believe that children should not be exposed to parental conflict, and therefore as a matter of principle not share with them my disagreements with their mother, my more foundational norm is to provide children with a loving and nurturing home. If I have sometimes expressed frustration with my ex-spouse to my children, I may have violated behavioral guidelines but not necessarily my foundational norms. The distinction between these is often essential to helping parents work their way through conflict.

- *Existing at different levels of generality.* Some principles are couched in very specific language or meant to apply to a limited set of circumstances; others are framed in more general terms and meant for more universal application. Understanding the appropriate level of generality or specificity is often the key to achieving a more constructive approach to value disputes. For example, there is a difference between the very general belief in the "sanctity of life" and valuing people's right to "die with dignity," which applies to a more specific set of circumstances. I may broadly believe in "preserving the natural environment of our planet" and also believe in the value of protecting wetlands from destruction. Both of these may be important values to me, but they are not equivalent in the breadth of their scope.

- *Systemic and interactive in nature.* As opposed to thinking of principles as existing in a hierarchy of importance or as offering a clear guide to action, we can view our values as operating in dynamic and evolving interaction with each other. Our principles are often inconsistent, and they frequently operate in opposition to one other, as was the case in the child welfare example earlier. Furthermore, how we resolve the tensions between our own values at any given time is very much influenced by the set of principles brought to the table by those with whom we are in conflict. For example, I may believe in the sanctity of life and the importance of acting decisively in the face of genocide (e.g., in Rwanda or Bosnia), but I find myself in a disagreement with someone who is committed to human rights for all and is a principled pacifist. For both of us, there is a tension within our own system of beliefs, and how we handle these in interaction with each other is very much influenced by how the other approaches this.

When we work with disputants on finding a way to honor their principles as they grapple with the compromises they have to make to give these principles life, we inevitably encourage a more nuanced approach. In doing so, we often start by helping people articulate the beliefs that are affecting their approach to a conflict:

"I am their mother. If he can't take care of the children during his time with them, then he should turn to me, not to some babysitter who hardly knows them!" Andrea and Pablo had been divorced for two years, and although their agreement specified a shared parenting arrangement, Pablo had been the primary caregiver for their two young children (ages six and seven) while Andrea finished her university degree out of state. Now she was returning to the town where Pablo and the children lived and wanted to move immediately to an equal parenting arrangement. Pablo thought any change in living arrangements should be gradual, and he wanted the children to live with him during the school week. They came to mediation to resolve this issue, but what Andrea seemed most focused on was the after-school care that was being provided by Pablo's friend Naomi. Andrea insisted that she, the children's mother, be the afterschool provider as a matter of principle. This was further complicated because Andrea lived about an hour away from the school and the only

practical way of her providing after school care would
be in Pablo's home, which he was unwilling to allow.

At first I thought this issue was representative of
the broader question of living arrangements, but they
were able to reach an agreement about that fairly easily.
Though Andrea did not seem ready to take on a primary parenting role, she was adamant on the issue of
child care. I wondered if she was worried that Pablo
and Naomi might be more than friends, but this did
not seem to be the case. Andrea insisted that this was a
matter of principle, that it was just not "right" that they
should be with a babysitter instead of her, and that the
consequences of the current arrangement devalued her
role as a mother.

When I hear value-laden language like this, I
generally assume that people are expressing principles
that are important to them but that are limiting their
flexibility. I inquired about their concerns about after-
school arrangements. Pablo worried about boundaries,
sending confusing messages to the children, and
Andrea's presence in his life. Andrea reiterated that it
simply was not right for Pablo to be using a babysitter
(at any time, not just after school) if she were available.

It became clear to me that I had to focus on the
principle underlying her stance. I started using the language of values and asked her what her beliefs were
about parenting. Some were fairly standard—access to
both parents, security, love, consistency, and insulating
them from parental conflict. One principle, however,
jumped out at me. Andrea said, with considerable emotion, that "the most important thing is that the children
know that their parents really love them." How could
this be conveyed to them? Andrea said that parents
needed to show the children that they "would go out

of their way to be there for them." Taken in conjunction with her relative absence during the past couple of years, this seemed very poignant and opened up a whole new line of discussion, including a consideration of "making up for lost time" and "looking toward the future." Andrea could not give up the basic principle, but she was gradually able to land on a more general formulation of this (demonstrating commitment to the children), which enabled her to be more flexible about specific arrangements.

It is rare that one specific intervention makes all the difference in significant conflict interactions. It seemed to help to work with Andrea on the level of generality with which she understood the principle she was espousing; however, it was also important for her to look at her underlying system of values. This enabled her to understand the importance of focusing on the future and minimizing conflict, even though that required her to start rethinking her stance. No doubt it also helped to discuss her feelings about having been relatively absent during the past couple of years. Perhaps simply holding out for a while was a means of demonstrating her commitment to the children, and by honoring her principles in that way, she could then compromise. In the end, it seemed she realized that to "be there for her children" required that she compromise and, in particular, that she give up trying to make up for her past absence.

Principles Are Pragmatic

When I hear someone say, "Let's get real," I think, "I am about to hear a very self-serving version of reality." Disputants often try to corner the market on the right to articulate reality. But just like reality TV is not real, no one person's version of reality is truly reality. What often goes along with these assertions of what the "real world" is like is an assumption that principles are not pragmatic, that when someone "stands on principle" they are not being realistic, and that being principled is not how you get things done in the world we actually live in, as opposed to the world we might wish existed.

Just as principles without compromise are not truly principled, compromise without principles is not effective, practical, or realistic. Our principles give us power. They help us mobilize our energies. They focus us on what we are really trying to accomplish. They help unify our allies and provide our team with a common purpose. Perhaps most importantly, they help us evaluate the true costs and benefits of the compromises we are considering or are being asked to consider.

Disputants may seldom admit to operating without a set of guiding values, but when we see people floundering with no clear sense about how to evaluate next steps or how to consider potential compromises, they are likely in need of some grounding in a set of principles. Similarly, when we see people rigidly adhering to a position for no other reason than their desire for a particular outcome, we can at least hypothesize that they are not operating from a grounded set of principles.

When we see that people are confused about the choices they face, one of the most useful things we can do as conflict interveners is to work with them to consider the principles that are important to them. So whether we are trying to help people who are unable to consider "compromising their principles" or people who seem to be confused about what compromises to suggest or accept, helping disputants focus on principles is an important place to start. This is not a new concept; it is one of the key insights in Getting to Yes (Fisher and Ury 1981) and is promoted by many other approaches to negotiation as well. It highlights the pragmatic value of a principled basis for our actions in conflict.

Two overlapping concepts are related to the role of principle in guiding us through conflict—interests and objective criteria.

The line between *interests* and *principles* is porous and subtle, but essential. Although we may have an interest in adhering to our principles, our interests are reflections of our needs, while our principles derive from our values or our beliefs. Sometimes the difference may seem semantic; indeed, the way we express something can make almost the same words sound like an interest or a principle, but they are very different in terms of the challenge they present for disputants. It is not "unprincipled" to compromise on our interests, but by definition, compromising on principles presents a different kind of challenge. It is interesting how seldom our principles guide us to act against our interests, but they often should and sometimes do (e.g., when we turn down a lucrative and interesting job because we do not approve of some of the environmental practices of the company).

Because of the relationship between interests and principles, one way in which we can handle value disputes is to focus on the interests or needs people have that give expression to the values at stake (Moore 2003). For example, if the principle is "equal pay for equal work," then we can focus on how to maximize the equality of pay across gender, race, age, or other characteristics. It is easier to be more flexible about the interest than the principle in coming up with specific solutions; however, the measure of the outcomes achieved will be based on how they advance the principle.

Disputants who strongly embrace a principle may find any compromise that falls short of achieving it difficult to accept. That is why it is often necessary to do the reverse of what Moore (2003) suggests—to travel back from an interest- or need-based discussion to a consideration of the principle itself and how it can best be advanced.

With *criteria* and *principles*, we are also dealing with related but different concepts. Principles are important criteria for evaluating the compromises we are called upon to make during conflict. But they are hardly objective. Our values are some of the most subjective elements we bring to conflict. They are not derived from an objective set of standards but from the beliefs that we hold dear. Their power lies in our commitment to them, our willingness to sacrifice for them, and our intention to adhere to them across a broad range of circumstances. In other words, it is the subjectivity we bring to our values that makes them powerful. We may use objective criteria to assess whether our values or principles are being upheld (e.g., are men and women in the same job category with the same amount of experience being paid the same salary?), but the principle itself is not a formula. When negotiating the price of a car, we may use the "bluebook value" as an objective criteria, but it is hardly a principle in and of itself. Criteria are methods for assessment; principles are our most fundamental guides through life.

Subjective though principles may be, the absence of them makes us less effective in achieving our interests, developing meaningful criteria, or navigating our way through the difficult choices that conflict engagement presents. Moreover, when we are clear about our principles and find clear and constructive ways of articulating them, we often find areas of agreement where previously we saw only an irresolvable value conflict. This was brought home by a late night call that led to my immersion in municipal finances:

"You have got to help us! We are getting nowhere, and if we don't succeed, all that money will go!" A sales tax was expiring, and two separate groups had gathered enough signatures to put a renewal of the tax on the ballot—but for very different purposes. One called for dedicating the revenues to human services—mental health, housing, emergency family assistance, domestic violence services, and related programs. The other was for an expansion of recreation and athletic programs. With both petitions on the ballot, neither would succeed, which would have been fine with the city council, because they preferred a non-dedicated tax to give them maximum flexibility in spending.

I agreed to work with the two groups on developing a jointly sponsored initiative. At first, this seemed like a simple matter of separating the positions they had taken from what they were really trying to accomplish—additional funding for two worthwhile programmatic areas. However, the negotiations had been cast as a value dispute—services for the needy versus facilities for the entire community; or, to put it negatively (as the participants in this discussion were wont to do), more funds for a very small part of the population who were already well served in this community, versus more facilities for the rich and the elite.

To deal with this, the group had to depersonalize the discussion so that individual motives were not the focus. We also focused on the specific needs that each group wanted to address. But we could not have made genuine progress without delving into the principles that each group espoused. There was no significant disagreement when we stated these in positive terms— providing services for the needy in a wealthy community versus providing resources that would address the needs of youth, and really, the entire community.

The problem was that people from each side felt that the more they agreed to accommodate the other side's needs, the more they were compromising their own principles. So we engaged in a discussion of why this particular sales tax was so essential to standing up for their principles. As is often the case, there was an underlying belief that both groups shared—that funding for what they saw as essential needs should be dedicated, and not dependent on annual decisions by elected officials whose priorities were likely to change. With some clarity about this jointly shared belief, it was easier to arrive at a compromise on the overall package.

The real value of centering the parties on the principles that were guiding their decisions became clear after the joint proposal narrowly failed. It did so because the city leadership asked that this initiative be voted down so that the needs of the entire city could be examined. The city manager promised to convene a stakeholders' group to look at the overall financial needs of the city—and to put any jointly arrived at proposal on the next ballot.

And so the Municipal Finance Strategy Committee was born. This time, a wider group participated, including the city manager and certain other city officials, representatives of the business community, youth program leaders, as well as the original participants. The city wanted to renew the tax with the support of this group but did not want to have its hands tied by a fixed formula of allocation, which was counter to the most important common value of the two original groups. In the end, the committee agreed to an allocation formula with a certain amount dedicated to the general fund but with most revenues dedicated to human services, youth programs, and parks and recreational services. The city council agreed in principle to the proposal but wanted to put only the general tax on the ballot. Now the guiding principle that had motivated the groups brought them together to demand not only the renewal of the tax, but also the allocation formula they had agreed on.

On the ballot, voters were presented with a complicated ballot that asked two separate questions: should the tax be renewed and should the allocation formula be required? Both proposals passed overwhelmingly. Without a clear focus on principle, the initial compromise could not have been achieved, nor could the proposal be brought to fruition.

The Power of Principle and Compromise

Approaching conflict with a principled stance is empowering. Whether we understand this as the power of truth—*satyagraha* as advocated by Mohandas Gandhi (2008) and Martin Luther King Jr. as the power of acting in a moral manner, or as the power of fighting for something we believe in, we can readily see that principles are powerful. When we believe we are working for a higher good, we are better at mobilizing our energies and our supporters and withstanding efforts to coerce us to sacrifice what is important to us.

But we should not lose sight of the power of wise compromise as well. One reason why compromise is essential to maintaining our principles is that it helps bolster and enhance the power of those principles. Rigid adherence to principles can be empowering up to a point, but when such adherence produces no discernible advancement of the principles, then inflexibility actually diminishes power.

The debate around the Affordable Care Act shows this dynamic in action. During the initial debate about the proposed legislation, President Obama was criticized from all sides for either compromising too much or not enough. Should there be a "public option" (a government-sponsored health insurance)? Should a "single-payer system" (the Canadian and British model—one government-sponsored health insurance for everyone) be seriously considered? How much effort should be put into compromising with Republicans, who were themselves under pressure both to compromise and to stand on principle? In the end, considerable compromises were made to institute the ACA, even though this bought almost no Republican support. Arguments are made to this day about whether we would have achieved better, worse, or no changes in the health care system had the Democrats not agreed to significant compromises.

And the issue continues. Changes have been made to accommodate new challenges and political realities. As of this writing, Republicans have by and large continued to stand against the whole bill in principle rather than enter into a serious effort to work with the administration to modify it. The results have been both empowering and disempowering to all sides of the issue. By compromising as much as he did, President Obama *did* succeed in getting the ACA passed, providing the first major overhaul in the US health care delivery system in a very long time. This has been the signature domestic achievement of his administration. Despite repeated efforts to discredit and repeal the ACA, it is gradually becoming ever more deeply embedded in the American health care system, thereby making efforts to undo the law increasingly unlikely to succeed. On the other hand, by standing on principle, the Republicans have been able to mobilize their base, particularly in off-year elections, which has led to considerable gains in their legislative power. It also led to the birth of the Tea Party movement, whose reliance on principle and abhorrence of compromise have both enhanced and limited its power.

We can see this same dynamic play out in smaller-scale disputes, as well as those that play out on a broader social level. Every time someone "stands on principle" in a dispute, they are to some extent playing a power game, whether or not they mean to. The power dimension of this dynamic is always present, whether this involves a business partner demanding that every management decision the organization faces, no matter how insignificant, be achieved by consensus; a union negotiator arguing that there should be no changes in retirement benefits despite the impending bankruptcy of an employer; or a parent insisting on the principle of exactly equal parenting time as an ex-spouse.

Let's consider several specific elements to this interplay.

- *Disputants stand on principle because of the importance of the principle, because they feel powerful, or because they feel powerless—or sometimes, because of all three.* When I hear disputants cling to a principle, I first respect their commitment. But I almost always ask myself whether this stance is encouraged by a sense that they are in a powerful enough position to feel that no compromises are (currently) necessary. I wonder whether they are afraid to compromise because they feel disempowered, and therefore are concerned that once they open the door to any compromise, they will not be able to stand their ground at all. I also ask myself whether they are primarily motivated by furthering a principle or by advancing their interests, and whether their standing on principle is truly a matter of adhering to their values or is essentially a power play.

- *Compromising may be a sign of weakness, but an effective approach to compromise requires confidence.* When people seem to be compromising without getting much in return—and, in doing so, relinquishing a significant principle—they can easily seem weak. In this case, holding to their principles may be essential to their credibility. But rigidity can also be a sign of vulnerability. Effective compromising requires the confidence that we *can* hold the line when we need to, but we do so as a strategic decision, not a defensive default.

- *Taking a principled stance may enhance distributive power but undercut integrative power.* There are many different types of power, and enhancing one kind may undercut another. Distributive power ("power over") refers to the ability to claim a greater share of a limited pie, and integrative power ("power with") denotes the capacity to use our power in conjunction with that of others to increase the size of the pie. I may be able to claim a higher percentage of a limited salary pool for myself by exercising distributive power (for example, by threatening to quit), or I may be able to work with others to ask that the amount of money being allocated for salaries be increased (by joining with others to pool our power—for example, through a union).

Standing on principle may encourage others to join with me and thus may contain a significant integrative potential. However, this approach often makes it harder to consider how to address others' needs that are seen as being in conflict with our principles. This can make genuine efforts at employing integrative power more difficult. The trick to standing on principle in an integrative way is to work with those we are in conflict with so that they, too, can stand on principle.

- *Compromising on one principle may enhance the ability to pursue another.* As a preceding point suggests, we seldom operate with just one principle or just one kind of power. For example, I may believe that we should each receive a salary based on our contribution to the organization, but I may also believe that we are all in this together and that we therefore should unite in the face of inevitable demands to cut our benefits. The decisions we make about which principles to emphasize and what kinds of power to exert on their behalf is the crux of what much of our strategizing about conflict involves.

- *Standing on principles provides disputants with an emotional boost that enhances their power.* But without compromising appropriately, that energy can dissipate. One source of personal power is the emotional resources and commitment that people can bring to a conflict. The more focused, confident, and energized we are, the more empowered and better able we are to bring our power to bear. One of the reasons a strong, principled stand can enhance our power is that it helps us mobilize our emotional resources and those of our followers. It's difficult to rally people behind the wisdom of compromise. But over time, we need to believe our efforts are making a difference to maintain this emotional commitment. And this usually requires some compromise.

Values, Interests, and Resources

Related to the tension between principle and compromise is the interplay between resource disputes and value disputes. Resource disputes arise from a desire to achieve the maximum available amount of a limited resource or to minimize the loss of a resource. Resources may be tangible items such as money, goods, services, or property, but they can be less tangible as well, such as power, public recognition, or access to decision makers. Value or normative disputes are based on our beliefs and principles—disputes over abortion, protection of endangered species, or gun violence, for example. Normative disputes may also have a significant procedural element. For example, I may believe that decision making in an organization should be based on consensus, whereas someone else may believe that leadership requires decisive and often unpopular action. Struggles for leadership in an organization, perhaps a political advocacy group or a charitable organization, may be cast as value disputes, but there is almost always a significant resource conflict as well, having to do with who will be able to exert the most influence or have access to higher-level decision makers.

The problem that conflict interveners face is that resource disputes can masquerade as value disputes, and value disputes as resource differences. For example, let's say I want more pay for the work I am doing. Rather than focus on my need for more resources, I may instead argue that I am being discriminated against based on age, ethnicity, or gender. However, if I feel that I have been a victim of discrimination, I may become very fervent in my advocacy for a promotion, framing this in terms of my desire for career advancement. Most conflict involves both resource and value disputes.

Although compromises about resource disputes are common (in essence, this is how the market operates), compromises over values are much more complicated—some would say impossible. Some conflict theorists (Aubert 1963, Moore 2003) have suggested that, rather than working to achieve a compromise about normative differences, it is more effective to identify the resource issues and interests involved in a conflict and work on these. Moore suggests also looking for "superordinate" values that all parties can agree to.

This does not necessarily mean that compromise is impossible in principled disputes or that the only viable approach to these is to focus on the underlying interests and/or resources and thereby avoid a conflict over principles. Rather than avoid value differences by looking for a way of resolving the resource issues, it is generally more effective to encourage people to affirm their values, to discuss them (in positive terms—what we believe in rather than what we are against), and then decide how best to honor them in a conflict. While we should never ask others to set aside their most important values, we have to pose the question of how best to further those values. It is in this sense that understanding the resource issues and interests involved is important.

Although the nitty-gritty of negotiations may focus on resources or interests, the essence of the challenge is often a principled one—how to further our principles by compromising. Negotiations of this sort happen all the time. We work on resources by focusing on the values we are committed to; we make progress on our values by discussing resources. Staying true to our values while negotiating compromises over resources are inseparable processes. Consider for example, Johanna's experience with the medical system:

> Johanna went to the emergency room complaining of severe pains and some bloating in her side, which the medical staff diagnosed as gastroenteritis. She was given intravenous fluids in the ER and was sent home with instructions to stay hydrated, to eat regularly but in small amounts, and to drink fruit juices and eat bananas. This seemed to help for a short while, but the symptoms soon returned. Subsequent visits to the hospital and to her doctor, whose practice was attached to the hospital, caused her to undergo tests for celiac

disease and a variety of other disorders. After a couple of months of what she believed to be a runaround, she was referred to a specialist and was found to have a tumor on her ovary that had escaped earlier detection. By now the tumor had advanced, the prognosis was worse, and her medical expenses had escalated.

Johanna made a complaint against the hospital where she had received the early misdiagnosis. What most infuriated her was the supercilious way in which she felt the hospital staff had dismissed its error—insisting that no harm had really been done and that they had followed normal medical procedures.

In the meeting that followed, Johanna and her partner asked for an apology, for better diagnostic protocols to be implemented, and for compensation for loss of work and additional medical expenses that she believed she had incurred as a result of the misdiagnosis and failure to refer her immediately to a specialist. Representatives of the hospital initially treated this as if it were simply a matter of resources and attempted to find out how much money Johanna wanted. They offered what Johanna considered an inadequate apology: "We are sorry for the pain you have endured and for our failure, despite following normal protocols, to detect the source of the problem during your initial visits." They also asserted in a nonspecific way that they were reviewing the incident with an eye to refining their protocols. Johanna and her partner were very upset with this response and dealt with it by increasing their financial demands, which reinforced the hospital's view that this was primarily a resource issue.

In a subsequent mediated session, which now included the chief medical officer of the hospital and Johanna's own physician, Johanna was able to express the underlying values that were impelling her—why it was important that the hospital take genuine responsibility for what had happened, be more concrete about how it was going to change its procedures, and recognize the genuine damage that had been done to her. Johanna felt that her doctor was able to acknowledge what she had been through in a meaningful way. The medical director was clear about the fact that the hospital did bear significant responsibility for this and laid out an explicit plan for how the protocols would be reevaluated. These admissions both enabled and were facilitated by a discussion of the principles that would be used to arrive at an appropriate settlement. (The specific amount was negotiated in a separate discussion involving the hospital's attorney and insurance carrier.)

This negotiation involved a bit of a dance between a resource focus and a discussion of principles. Each element informed, at times exacerbated, and at other times facilitated the discussion of the other element. They were distinct but inseparable.

Compromising with Evil

Let's take this discussion one step further. How can we hold on to our principles when we engage with those who we consider evil, immoral, untrustworthy, and dangerous? How do we avoid the peril of "another Munich," the agreement among Germany, France, Britain, and Italy (but not Czechoslovakia) in 1938 that allowed Germany to annex the Sudetenland, which had been part of Czechoslovakia? This agreement, meant to bring "peace with honor" and "peace in our time" (in the words of British Prime Minister Neville Chamberlain), instead paved the way for further German aggression and has since been viewed as an unprincipled act of appeasement.

But there are also dramatic examples in which people have chosen to negotiate with oppressors, and those have been regarded as acts of heroism. Nelson Mandela negotiated from prison with the government that brought apartheid to South Africa and murdered people engaged in peaceful protests against discrimination. Mandela was criticized by many of his supporters at the time. Now, however, his actions are widely regarded as examples of moral courage and wisdom, for which he was awarded the Nobel Peace Prize. Or consider the negotiations in Northern Ireland that led to the Good Friday agreement that required those on all sides to negotiate with people they considered evil. On the other hand, Winston Churchill's refusal to negotiate with Hitler in 1940 when it appeared that Britain might soon be invaded is widely hailed as an example of moral courage. The moral calculus involved in decisions about standing on principle and considering compromise when we believe we are dealing with evil is not as straightforward as we sometimes assert it to be. And, of course, whether an action is seen as an example of moral courage or cowardice depends in part on how things turn out over time.

We don't run across evil of that kind in our everyday lives, but we often encounter situations in which we feel we are dealing with unscrupulous people, such as

- An abusive ex-spouse

- A dishonest salesman

- A bullying co-worker or boss

- A corrupt politician

- A proponent of discrimination

Although we might like to take a purely principled stance in such situations by refusing to enter into any agreement or compromise, sometimes this is simply not possible. The ethical dimension here, as with the challenge of conflict avoidance discussed in chapter 4, is of paramount significance. But simply refusing to negotiate or enter into any compromise under *any* circumstances may not be the best way to counter the behavior or protect potential victims. We may not have the power to punish, victims involved may not be able or ready to speak openly about their circumstances, and the quickest way to end behavior may be through negotiation. And even though someone might act immorally, they may still have legitimate concerns that ought to be addressed.

In 1993, when a reporter asked the former prime minister of Israel, Yitzhak Rabin, how he could enter into an agreement with Yasser Arafat, a man he had repeatedly condemned as a terrorist, he replied, "You don't make peace with friends. You make it with very unsavory enemies" (http://articles.chicagotribune.com/ 1993–09–15/news/9309150118_1_rabin-israeli-yaron-ezrahi). But acts of evil are not challenged by compromise. Sometimes we need to take principled, even dangerous, stands against immoral behavior, because otherwise that behavior can be potentiated and vulnerable people can be left unprotected. Sometimes the immediate result of a principled stance is a dangerous escalation or further victimization, but we won't make progress over the longer term if we don't risk those results. Those who have stood up to sexual harassment or bullying behavior in a workplace, for example, have often paid a heavy personal price, but without their principled stance, the behavior would have been tolerated and would have continued. The lesson of Munich may well be that we have to risk violence to forestall violence. But if we apply that lesson indiscriminately, we will lose the message that Nelson Mandela or Yitzhak Rabin have to offer as well.

In his book *Bargaining with the Devil* (2010), Robert Mnookin proposes a series of questions that we should consider in deciding about whether to enter into negotiations with those we consider evil or immoral. He applies these to a wide range of circumstances, from international disputes to interpersonal conflict. He suggests we consider the following:

- What interests are at stake?

- What are the alternatives to negotiation?

- Are there possible negotiated outcomes that would meet the interests of the parties?

- Is there a reasonable possibility that these outcomes might be carried out?

- What are the costs of negotiating or of not negotiating?

- Is there a legitimate and morally acceptable alternative to negotiation, and how effective might it be?

While Mnookin does not suggest that these questions provide a simple algorithm for determining whether negotiating or fighting (which might include military action, going to court, or going on strike, for example) is the right choice, he proposes that we ask ourselves these questions as we consider this decision. He also discusses the traps we often fall into that may lead us to want to fight when negotiating may be the wiser course, or to negotiate when fighting may be the more effective alternative. For example, moralizing and demonizing may push us to fight, whereas commitment to win/win outcomes or rationalizing behavior based on context may push us to negotiate.

Mnookin's analysis is thought-provoking and opens up some interesting lines of inquiry, but as with many of the conceptual frameworks we bring to conflict, it offers a dualism that we need to beware of. Seldom are our choices either to fight or to negotiate, to stand up for our principles or to compromise, to confront evil or to compromise with it. The mistake at Munich was not that compromises were made but that important principles were abandoned, and the compromises were themselves unprincipled.

We experience the principle–compromise paradox much more dramatically when we are dealing with behavior that we not only consider wrong but intensely evil. However, the dynamic is not really different in kind from what we see in less extreme or exten-sive conflicts. Whether we are contending with an abusive boss, a cheating business partner, a bully, a plagiarizer, or whatever partic-ular form of immorality we are contending with, we still have to act in a principled way, realizing that this often requires compromises that we might prefer not to make.

Reflections from Practice

As almost all graduates of a social work program can attest, one of the incessant discussions that permeated their education was whether the work that social workers do is merely a Band-Aid or a part of a genuine effort to improve society. As a social work student at Columbia University from 1968 to 1970, I experienced this as a question of paramount importance. Of course, it has no conclusive answer. Any professional role we might occupy—architect, doctor, banker, lawyer, teacher, or mediator—is partly about contributing to the social good and partly about maintaining a social structure with all its flaws and possibilities. The concern about the tension between these roles seems more prominent in some professions than others. In social work, which defines itself as a helping profession, and perhaps particularly in the politically tumultuous years when I was a student at Columbia, this seemed like a crucial issue. For many years, I argued that all professions, as socially sanctioned structures, were part of a system for maintaining the status quo rather than changing it. I could provide beneficial services to individuals and groups, but my professional work would not be directed toward fun-damental social change. I would advance that goal by participating in social or political movements.

Over the years that I worked as a social worker, primarily in mental health, child welfare, and substance abuse, I felt that much of my work was worthwhile on an individual or small group level but not really relevant to changing society. But at the same time, I participated in a variety of political and social movements that were aimed at social change. I was trying to put into practice the analysis I had developed as a youth growing up in the turmoil of the sixties. In a sense, what I was doing was bifurcating principle and compromise. If my professional life was about compromise, my political life was about principle. If in my professional life I was helping people adapt to a social system riddled with inequities, my political life was about changing that system. Now viewed from the perspective of more than forty-five years of professional practice, this division seems well-meaning, but naive.

My introduction to conflict work came as a result of my participation in political action. I started acting as a trainer in nonviolent social change in conjunction with a series of actions at a nuclear weapons plant near Boulder, Colorado (Rocky Flats). I was introduced to this work by Christopher Moore, who soon became one of my long-term partners at CDR Associates. For the first time, I felt my interest in personal growth and in social change came together, which was exciting and energizing. When Chris developed an interest in conflict resolution and mediation, I followed him down that path, and I have stayed on it for more than thirty-five years. I continue to believe that this work allows me to integrate my commitment to social change and personal growth—although by no means seamlessly or perfectly.

I have learned that there is a fundamental problem with trying to separate these two goals, no matter what our career path. Working for social improvement and having a fulfilling career are intertwined, as with all the dilemmas discussed in this book. In essence, tension around our vocational choices is about principle and compromise. We make compromises to earn a living, to live within the business and ethical boundaries of our professions, to market our services, and to function within the institutions that employ us. But if we compromise to the point that our work is no longer congruent with our values, we are likely to be less effective, productive, motivated, and energized. Of course, people bifurcate their approach to principle and compromise all the time, and finding a vocation that not only pays our bills but also contributes to our purpose in life is in many ways a class privilege. We should never forget that most individuals have little choice in this regard, and that is why so many people feel alienated from their work. Contributing to society and developing a meaningful working life are inextricably bound together.

One way I began to appreciate how the tension between principle and compromise manifests itself was through working as both a conflict skills trainer and a conflict intervener. Training is fundamentally about principles. Of course, we have always offered lots of practical examples, demonstrations, simulations, and exercises to make the training come alive and help students develop actual skills. But the frameworks that we teach and try to apply are essentially couched in the language of principles, such as the following:

- Frame the issue as a mutual problem to be mutually solved.

- Focus on why people want something, not just what they want.

- Empower people to solve their own problems.

- Focus on process, not outcomes.

- Remain impartial, authentic, transparent, and present.

Although we can view all of these guidelines as essentially practical approaches to encouraging constructive engagement, our commitment to them is often ideological in nature. They are not just practical approaches; they reflect values we have about how conflict engagement efforts should be conducted. But when we actually work on conflict, the process of intervention always requires compromising in some way on the principles we teach, even if we do not always own up to this. Sometimes we focus on how to compromise among competing positions without delving into the underlying interests. Sometimes we do not feel at all impartial, and trying to act as if we are is impossible. Sometimes we suggest potential agreements, and we even advocate for these. For every principle that I have taught, I have been forced to make many compromises when putting it in practice.

So as I have tried to help disputants deal with the tension between the principled basis of their stance in conflict and the compromises they are of necessity considering, I am applying what I teach to what I do. Often this has led me to alter what I teach—to modify my "espoused" theory and the principles governing my practice. For example, I don't view interests and positions to be different in kind the way I used to. This is a core element of being a reflective practitioner. Hopefully, while I have often had to compromise to be effective, I have hopefully never made unethical compromises. I continue to act on the basis of the essence of what I believe—but although essential, integrating principle and compromise is not easy.

I used to say, partly (but only partly) in jest, that the thing that scared me the most as a supervisor was when someone did exactly what I told them to do, because circumstances are always different and the best approach interacts and is influenced by what is happening in the moment. Furthermore, all practitioners are different—and what will work for me won't work for others. This is why principles are at the core of what we teach rather than specific intervention tactics. It's also why compromise is essential to practice.

It is an enormous challenge for disputants to find a way to adhere to their principles and simultaneously search for compromise, as they often must. And it can be aggravating and painful to work through this tension. This is one of the reasons people want to avoid conflict. Because we cannot escape this dilemma, however, we had better face it. Grappling with this challenge has provided some of the most challenging yet moving moments I have experienced in my work in conflict. These have generally come when I have encouraged people to face the dilemma and to articulate it, rather than trying to find a way of minimizing or avoiding it:

> "I swore I would never work with him again after how he treated me and others, and now he is supposed to come back and serve as my supervisor? No way!"

Terry had worked on Roscoe's team two years before and felt that Roscoe had taken an intense dislike to him. Terry assumed that this was because he had been active in the union and had worked with several others to file grievances against management, of which Roscoe was a part. Whatever the reason, Roscoe was very critical of Terry's attitude toward his work, gave him poor performance reviews, twice threatened to suspend him, and had refused several requests for schedule variation to accommodate Terry's co-parenting obligations. When Terry accused Roscoe of being "an abusive manager, and an incompetent one to boot" in front of several other workers, Roscoe exploded. He called Terry a "troublemaker who was more interested in making life miserable for management than in doing his job." He suspended Terry for the rest of the day, and Terry in return filed a grievance. In response to this, the management agreed to transfer Terry to a different department (which actually worked for Terry); in return, Terry agreed to suspend his grievance.

Two years later, Roscoe was transferred to take charge of Terry's unit. Terry immediately filed a grievance that repeated the concerns he had raised two years earlier and contended the management was reneging on its agreement with him. Management responded that this had been an informal agreement and that they had never promised that it would continue "until the end of time." They offered Terry the option of switching to another unit or working the night shift. While Terry was considering the night shift, he did not feel that he should be punished for the way he had been treated in the past. At this point, the case was referred to me for mediation.

Terry's initial understanding was that he would meet with the head of labor relations for the facility in which he worked. It seemed that both Terry and management were trying to negotiate a way that would avoid Terry having to work under Roscoe's supervision. But it became clear that for Terry this meant making sure Roscoe did not take over supervision of his unit, while for management it meant that Terry would either transfer or that there would be some mechanism for putting him nominally under someone else's supervision.

I felt that everyone was talking the language of compromise, but no one was talking the language of principle, and I decided to take a risk. I suggested that Terry and Roscoe talk directly with each other, with my help. Roscoe was willing, but Terry was reluctant and delayed until almost the last possible moment before the case would have to go to arbitration before deciding to give this a try.

In private meetings, Roscoe admitted that Terry had gotten under his skin and that he found him "incredibly irritating," but he also said that Terry was a good worker and that he had overreacted to Terry on a couple of occasions. Terry said that he was being manipulated "yet again" by management, and he did not think it was fair that he was put in this position. However, he also acknowledged that Roscoe was not the only manager with whom he'd had problems. When we met together, I asked both Roscoe and Terry to state the principles at stake for them in this issue.

Terry was very eloquent in talking about the right of workers to be treated with respect, and the importance of management being held accountable for following through on their agreements, informal or otherwise. Roscoe said that he supposed for management an important principle was their right to deploy supervisory staff as they saw fit, but then he said, "That's not my issue, however. I think everyone should treat everyone else with respect, management or union. I also think we should be willing to give each other second chances. Terry, I think you often treated me like I was your enemy just because I was management. But I also lost it with you on a couple of occasions. I don't blame you for being pissed off with me. I hope you get why I sometimes got pissed off with you. Let's try again. I can do better. I hope you can, too."

This statement had a very positive impact on Terry, who said he appreciated it and he might be willing to give it another go with Roscoe, but it really irked him to let management off that easily. I asked him to talk about the principle involved with this. He reiterated previous comments about holding management accountable. I said that I understood how important that principle was, but then asked whether it was the most important one to him in this case. He thought for a while and then said, "No. The most important one is that workers—well, everyone—should be treated with respect and kindness." He then said to Roscoe, "Let's give it a go. Maybe we should go out to coffee first and see if we can't get on better terms with each other." That is how the mediation ended, and that is the last I heard from them.

I have no idea if things worked out in the long run. I know that Terry in particular really struggled with whether he was compromising essential principles, and that he resented being put in this position. But I also felt that in the course of discussing their principles and delving into what was essential to each of them, both men found the maturity and strength to face the challenge of adhering to their values and accepting compromise. Having them deal with each other directly seemed necessary to enable them to confront this dilemma. I suspect that they faced some rocky moments as they adjusted to working together again, but they went into this committed to trying and recognizing that this path would continue to be challenging.

Although it would be nice to end this chapter with an example that shows how we can fully defend our principles while making the compromises necessary to achieve meaningful and durable progress, that would be misleading. This story seems more typical to me. As with all genuine dilemmas, we can make progress and work on them at ever more sophisticated levels, but the essence of the paradox remains. Principles are essential; so, too, are compromises. They are interwoven and inseparable. The process of working with this is difficult and the results are often ambiguous, but embracing the dilemma is the most genuine path to constructive engagement.

chapter six

emotions and logic

One ought to hold on to one's heart; for if one lets it go, one soon loses control of the head too.

Friedrich Nietzsche, The Portable Nietzsche

I never wished to set emotion against reason, but rather to see emotion as at the least assisting reason and at best holding a dialogue with it.

Antonio Damasio, Descartes' Error

Our thinking about the tension between emotions and logic, between feelings and reason, is inconsistent. As the previous quotes suggest, we sometimes favor one and sometimes the other. This bifurcated way of viewing emotions and logic is not a recent development; rather, it reflects the age-old effort to understand the relationship between the body and the mind.

We tend to view emotions and logic as opposites. We differentiate between them in terms of their source, their location in our body (heart and brain), the neural pathways that characterize each (neocortex and amygdala), even their gender characteristics. One popular misconception is that logic is a left-brain phenomenon and creativity and emotion a right-brain one. But as the work of neuroscientist Antonio Damasio (2003, 2005) suggests, they are essential to each other. Without emotions, logic may lead us to illogical conclusions, while our rational system is necessary to allow emotions to do their most important work. The conflict field has largely bought into this division of emotion and logic, and conflict professionals tend to view these as very different processes. The techniques that we advocate for dealing with conflict are essentially rationalist in nature. We urge "separating the people from the problem," looking for the interests prompting disputants' demands, breaking issues into their specific components, and identifying "agreements in principle." We offer a variety of tools for analyzing conflict and for framing issues in constructive ways. These tools are often very effective in promoting a more productive approach to conflict, but they are presented as logical, rational, analytical approaches. Yet we also know that people often act on the basis of intuition, instinct, emotions, and hunches when they are in the midst of conflict. A complete approach to conflict cannot simply be a rational one, but neither can we work our way through conflict merely by exploring and expressing our emotions.

Constructive conflict engagement is neither an encounter group nor an exercise in logic. It is an integration of rational analysis and emotional energy. Fortunately, we are working in a time when there has been significant progress in our understanding of the relationship between emotion and logic. As a result, we stand to benefit greatly from this as we try to understand what is actually going on in conflict. But let's start by looking at how we typically managed the interplay of emotions and logic in conflict.

The Response of Conflict Specialists to the Emotion–Logic Paradox

As stated previously, conflict specialists usually understand—and therefore describe—emotions and logic as separate processes. We tend to believe our job is to work on emotions *just enough* to allow more rational approaches to take over. Once we have listened, affirmed, and helped people to express their emotions, we can then help them engage in a more rational problem-solving process.

But this approach does not really embrace either the challenge or the opportunity that the emotion–logic paradox presents to effective conflict work. If we don't access our own emotions when we are in a conflict, we can't engage effectively, make decisions, or move the dispute forward in a constructive way. However, emotions also provide the fuel that escalates conflict, that encourages us to be more certain than we ought to be, and that leads us into poor decision making. Emotions are essential to us, yet they often lead us down unproductive paths. Our challenge in conflict is therefore to access our emotions and to provide space for others to do the same—to experience them, use them, and recognize the powerful role they play in our cognitive processes, yet monitor them and keep them in perspective. This is no easy trick, especially since conflict is both a product of emotions and a catalyst for them.

One of the foundational texts of the modern conflict field is *The Functions of Social Conflict*, by Lewis Coser (1956). Coser argues, with reference to the earlier work of George Simmel (1955), that social conflict provides essential bonding mechanisms for society. Coser differentiates between what he calls "realistic" and "unrealistic" conflict. The realistic component refers to the aspect of conflict that is related to the desire for different outcomes and is therefore, in his view, amenable to a rational negotiation or conflict resolution process. If disputants can find an alternative means to satisfy their needs, they can address this element of the conflict. The unrealistic component refers to the tension, aggression, or anger that a disputant is experiencing. This element requires some sort of energy discharge or release and cannot be satisfied simply by an alternative solution. Coser's formulation is sophisticated, but it is easy to draw the conclusion that emotions require expression, whereas conflict among interests requires problem solving. Some variation of this view is embedded throughout our field.

In *Getting to Yes* (1991), authors Fisher, Ury, and Patton provide an essentially rationalist approach for dealing with conflict, and their prescription for how to deal with the emotional dimension is to separate the people from the problem. We can do this by framing the issue as a mutual problem to be mutually solved, by looking for joint interests and for interests that can be traded, and by identifying objective principles or standards that can be used for analyzing potential solutions. The authors also suggest that we give people an opportunity to let off steam in order to make it easier for them to deal with an issue rationally. In *Getting Past No* (1993), Ury suggests that we should "go to the balcony" to gain a wider perspective when we are wrapped up in our emotions and feeling stuck. The implication is that we must acknowledge our emotions, but not let them impede finding a resolution. Moore (2003) suggests that mediators sometimes need to find a way to allow people to express their emotions, but that they ought to keep emotions out of the process entirely at other times. He offers a variety of suggestions for how to do both, including active listening, caucusing, setting ground rules about behavior, and—echoing Fisher, Ury, and Patton—encouraging parties to vent about interests, not people.

In *The Promise of Mediation* (2005), Bush and Folger's criticism of outcome-oriented mediation can be understood in part as a call to address the emotional and relational elements of conflict. They argue that we can realize mediation's truest and highest potential only if we look for opportunities for empowerment and recognition, which they describe as an essentially emotional phenomenon. They take a step toward an integrative framework but then undercut this by insisting that the transformative approach they advocate is of a nature entirely different from other approaches, such as facilitative mediation, which might pursue both relational and problem-solving goals.

In each of these treatments of conflict, there is a clear understanding that you cannot ignore the impact of emotions (although some conflict interveners may try to do just that by focusing on the substance of the dispute, defaulting to a process that keeps disputants separate rather than bringing them together, and by focusing on rights-based arguments). Instead, these approaches tend to *separate* emotions and logic—to assume that if they are not opposites, then they are at least very different.

One interesting and more integrative approach to the role of emotion and logic in conflict work is offered by Daniel Bowling and David Hoffman in their book, *Bringing Peace into the Room* (2003). They suggest that a key element of successful mediation is the degree to which mediators are "present." In their view, presence involves self-awareness about our emotional reactions to our clients and theirs to us. By attending to this emotional space, experiencing it, and remaining aware of it, we are better able to help disputants through conflict.

I believe that to embrace and work with the paradoxical relationship of emotions and logic, we need to view them both as part of the same overall process. Both are tools for making sense of the world. At different stages of an interaction, we may focus on expression or analysis, on venting or more measured discourse, but emotions and logic both operate at every step along the way and are essential to each other.

We know this on an experiential level. We can be upset, angry, and fearful, and still try to reason our way through a dilemma. The emotional intensity we are experiencing creates special challenges, but we can no more put our reasoning on hold when we are upset than stop feeling when we reason. When emotions run rampant, we may make bad decisions, but without our emotions operating, we can't make any decisions (Damasio 2005).

Emotions, Logic, and Decision Making

Neuroscience has become a popular topic at conflict resolution conferences, in part because it has received a great deal of recent attention in our popular culture. Malcolm Gladwell's bestselling book *Blink* (2007) argued that many of the most important—and often best—decisions we make are those we make quickly, without thinking too much. We do this, he argues, by focusing on very limited data and ignoring, filtering out, and never bringing to consciousness the rest. Gladwell calls this process "thin-slicing." He suggests, for example, that all of us are prone to decide very quickly which political candidates we like, which movies we want to see, and how friendly someone we encounter is. The capacity and the urge to react in this way makes sense from an evolutionary point of view, because our survival has often depended on rapid decision making.

However, this carries with it considerable dangers. Thin-slicing often ignores important information, and once we make decisions or form impressions, we are apt to pay attention to new information or inputs that support those impressions and ignore information that does not support them. If, for example, I have developed a positive impression of a public figure, perhaps a political leader, I will likely be very interested in information that supports that position (positive reports, analyses, polls, and anecdotes) and will overlook or discount more negative ones. In fact, I might not even allow the negative information to enter my consciousness. This confirmatory bias can get in the way of making important decisions, however. We make most of our everyday decisions without slowing down our decision-making process long enough to check our biases or consider new information. If we did, we would be paralyzed.

Daniel Kahneman, a psychologist who was awarded the Nobel Prize in economics for his work on decision making, offers a related but more sophisticated approach to this in *Thinking Fast and Slow* (2011). Kahneman describes two approaches to decision making, which he characterizes as entirely different systems of thinking. "Fast thinking" is our workhorse. We make most decisions using this method, which we can call intuition; this is akin to Gladwell's concept of "thin-slicing" and psychologists refer to it as "System 1" thinking. We cannot "turn off" this type of thinking. It operates all the time, but it is undisciplined and very prone to confirmatory bias.

Kahneman describes System 1 thinking as operating "automatically and quickly with little or no effort and no sense of voluntary control" (p. 20). He further says this of intuition:

> Each of us provides feats of expert intuition many times a day. Most of us are pitch-perfect in detecting anger in the first word of a telephone call, recognize as we enter a room that we were the subject of the conversation, and quickly react to subtle signs that the driver of the car in the next lane is dangerous. (p. 11)

We are able to make these distinctions by drawing unconsciously from a broad set of stored information and past experiences. A key aspect of our ability to do this involves the emotions that we have associated with that information.

Thinking slow, or "System 2" thinking, is more deliberative and intentional. It can control for the mistakes of fast thinking but takes a lot of energy (literally—the brain uses up a great deal of energy to begin with and this is an especially energy-intense activity). Furthermore, Kahneman describes System 2 thinking as lazy—as trying to avoid working by relying on System 1 whenever it can:

> System 2 allocates attention to the effortful mental activities that demand it, including complex computations. The operations of System 2 are often associated with the subjective experience of agency, choice, and concentration. (p. 21)

The relationship between these two systems, which do not occupy specific locations or systems in our body or brain, is symbiotic. They are essential to each other, as Kahneman explains:

> [System 1 thinking is] effortlessly originating impressions and feelings that are the main sources of the explicit beliefs and deliberate choices of System 2.

> The automatic operations of System 1 generate surprisingly complex patterns of ideas, but only the slower System 2 can construct thoughts in an orderly series of steps. (p. 21)

Fast thinking is unreliable when it is essential that we counteract our tendencies to jump to conclusions, when we need to guard against selective perception and confirmatory bias, and when we need to engage in complex and orderly calculations. But even in what might appear to be a clear case for System 2 activities, System 1 might still prevail.

A good illustration of the tendency of System 1 thinking to prevail is a simple mathematical problem we used in our training programs at CDR Associates. The purpose of the exercise was to illustrate how easy it is to interpret the same data differently. We asked people to calculate the net loss or gain someone would accrue if they bought something (for example, a horse that was very underpriced) for $200, sold it for $300, bought it back for $400, and sold it for $500. We could count on the fact that the answers would be all over the map, no matter who we were training—managers, lawyers, even accountants would come up with a spread of answers (we did tell the story in a rather elaborate way, but the facts were clear and were written on a flipchart). There is a right answer if you don't bring in additional facts, such as transaction costs—but I will leave it to you to figure that out.

One particular response to this puzzle stands out for me. When we asked participants in one workshop to explain their answers, each one replied with what sounded like a reasonable System 2 approach to their calculation—all except for the one person who got the correct answer. She said, "I work with numbers all the time," and that answer "just felt right—I just knew it was right." This fits with Kahneman's hypothesis that the more familiar we are with an area of knowledge (say, medical diagnosis or structural engineering), the more we are able to rely on our intuition.

Kahneman describes slow thinking and fast thinking as separate but intrinsically related processes. Damasio (2005) goes a step further and describes emotions as part of cognition, as essential to our ability to make any decision at all:

> Certain aspects of the process of emotion and feeling are indispensable for rationality. At their best, feelings point us in the proper direction, take us to the appropriate place in a decision-making space, where we may put the instruments of logic to good use. (p. xvii)

Damasio drew this conclusion from studies he and others conducted with a number of patients who had suffered injury to the part of the brain that allowed them to experience emotion, but whose memory and logical capacities were not impaired. The fascinating conclusion drawn from this research was that it was impossible for these patients to make decisions without the capacity to experience emotions. They could weigh the pros and cons of the alternatives—for instance, Damasio gives an example of someone trying to decide which restaurant to go to—but they could not actually *decide*. This led Damasio to view feelings as part of our cognitive process, just as perception and logic are. He understands intuition to be a form of rapid cognition based on history and emotion: "Intuition is simply rapid cognition with the required knowledge partially swept under the carpet, all courtesy of emotion and much past practice" (2005, p. xiii).

Another very popular take on the relationship of emotion to rationality is the work of Daniel Goleman, whose best-selling book, *Emotional Intelligence* (1995), argues that we take too narrow a view of intelligence. Goleman maintains that intelligence is not as genetically determined as we are prone to think, and that a critical element is emotional. Emotional intelligence has an enormous impact on our ability to function successfully in the world, to be fulfilled, to engage in meaningful relationships, and to deal with conflict. Furthermore, he believes that emotional intelligence can be taught. He identifies emotional awareness, emotional regulation, empathy, and the capacity to manage relationships as critical components of emotional intelligence. His classification of "EQ" as an essential part of intelligence has been criticized on a conceptual basis; for example, Locke (2005) argues that emotional intelligence is really standard intelligence applied to a particular area—emotions. However, the skills Goleman describes are clearly essential to our ability to function in the world.

Goleman also describes how an inability to regulate our emotions can overwhelm our ability to think clearly. Signals of strong emotion create "neural static" that can disrupt our working memory, and that is why, he says, when we are extremely upset, we "just can't think straight" (p. 27). This is further evidence of just how intimately connected our emotions and our thought processes are:

> The connections between the amygdala (and related limbic structures) and the neocortex are the hub of the battles or cooperative treaties struck between head and heart, thought and feeling. This circuitry explains why emotion is so crucial to effective thought, both in making wise decisions and in simply allowing us to think clearly. (p. 27)

Emotions and Logic in Conflict Work

Goleman, Kahneman, Damasio, Gladwell, and others (e.g., de Sousa 1987, Elster 1999) provide powerful testament to the essentially interconnected nature of emotions and logic. Mr. Spock and Captain Kirk really do need one another.

Yet, as I discussed earlier, the predominant approach in the conflict field still seeks to separate the two. We are encouraged to deal with feelings so that the more valuable logical-rational work of problem solving can go on. But the real challenge—no matter what our specific approach—is to view emotions not as an *interference* with the rational work of problem solving, but as *essential* to it. One way in which this has become apparent to me is through working on public dialogues on difficult issues, where the standard reaction to emotional outbursts is to try to shut them down:

"If you let her take over the meeting, it will go to hell in a hand basket." The parks department's fear of Delaney was likely why I was hired to facilitate a neighborhood meeting to review plans to redesign a popular city park. Delaney was the most outspoken opponent of a plan that would require changes in parking, road alignment, and a variety of other features. The department felt these changes were necessary to refurbish the aging facility and to diminish congestion. Those who lived close to where the new parking would be located were very concerned about the impact on them. The city was willing to negotiate specifics but believed some changes were essential. Furthermore, the city had been promised state funding to make these changes, which would be withdrawn if it was not used. Delaney was a very strong personality and was furious at the city, because she felt officials had been withholding information and manipulating her. When she spoke, she often accused city staff of being deceitful and of violating their own rules.

After a series of unpleasant interchanges in which city officials had gone to great lengths to prepare requested information—only to have Delaney accuse them once again of dissembling—they had become increasingly hesitant to interact with her. Their tactics included trying to avoid Delaney, flooding her with information, and asking her to restrict her comments to three minutes. None of this seemed to help, so I was asked to facilitate the next meeting.

Sure enough, Delaney responded to a slightly revised parking plan by accusing the city of not taking her and her neighbors' concerns seriously and of suggesting only "cosmetic changes." I let her go on until she was finished and then asked a couple of clarifying questions. I then said that I would like to hear more about her concerns in a minute. But first I turned to Renee, one of the city officials, and offered her a chance to respond—specifically, to react to the anger that Delaney and some others had expressed about whether their concerns had been taken seriously. I told Renee she did not have to defend herself, but if she had a reaction to what was said, she was welcome to share it. I don't think anyone—city staff or the neighbors—were expecting this. The unwritten rule was that while neighbors were allowed to be angry, city employees were not. Of course, I took a risk in doing this, but I had the sense that Renee could pull this off if I asked her the question in the right way. I did not ask her "How do you feel," but rather, "What is your reaction?" which could lead to a discussion of her emotional reaction, her analysis of the situation, or both.

Renee said, "I wish you could see the amount of time some of us put into trying to accommodate your concerns and still deal with the serious infrastructure problem we are facing. We may not have produced exactly what you wanted, but we have tried very hard, and I wish you could understand this." She said this with an air of resignation and slight exasperation, but not with much anger. I said nothing in response, and there was what I experienced as a moment of very productive silence. All present seemed to be holding their breath, waiting for what would happen next. Then Delaney said, "You may have tried, but you did not succeed. Let's keep trying." Not as great an affirmation as I might have hoped for, but there was not much emotional "oomph" behind her words, and the request to keep trying was a very different kind of statement from what had preceded. Renee responded, "Sure, let's." And we went on to have a more productive interchange.

It's not as if this single interaction turned everything around. Delaney was still outspoken and the city defensive, but the nature, or at least the tone, of the discussion became more constructive. There were two elements to my intervention that seem significant in retrospect. One was that instead of trying to stop Delaney from expressing her anger and even disdain, I invited her to say more, although my questions were requests for her to *explain* her thinking rather than emote. The other was that I did not ask the city staff to respond to Delaney's questions or accusations, but simply to react. This gave Renee the space to bring her emotions into the equation if and as she chose to.

I did not take this approach because I was thinking, "Find a way of bringing feeling and thinking together, of overcoming the bifurcation between emotions and logic." This and similar interactions occurred long before I had begun to think in those terms. It just seemed like the right thing to do to change the interaction's dynamic. In other words, I confronted my own fear of this "going to hell in a hand basket" and consciously decided not to let the city staff's fears become my own. Instead, I let my own feelings inform my thinking.

I also felt that I had to show enough trust in the participants to give them the space to let their emotions rise to the surface as part of their deliberative process. This was definitely "thinking fast," as most of our interventions in conflict are—and, like everyone else,

I sometimes err when I do this. But if we at least give our intuitions a moment to surface, they can do important work. We can then bring a bit of System 2 thinking to bear to examine what our "gut" is telling us.

What we may not realize—especially if emotions are not clearly expressed or demonstrated—is that we are always making decisions about how to focus on the emotional content and rational component of an interaction, because both are always present. Most people's default position is to gravitate toward the logical, rational, problem-solving element, because emotions seem unpredictable, chaotic, energy-draining, and sometimes just plain scary. We often don't have the skills, self-confidence, or even the language to take on intense emotions. So we prefer to keep a conversation calm and rational if we can. But trying to maintain a logical demeanor does not mean that emotions are not playing a role. They always are. The question is whether or not we deal with them intentionally.

How can we counteract our tendency to divide emotions and logic? We have been educated, socialized, and taught very basic language that promotes this dichotomy. We have complex and inconsistent values about being emotional and being rational, as the epigraphs that opened this chapter demonstrate. We believe it is important to be in touch with our feelings, yet sometimes we dismiss efforts to do so as self-indulgent, soft, and a means of avoiding hard realities and difficult problems. On the other hand, being rational and reasonable under stress is a widely admired capacity, but sometimes it is equated with being detached, cold, and uncaring.

We are up against a lot in finding ways to move ourselves and others beyond this dichotomy. But it is also natural to try to find an integrative approach. The metaphor of the left-brain/right-brain dichotomy—although wrong as science—suggests the importance of trying to bring together these two elements of our cognitive structure. Let's consider a few ways that we do this, whether intentionally or not.

The Language of Feeling and Thinking

We use both feeling and thinking language to ask questions, relate events, propose actions, and react to what others have said, and we often frequently substitute one for other. For example, if we are inquiring about how someone reacted to a criticism, we might ask, "How did you feel when he said that?" or "What did you think about what he said?" or both—"What did you think and how did that make you feel?" In the preceding example, I asked Renee, "What were your reactions?", which had the potential to open the door both to feeling and thinking responses. It often helps to change our wording from one framework to another to encourage a more constructive interchange.

Feelings About Thoughts, Thoughts About Feelings

One way in which we use language to help people take an integrative approach is to ask them what their feelings are about thoughts and what they think about feelings. I often ask people to explain how they feel about something. For example, if someone is clearly angry at something that has been said, I might say, "You seem angry or upset at the way this is being presented. Can you explain this to us and tell us why?" In some respects, this is unfair, because feelings are not necessarily explainable. However, people can usually identify what stimulated their emotional response.

This is not the same as encouraging people to vent, which is essentially a means of catharsis, of expressing emotions to release them. Venting is a metaphor—an actual vent takes something (such as hot air) out of a room. We are not in this case asking someone to remove the emotional content, but to bring it into the interaction in a constructive way. The counterpart to this is to invite people to express how they feel about an interaction that appears based in measured, logical, rational statements. Often, we go back and forth between both approaches as occurred in this court-ordered mediation:

Les owned a plumbing company and had been called in during one of the coldest days of the winter because Barrie's pipes had frozen. Les tried to unfreeze the line but in the end had to replace it. Replacing it cost about $500, but the time Les and one of his employees put into trying to thaw the line cost more than $1,000. Barrie was very upset, because he felt that it would have been much cheaper if they had just done it the "right way" to begin with.

In a small claims court mediation over this conflict, Les said, "Our standard practice is first to try to thaw the line, because often we can solve the problem immediately that way. It did not work this time. Sorry. So we charged you for time and materials, plus a 5 percent overhead cost. That is standard, too. In hindsight, it would have been wiser to go straight to the replacement, but in hindsight we all should have bought Apple stock twenty years ago."

Barrie did not like this response, and he seemed ready to give a detailed counter argument. The mediator asked, "How do you feel about this line of argument?" Barrie responded, "It pisses me off," and proceeded to give a counter-argument, which indicated that he really did not like the Apple analogy. The mediator interrupted him by saying, "Comparing this to an investment decision seems particularly annoying. Can you explain why?" Barrie responded, "Because I know when I go into stocks I am speculating. I hired Les because of his reputation and supposed expertise. He is supposed to know what he is doing and not just run up my bill. Some time on thawing efforts makes sense, but not six hours at his rates."

Les responded that he could understand why Barrie felt that way and offered to cut a deal, which Barrie accepted.

The mediator in this interaction—perhaps intentionally, but perhaps not—moved both Les and Barrie back and forth between explaining their feelings and soliciting their emotional reactions to the logical arguments that were being presented. We can't know for sure that this was critical to achieving a positive outcome, but what is clear is that the disputants were responsive to this approach.

Sequences and Iterations

We may not be able to combine the emotional and logical dimensions in one question, statement, or reflection, but we can go back and forth between both dimensions in an iterative manner. Instead of trying to focus first on one element and then switching to the other, we can move, sometimes rapidly, between both. This was more or less what happened in the interaction between Les and Barrie.

Narratives

Conflict communications are conducted in large part through the exchange of narratives. Barrie and Les exchanged their stories, and as with all narratives, their stories had certain characteristics. In this case, Les put forward a narrative of inevitability—that is, what happened could not be helped. Barrie's narrative was one of responsibility. Furthermore, each narrative emphasized a cognitive style, with Les's being rational ("This is how we proceed and why") and Barrie's being more emotional ("I am pissed off because the bill is unfair"). We can often work with the narrative to try to find an overlap between the fundamental stories, thereby bringing together the different elements of their cognitive styles. So Barrie, Les, or the mediator might have said something like this:

> No one expected a "polar vortex" that would create temperatures like we have had. I am sure that Les's business was overwhelmed and they were trying to do the best they could to keep up with demand. That was probably stressful. On the other hand, that also suggests that

"normal operating procedures" might not have been as useful as they sometimes are, and perhaps that was the case here as well.

Of course, we can't know the impact this might have had, but it does illustrate the combination of narratives and the way in which the emotional and logical dimensions could be reallocated, as it were, between the disputants.

Observations

I have often restricted my interventions to simple observations about what is going on, waiting to see where the disputants then take the discussion. This is probably the most frequent intentional intervention I make as a third party with regard to this paradox. Following are some paraphrased examples of observations I have made to people I have worked with in conflict:

- "June, you are speaking about how you feel about what happened, and, Janet, you are talking about what you think we should do now. It seems like you might be talking past each other a bit."

- "Your team [one side] is upset and wants to say so in no uncertain terms, while your group [the other] is focused on why you did what you did and would like this to be acknowledged."

- "Every time one of you talks about feelings, the other responds about what makes logical sense. I am guessing this has crossed you up before."

Sometimes these comments have helped, and sometimes they have not. But they have almost never hurt. If I am off in either my observation or the timing of my comment, or if they really do not want to take this on, they usually just ignore me.

Identifying Feelings and Thinking

Another common approach is exploratory—to inquire about people's feelings and thinking, which we can do by way of counterbalancing the tendencies we detect or by reinforcing them. For example, when people employ the language of logic, I can ask for their feelings about the situation, or I can ask them to say more about their reasoning and how they developed it. One approach tries to bring in the missing element; the other builds on their area of comfort and also may encourage them to bring in the other dimension of their own accord.

Venting

We sometimes misuse or overuse this approach. Though it may temporarily feel good, venting can reinforce itself and does not necessarily lead to a reduction in anger (Goleman 2011). However, venting is sometimes helpful—usually when people simply cannot go on until they have given full expression to their upset or anger. Unless we are willing to accept a forceful expression of emotions without trying to tamp them down, we may be avoiding a key element of the conflict and effectively shutting down one of the parties. The challenge we often face is how to do this in a way that keeps people safe, does not reinforce an abusive power dynamic, and does not shut down subsequent communication. This gets us back to the issue of avoidance and engagement, discussed in chapter 4.

Making Use of Tension in Our Own Experience of Emotion and Logic

Naturally, we experience this tension as interveners, as well as when we are disputants. My first response to almost all displays of strong emotion is to become analytical, and I sometimes have to work very intentionally on staying with the feelings. On occasion, we can use this tension to help others in conflict—first by being aware of it and second by sharing it. For example, I may say to disputants, "My natural tendency is to want to calm things down and stay rational, but I suspect that is not what people need at the moment." Or I might remark, "The nice, rational discussion we are having at the moment is comfortable to me, which makes me think we may be avoiding some of the deeper feelings that are driving this conflict." The conscious determination of how to proceed then becomes everyone's responsibility, not just mine.

Follow Others' Lead

Finally, we can follow the lead of those with whom we are working, without trying to influence their direction. This is akin to what Bush and Folger (2005) refer to as "following the parties around the room."

What We Feel, How We Think

Although there are common patterns in the neurobiological basis of our emotional and rational life, everyone has their own unique cognitive and emotional process. This means that how we integrate our feelings and our thinking is also unique to each of us.

We vary in how expressive we are with our feelings, how in touch we are with what we are experiencing, which emotions are acceptable and which we are more likely to suppress, how well we can manage our feelings, and how quickly we move from one emotional state to another. Our rational processes are also extremely varied. We are more or less methodical in our thinking. We may be prone to focus on facts and logical deductions, and to break issues apart into their component parts, or we may be more inclined to look for broad patterns, generalizations, or overriding concepts. There are areas of reasoning we are more comfortable with and others with which we are less adept. Under stress, some of us become more analytical and others more emotionally expressive.

And we always operate in a relational space. For example, I may be much more prone to emphasize a quiet, logical approach in interaction with someone who is very emotionally labile, while being more likely to articulate my emotions when interacting with someone who is constrained in their emotional expressiveness. So we need to be careful in generalizing how people respond to the interaction between emotion and logic.

Many taxonomies and personality inventories have been developed to provide information about how we approach decision making, conflict, and more generally the challenges of everyday life. Most of us have used one or more of these inventories, taken them ourselves, and/or studied them. They commonly consist of scales that measure where we fall along a variety of continuums, defined by either cognitive or emotional variables. One of the most popular of these tests is the Myers-Briggs Type Indicator, or MBTI (Myers 1962, Myers et al. 1998). Based on the theories of Carl Jung, particularly his 1921 book *Psychological Types* (reprinted in 1976), the MBTI attempts to measure our tendencies on four scales defined by dichotomous variables meant to indicate how we perceive the world around us and how we make judgments based on those perceptions. The specific variables in the MBTI are introversion–extroversion, sensing–intuition, judging–perceiving, and thinking–feeling. The thinking–feeling dichotomy in particular suggests that we make decisions and analyze information either through a logical, fact-based, systemic, and deductive process *or* through a consideration of our likes, values, and the impact our decisions will have on others (Quenk 2009).

The MBTI and other personality inventories—such as the Minnesota Multiphasic Personality Inventory (Hathaway and McKinley 1989), the Strength Deployment Inventory (Porter 1971), and the Neuroticism Extraversion Openness Personality Inventory (NEO-PI) (Costa and McCrae 1992)—can prompt us to look at our characteristic ways of understanding the world and responding to different types of challenges, but each of these has been criticized for its methodology and underlying presumptions. For example, the MBTI has been criticized because its variables, expressed as dichotomies, are not clearly connected to common patterns of behavior. If the variables truly measured different types, we might expect a bimodal distribution—that is, a peak of people would measure high at each end of the continuum of each variable. But instead, there is close to a bell-shaped distribution with a peak at the center of each variable (Pittenger 1993; Stricker and Ross 1962, 1964).

I believe that the dichotomous framework that underlies the MBTI and other inventories of personality or cognitive style limits their effectiveness. When we try to understand how people react to conflict, we should not think of approaches characterized by emotional expressiveness as independent or in opposition to those characterized by logic. Although we each have individual ways in which we use emotions and logic, we do not choose between them—rather, they are both present in everything we do. Furthermore, how we use emotions and logic in any given context always takes place relative to how others are dealing with this same dynamic. So what might appear to be a disputant's very reserved or very emotive style might only be the case in interaction with a style exhibited by someone else or in a particular context.

Until we develop a more sophisticated analytical framework, it is probably more helpful to use a series of considerations or questions that illuminate how we use feelings and logic, rather than to search for or rely on a supposedly comprehensive taxonomy or inventory of styles. Some potentially useful questions to ask ourselves, or to put to those with whom we work, include the following:

- What language are people using—both to describe their own conflict experience and to characterize those with whom they are in conflict? Specifically, are they using the language of thinking, feeling, or action? For example, do they describe an incident in terms of what they thought, felt, or did?

- How emotionally expressive are the people involved, and which particular emotions are they most likely to identify with or to demonstrate?

- What is likely to trigger a disputant to be more emotionally expressive, and what is likely to lead to a less expressive response? For example, as stress increases, are people likely to adopt the language and posture of a more logical or a more emotional response?

- How do people use emotions and logic to avoid conflict and to engage in conflict?

- How consistent and how variable are people in their use of emotions and logic?

- What is the nature of the argument that people are making or the narrative they are employing? Is it analytical? Logical? Evidence-based? Emotional? Rights-based? Focused on values?

- As people become more emotionally expressive, do they speak the language of emotion more or the discourse of logic and rationality? For example, if I get angry, I am likely to listen less and to argue more, but my argument will be conducted using the paradigm of logic and rationality (even if what I say makes no sense whatsoever).

- What is the impact of one person's use of emotions and logic on how others manage this dynamic? How comfortable are people in interacting with those who have a very different way of employing emotions and logic?

Although this is not an exhaustive list of questions, I present them as an indication of what we might consider in observing the different ways in which people (including ourselves) approach this paradox. For example, consider how some of these questions might be used better to explore and understand this unpredictable turn of events in a divorce mediation:

> Geneva and Roland had been married for about twelve years and had three young children when they mutually decided to end their marriage. Geneva had recently resumed her career as a dental hygienist. Roland was a civil engineer employed by a large construction/development firm. Though this was ostensibly a mutual decision, Geneva seemed relieved and Roland tense. Just as there had been a somewhat typical role division in their marriage, with Geneva staying home to rear the children and Roland working, there also appeared to be a stereotypically gendered division in their resort to emotion and logic. Geneva was much more free in expressing emotions—mostly anger about the past and fear about the future—in the mediation, whereas Roland presented himself as the logical, rational engineer who was focusing on facts. The more logical Roland's presentation, the more emotional Geneva's became.
>
> At one particularly tense moment, Roland abruptly jumped up from the table and started rapidly pacing around the room. He delivered an energetic rant: "This is the age where we are all supposed to express our emotions, right?! Well I am going to express my emotion! This is all bullshit. What Geneva is asking for is totally unreasonable and it pisses me off!"

And on he went for about five minutes, while Geneva just smiled and my co-mediator and I watched and listened. Geneva seemed thrilled—as if she had won a victory by getting Roland to get angry. Roland seemed pretty pleased with himself as well, as if he had finally done something right. After this incident, he returned to his seat and resumed his ostensibly logical manner, and the two of them concluded their negotiations fairly quickly. They continued to be negative about each other, but the tension level had at least temporarily dissipated. I thought that Roland's language and the relationship he identified between emotions and logic were especially interesting. Three things in particular stood out: First was his statement, "We are all supposed to express our feelings." In other words, he believed that it was normative in this circumstance to act differently from his usual inclinations and OK to get upset. Second, he claimed to be angry because Geneva was being unreasonable; in other words, her failure to abide by his norms about decision making meant he could employ hers. But in reality his presentation was still very logical in nature, even though his affect was angry and upset. Finally, although Roland said he was going to express his feelings, the feelings he showed were anger and exasperation. He did not express his feelings of sorrow, fear, regret, or caring—even though these were clearly part of the picture.

The impact on Geneva was also surprising. She not only thoroughly approved of this outburst, she actually seemed comforted by it. She appeared to feel vindicated to some extent in her own more overtly emotional approach, but perhaps even more significantly, she felt empowered by her ability to "get to him." I suspect this dynamic was not new to them.

Gender and Culture, Emotions and Logic

The belief that women are more emotional and men are more logical is widespread. So are many stereotypes about cultural differences in regard to emotions (for example, that Italians are emotional, Norwegians reserved, and Navajos stoic). We see these beliefs perpetuated in almost all forms of popular culture. But are they true?

There is no consensus on this, and the question itself is overly broad and misleading. Emotions are an important part of what drives *all* people, regardless of gender or culture. If instead we ask three related questions, we can at least take a more nuanced and meaningful look at variations in people's emotional experience across genders and cultures:

How are emotions *experienced?*

How are they *expressed?*

How are they *managed?*

For example, there may be less difference in how "emotional" men and women are in terms of the intensity with which they experience emotions, more difference in how they express emotions, and further difference in "emotional intelligence"—particularly, their ability to empathize or experience others' emotions (Goleman 2011, Karafyllis and Ulshöfer 2008). But these are differences in degree rather than in kind.

Deborah Tannen reports on the difference in linguistic styles between boys and girls, as well as between men and women, in a number of her writings, most notably in *You Just Don't Understand: Women and Men in Conversation* (2007). She concludes that there is a significant gender difference in communication styles in the populations she studied (US English speakers). Men are more likely to employ conversation to exchange information and to establish hierarchy, whereas women employ conversation to establish emotional connection. This difference occurs from a very early age. It is related to the difference between what Tannen calls the "message" (the actual content of a communication) and the "metamessage" (its unspoken implications); women tend to be more tuned into the metamessage, men to the message. In our example, Roland's main message was that he was angry and going to say so. For Geneva, the metamessage—that she had power over Roland—was equally important.

There are very strong norms in many cultures governing which emotions are appropriate for men and for women to express, and even to feel. For example, it's often more normative for men to express anger and for women to express fear or hurt. If men express fear, it may be considered "unmanly," and if women express anger, they may be viewed as "emasculating." But this does not mean that men do not fear as much as women or women do not get angry as often as men. It just means that some emotions can be expressed, while others must be suppressed to maintain social norms. The consequences of these gender biases are often very severe, perhaps leading to greater rates of depression for women (anger directed inward) and violence (fear externalized) from men.

Similarly, we see significant differences across cultures in the ways that individuals express and regulate emotions, as well as which emotions are considered acceptable, but not necessarily in which emotions are experienced. Some studies have shown that facial expressions displaying anger, happiness, disgust, sadness, and fear are interpreted similarly across quite a range of cultures (Ekman 1972; Izard 1971). This suggests that these emotions are also experienced similarly—at least on a physiological level—across a wide range of cultures. However, cultural norms about what kind of emotional expression is acceptable and the appropriate context for doing so vary greatly. For example, displaying emotions in formal negotiations is common in some cultures, but in others, negotiations are expected to be conducted by logical analysis and argumentation (Moore and Woodrow 2010).

As with all our attempts to generalize about cultural or gender variables, it is important that we remember the enormous variation within culture and gender (just think of the differences among your siblings or your children). At best, there are different tendencies, and perhaps these differences are themselves artifices of our norms and beliefs about emotions and logic. Although it seems clear that important differences in norms about emotional expressiveness and the presentation of a logical approach exist across cultures and genders, it is far less clear that people experience emotions differently or think differently. Furthermore, the idea that emotions and logic are separate entities is likely a cultural artifact as well, and perhaps a recent one.

As conflict interveners working across cultures and genders, we do best, I believe, by accepting that everyone struggles to integrate the emotional–logic polarity and that most experience a similar range of emotions with a similar range of intensity. What varies is the degree to which people allow this experience into their consciousness, the types of emotions that they feel permitted to express, the manner and intensity with which they express it, their ability to understand and empathize with others' emotions, and their capacity to regulate and manage their own. Similarly, I believe everyone strives to find their own logic or rationale for how they understand a conflict and the actions they choose to take. What may seem illogical behavior from the outside makes sense to the person who is behaving that way.

Whether we are "thinking fast" or "thinking slow"; acting on the basis of emotions, instincts, knowledge, experience, or habit; or using a more evolutionarily advanced or a more primitive part of our neural system, both emotions and logic are always playing a role. This means that no matter how logical and rational our own actions or decision-making process may seem, they do not occur independently of our emotional process, so actions or decisions that seem totally reasonable to us can seem unreasonable or emotionally driven to others. When one person accuses another of acting on the basis of emotion, not reason, the accusation is always half right—and half wrong.

This is true regardless of gender or culture. While such factors may encourage or reinforce socially constructed tendencies and preferences, any claims to simple dichotomies (e.g., "women are from Venus, men are from Mars") is misleading. Self-awareness is crucial here. If we can access our own emotional drivers and our own thought processes, we can increase our understanding of ourselves, our empathy for others, and our ability to engage in constructive interactions (or to be clear why we don't want to interact).

Reflections from Practice

Over the course of my work as a conflict specialist, I have come to realize that although agreements might be more readily attained by promoting a rational, logical exchange, their depth and durability require a deeper mining of the emotional content of the disputes they are meant to resolve. This is not about encouraging people to release their feelings or transform their emotional experience, which is neither possible nor necessary in most conflict interventions. Efforts to focus directly on emotional expression to the exclusion of logic or analysis are just as limited as approaches that attempt to avoid the emotional content. Sometimes, conflict engagement efforts precipitate an emotional release or exchange that transforms the nature of conflict, the relationship, or the disputant, but this seldom happens because of intentional efforts to accomplish such a transformation. But if we avoid engaging the emotional dimension, then we are likely to end up with a more superficial and brittle outcome.

In previous writings (Mayer 2012a), I have suggested that we consider three fundamental but overlapping components of human needs as drivers in conflict: interests, identity needs, and survival needs. To access all three of these levels of conflict, we need to bring to bear all elements of our cognitive capacities—emotional, intuitive, analytical, and logical. Many classic texts on negotiation (e.g., Fisher, Ury, and Patton 1991; Lax and Sebenius 1987; Moore 2003) emphasize a consideration of the interests of disputants. These may be substantive, procedural, or psychological in nature. The thinking goes that by focusing on these interests, we can open up a wider range of options for addressing conflict. This is essentially a logical process, in which the challenge is to make sure emotions are dealt with to the extent necessary to allow rationality to predominate. However, the most enduring aspects of conflict reside in our concerns about identity, meaning, values, and security. Although we can approach some aspects of these through rational processes, we cannot fully do so without accessing their emotional dimension.

I have had a sense of this from the beginning of my work as a conflict intervener. For one thing, the cues about how committed people were to agreements they reached seemed to be primarily emotional, not logical. It is not so much whether people said a resolution was acceptable or made sense, as how they said it, that led me to believe something important had happened (or had not happened). And it was also how I felt, whether I sensed that we had made progress or that we had just papered over differences. Sometimes minor or procedural agreements play a significant role in moving a process forward—but they do not accomplish this primarily by chipping away at the larger problem. The power of partial or short agreements lies in their ability to harness disputants' emotional engagement in trying to find a constructive path forward.

The logical challenge of finding an acceptable solution to a seemingly intractable problem is rarely the hardest part of our work with disputants. Finding the right way to respect, uncover, and use the emotional element is more often the most difficult thing we do as conflict interveners. Sometimes it is the overt expression of emotion that poses the greatest challenge—and sometimes it's the suppression of intense feelings.

> Two neighboring municipalities had long shared a number of facilities for handling waste, water, recycling, and trash. These had led to a number of conflicts over the years and to some pretty unpleasant public pronouncements by the leaders of each municipality. I was asked to mediate a dispute about a particular facility. Before scheduling joint meetings, I met in

private and in confidence with each town's city manager, mayor, and council. These discussions were mostly about the history of the dispute, the politics involved, and the legal framework. All were laced with considerable levels of emotion, but the issues were presented in a logical manner with lots of anecdotes. The predominant emotion participants expressed was something between frustration and weariness.

In the middle of a meeting with one of the councils, however, one of the members really let it rip. He started telling me exactly what he thought of the mayor of the other town (let's call her mayor of C)—and what he thought of her was that she was a liar, a manipulator, and a megalomaniac, and he expressed this using language that I do not choose to replicate here. He went on for more than five minutes, while his colleagues just watched. I decided that he had gone from venting to testing me to see what I would do. So I said that I believed I got his point and asked whether he thought, in view of his feelings about the mayor of C, that negotiations made any sense. He said he was very skeptical but thought it was probably worth a try. He almost seemed jovial after his outburst. The others said nothing, although several rolled their eyes, as if he were a pain in the neck to them, too, but one they were used to dealing with.

On the other hand, none of his colleagues were happy about the actions of the mayor of C either (whom I'd observed to be a tough but skillful negotiator). So I asked them to discuss their history and their thoughts about her. No one let loose in the same way, but each discussed his or her own misgivings about dealing with the mayor of C. I asked all of them the same question: "Does it make sense to negotiate, given their feelings, and could they imagine a realistic outcome that would justify the effort?" They replied that it did make sense and that they could imagine a justifiable outcome. So we went forward, and we achieved an agreement that has endured.

I had mixed feelings about the council member's outburst. On the one hand, I felt very annoyed at what seemed a misogynist and mean-spirited outburst, as well as a personal challenge to me. On the other hand, the emotions of this group might otherwise have been suppressed. I think his freely expressing his emotions somehow violated the sense most of those present had about their role and status as elected officials—and suppressed emotions could have interfered with the capacity of the group to reach a genuine agreement.

What is interesting to me about this situation, in retrospect, is my own reaction to it. All my natural instincts and some important values were urging me to close down the emotional outburst—and maybe I should have. I am not sure that letting this councilman have his say accomplished anything. He was well behaved and in fact very quiet during joint sessions, but perhaps he would have been that way no matter what happened. During the outburst, I wanted to shut him up, and I had to resist my impulse to do so. It would have been relatively easy to interrupt, reflect, and reframe and then move on to someone else.

Despite my years of attempting to become more comfortable with emotionality in conflict, my natural instincts remain. And I know they come from a decent place. I want people to be able to talk constructively, to engage on difficult issues, and to make progress if possible. Intense and overtly negative or hostile emotional expressiveness can interfere with this. For me, however, the struggle isn't to find a way to control or guide emotionality in a constructive direction; I can usually find a way to do this. Rather, it about letting the emotionality into the process to begin with—to create space, to ask for it, to receive it nonjudgmentally, and to give the disputants the opportunity to monitor and to react to this before I jump into the picture. I am not saying it is OK to allow people to abuse each other or to take over a process with emotional volatility, but as I have said, that is not usually the error I make. I am more likely to err by shying *away* from emotionality. Over the years, I have disciplined myself to make sure I do not behave as if I am the most uncomfortable person in the room with emotional expressiveness, and to err on the side of allowing this to go on too long, rather than shutting it down too soon.

Of course, integrating emotion and logic, or passion and reason, is not simply about letting people express their feelings. This process also requires that people continually think about their feelings and experience their emotional reactions to the ideas that are being discussed. It requires that we encourage people to use the entire range of their cognitive processes, emotional and logical, at all steps of a conflict process, and that we work on doing the same for ourselves.

A number of years ago I was involved in an intense conflict intervention process in which one of the key players was a union leader who had a way with words that reminded me of Yogi Berra (the Hall of Fame baseball player with a wonderful way of mangling quotes and still making sense). What the union leader said did not seem to make sense on one level, but on a deeper level it usually did. For example, I remember at one point him saying, "We kept interest basing at them, but they were positioning back at us." This articulation of the moral value we put on negotiating processes that are always a bit positional and a bit interest-based has always stuck with me.

One of the union leader's common expressions was, "I have a gut feeling in my head." At the time, my co-mediator and I had a hard time not laughing at this juxtaposition. But I think he got it right. Our gut feelings provide important cognitive information, and much of our reasoning takes place in our gut, just like our emotional life exists in our head. He naturally integrated emotions and logic, and that's what made him an effective leader.

chapter seven

neutrality and advocacy

We must always take sides. Neutrality helps the oppressor, never the victim. Silence encourages the tormentor, never the tormented.

Elie Wiesel, 1986 Nobel Prize acceptance speech

A mediator shall conduct a mediation in an impartial manner and avoid conduct that gives the appearance of partiality.

American Arbitration Association, American Bar Association, Association for Conflict Resolution, Model Standards of Mediator Conduct

Conflict specialists know there is something amiss in our reliance on neutrality as a fundamental self-defining feature. We are not neutral, at least in any clearly definable way. The concept itself defies easy explanation and also raises major ethical questions (Gibson, Thompson, and Bazerman 1996). Still, there is something about the idea of neutrality that is essential to our understanding of how we can help people in conflict, especially if we are functioning as third parties. Even when we act as coaches, advisors, or advocates, we value being objective and impartial, just as we do in the role of avowedly neutral third parties. But at the same time, our clients expect us to have opinions, values, views, and ideas, and they need to believe that we are committed to helping them accomplish their most important goals. And they are right to want this. Our work as interveners requires that we learn to function as both advocates and neutrals to fulfill our commitment to our clients and to promote a constructive approach to conflict. This is true whether we are acting in a third-party or an ally role.

The complex interaction between our functioning both as neutrals and advocates raises major questions about who we are and what we do. If we are not neutral, how can we differentiate ourselves from others who work on conflict? But if we *are* neutral, what does that say about our values about social justice, equality, peace, community, and autonomy? These are values that motivate many of us to do this work, and they fuel the commitment, passion, and energy that is essential to our effectiveness.

In an attempt to deal with this tension, conflict specialists sometimes draw a distinction between neutrality and impartiality (Cooks and Hale 1994; Moore 2003; Rifkin, Millen, and Cobb 1991), although we are inconsistent in how we differentiate between these. Neutrality is sometimes defined in terms of our values, whether we actively take sides, the impact we have on the substantive outcome of a conflict, or our previous relationship with disputants, whereas impartiality is seen in how we treat different parties, what are our feelings or beliefs about an issue, or how we conduct ourselves more generally. I find these distinctions confusing, and I use the terms *neutrality* and *impartiality* interchangeably. Moreover, the attempt to resolve this dilemma by differentiating between neutrality and impartiality misses the point. We really do find ourselves in a paradox here. Whatever we call it, the commitment we make to disputants—especially as third parties—to remain honest, transparent, evenhanded, and fair in our dealings with them—is essential to our self-concept and to the overt or implied contract we establish when we intervene in conflict. Yet it is also a commitment that is impossible to honor completely. We have values that affect how we conduct ourselves as professionals. Every act we take has an impact in some way on how a conflict progresses. We can't be effective and completely dispassionate. The contradiction in our commitment to neutrality and our capacity to be truly neutral is one element of this paradox.

The other element in the paradox is advocacy. Though we usually don't define ourselves as advocates, that's what we are. For example, we advocate for our explicit and implicit beliefs about autonomy, social justice, and equality. We advocate for outcomes that do not take unfair advantage of either party. We also advocate for particular outcomes—for someone to accept a compromise, to make a counteroffer, to move beyond an impasse. Were we not effective advocates, we would not be of much value to disputants.

Some argue that we should remain neutral about the substance of a dispute but should advocate for a constructive process. This, too, is an effort to deal with the tension that exists between our avowed identity and the reality of what we actually do. But this as well is a flawed distinction. Process and substance are inextricably intertwined. All of our interventions have an impact on both process and substance. We cannot make the tension between our functioning as advocates and our role as neutrals go away by relying on this distinction.

This paradox is so cogent because what we offer relies both on our commitment to impartiality and our effectiveness as advocates. Indeed, our commitment to neutrality is *enhanced* by our effectiveness as advocates. And our capacity to advocate is dependent on our ability to maintain an impartial stance. Yet we generally see neutrality and advocacy as incompatible.

What We Mean by Neutrality

Neutrality is a multilayered concept that is used to convey very different meanings. We are neutral if we do not take sides in a dispute. We can also be "in neutral," which means not being in any gear, not moving forward or backward; in this sense, being neutral can suggest doing nothing at all. In electrical or chemical terms, neutral means neither positive nor negative. Being neutral sounds vaguely like being a neuter (and has similar linguistic roots—both derive from the Latin words for *not either*). In our popular discourse, being neutral is easily equated with being weak, uncaring, uncommitted, uninvolved, and indecisive. Yet as conflict specialists understand it, neutrality takes a considerable amount of discipline, skill, and commitment.

What exactly do we mean by being neutral—as in maintaining our neutrality when we intervene in a conflict? Gibson et al. (1996) suggest three types of neutrality in their critique of the concept of mediator neutrality:

- **Impartiality.** A reflection of the mediator's lack of bias and his or her capacity to put personal feelings and opinions aside.

- **Equidistance.** The mediator's ability to provide equal weight to the views and needs of all disputants.

- **Discourse.** The mediator's capacity and commitment to provide an opportunity for all parties to articulate their stories in a manner that promotes the legitimacy of their concerns, and then to frame these in a manner that encourages parties to consider each other's viewpoints.

I have suggested five aspects of neutrality with regard to conflict work (Mayer 2012b): structural, behavioral, emotional, perceptive, and aspirational. I have further argued that the only element of neutrality that we can truly commit to is aspirational. I would now add a sixth element—cognitive. Let's look at each.

Structural Neutrality

Structural neutrality refers to where our position, history, or network of relationships locates us with respect to disputants. Clearly, if I am hired by someone to advise or represent them, I am not neutral. Nor am I neutral if I stand to gain if one party prevails in a conflict. These structural challenges to our neutrality are obvious, but what if I belong to the same church or country club as a disputant, have mediated or arbitrated previous cases involving a disputant, went to school with one of them, or represented one previously on an unrelated case? These less obvious examples are also challenges to our structural neutrality. Our personal characteristics (race, gender, religion, age, nationality, and so on) are also potential impediments to neutrality. Complete structural neutrality is impossible. Sometimes the best we can hope for is being non-neutral in this sense in relatively equal ways:

> Midway through a relatively smooth divorce mediation between Patty and Jerome, Patty turned to me and said, "Bernie, do you know we met at a party not that long ago?" Oops. "We did?" I replied, somewhat embarrassed at having no recollection of this whatsoever. "Yes, we were at Charlie's birthday party last year; she is my best friend." Fortunately, I did remember the party, and I did not recall doing or saying anything too embarrassing there. Charlie was a close professional friend of mine, but we had also worked together as political activists in the past. I turned to Jerome and asked if this newly discovered connection was a concern. He said, "No, I don't care. As a matter of fact, you know my brother." Sure enough, I did. His brother was another colleague and friend (their last name was very common and they did not look like each other at all). We were in business.

Most of us have had similar experiences, especially if we live in small communities. These connections are not generally problems as long as we are transparent about them and the parties are comfortable with them, but they do suggest the limitations on our structural neutrality. Some connections are clearly problematic, others are not a problem, and there's a gray area in the middle.

Whether our structural connections with disputants are problematic depends on the context in which we are working. I recall discussing proposed standards of practice for lawyer mediators in British Columbia in the mid-1980s. One standard suggested that lawyers who had previously represented someone, even on an entirely unrelated matter, could not act as their mediator. A lawyer from a small community in northern BC said that this meant he could not mediate in his community at all, since at one point or another he had represented just about everyone. The standard was modified accordingly.

Behavioral Neutrality

Behavioral neutrality concerns our actions—whether we act in a way that promotes one party's interests at the cost of another. Here, too, there are obvious non-neutral behaviors, such as arguing for one point of view and against another, revealing confidential information, or providing financial resources to one side only. But almost everything we do in a conflict, no matter our role, can empower one party at the expense of another, no matter our intention. Who I ask to speak first; what kind of eye contact, body language, or linguistic style I employ; the order in which I list issues; or the length of time I speak to different people are ways in which my behavior can affect the course of a conflict and its outcome.

One of the ways we serve disputants when we act as third parties is to act in a way that is partial to one party—sometimes we may even have an ethical obligation to do so. For example, if one person is quiet, intimidated, and anxious in a mediation and another is loud, domineering, and confident, we may very well choose to provide space and support for the more timid participant to voice his or her concerns, to consider options, or just to have air time. In part, this is in service of a more equitable and durable outcome. However, it may mean that the domineering person does not do as well, at least from his or her point of view, than might have been the case had we not acted to "level the playing field" (playing fields are never level).

Emotional Neutrality

Emotional neutrality is akin to what some refer to as *impartiality* or *lack of bias*. Do I feel more sympathetic to one point of view or one party? Do I like some people more than others? Do I hope that some participants will achieve their goals, whereas others will back off of unreasonable demands? In principle, I ought not to allow such feelings to affect my judgment or behavior; in practice, they frequently and inevitably do. I have heard mediators express two challenges related to this.

One challenge is to learn to control, question, and contain our emotional biases. The hope is that the more we work to appreciate all disputants' experience and pain, the more able we will be to contain our biases. On the other hand, sometimes we are fooling ourselves—we simply like some people more than others. We are human, no matter what our professional commitment. Furthermore, we are seldom *aware* of all of our biases.

The other challenge is to behave in a fair and appropriate manner (back to behavioral neutrality), regardless of our feelings or biases. The greater challenge here may be that of overcompensating—trying to correct our bias by being especially attentive to the parties we are less sympathetic toward, thereby acting unfairly toward those to whom we feel more connected. If I am aware of feeling extremely negative toward one party or point of view or positive to another, I can choose not to act as a third party, to withdraw from the case, or to work carefully to monitor my actions. In most interventions, however, my emotional reactions are less extreme and I may be less conscious of them, but they can still have a powerful impact, one which I am not always aware of.

Cognitive Neutrality

Cognitive neutrality is about how we think. Is our approach to how we make sense of a conflict or interaction, how we analyze alternative ways of proceeding, or how we assess potential outcomes more in line with some parties than others? For example, are we more likely to interact by telling anecdotes, throwing out multiple ideas, and putting forth intuitive judgments? Or are we more prone to a linear, analytical, and deductive manner for processing issues? When our cognitive style is similar to one party's natural approach, we may find that we can more easily communicate and relate to that person. Depending on our role in a conflict, we might structure an approach that is far more inviting to some than to others. The impact of this dynamic can be seen every day in courthouses, where people, often representing themselves, are often forced to operate in an alien cognitive framework. Mediation and other alternative approaches to conflict tend to operate within a cognitive framework that is more familiar to some disputants and agents than to others.

One of the challenges for conflict interveners is to develop mechanisms that allow for constructive interaction among people with very different cognitive styles. To do this, we often have to advocate for an approach that may be unfamiliar or uncomfortable to some of the parties. This is an example of how our capacity and willingness to advocate for a particular style of interaction may not be neutral but is essential to our ability to create a fair venue for interaction.

Perceptive Neutrality

Perceptive neutrality refers to whether others view us as being fair, evenhanded, unbiased, or impartial—as they understand these concepts. We often talk about avoiding the "appearance of bias." This is important, but it's also a moving target. In fact, appearing to be neutral may sometimes require acting in a way that is not neutral. And sometimes we have to risk being perceived as biased in order to help parties interact constructively. We may have to change the structure of interaction to accommodate the style of one party. We may have to put forceful limits on someone who is being disruptive. We may have to spend much more time preparing one party than another. This is one of the many ways in which one type of neutrality may be inconsistent with others.

Aspirational Neutrality

Aspirational neutrality refers to our intentions. We may offer only a narrow form of structural or behavioral neutrality, and we may not be able to offer emotional or cognitive neutrality at all. But we can commit to our intentions. As mediators, we can commit to our intentions not to advocate for one party's interests over another or not to behave in a way that promotes the needs of one side at the expense of the needs of another. As advocates, we can commit to trying to maintain enough emotional distance from a dispute that we can offer objective assessments. This commitment is about intention and best efforts, and the concept of transparency is related to this. We can never be totally transparent, nor would it be advisable (e.g., you don't really want me to tell you what I think of your children unless I really like them). But we can be transparent about any impediments to our neutrality that we are aware of and that we think people ought to know about.

How the Elements Interact: A Case Example

The elements of neutrality are always in play in conflict interventions, and they often trip over each other as we try to find a way to play a constructive role in conflict. This was the case when I dealt with the auditing department of a large government agency:

> Joshua and Simon, managers in a division of a state agency, had a long-simmering dispute that led Simon to refuse to attend meetings at which Joshua was

210 THE CONFLICT PARADOX

present. Because of this, Simon was suspended from his job, pending an investigation. Both were given the option of mediation, and I was asked to work with them to determine whether and how to go forward with the investigation. I scheduled phone calls with each. My conversation with Joshua lasted about forty minutes, during which he told me his version of what had led to this stand-off. He indicated that he was amenable to going forward, although he was hesitant to meet directly with Simon.

Simon called me before our scheduled phone call and said that before he shared his views, he wanted to check me out. He proceeded to interview me for about an hour, during which time he quoted back to me some things he'd heard in an interview with me that he had located on YouTube. He called a second time with some further questions about some work I had done that was published on a website. His questions were astute and to the point, but by the time he was ready to move forward with the mediation, I had spent considerably more time on the phone with him than I had with Joshua. This pattern continued throughout my work with them. I was somewhat uneasy about the time differential and, for that matter, about the amount of time in general, but I also sensed that without being willing to devote this amount of attention to Simon, this process was not going to go anywhere.

I was all over the place in terms of the categories of neutrality. I had no obvious structural connection to either man, although Joshua was about my age and from a similar ethnic background, unlike Simon. Further-more, it turned out that Joshua had participated in a one-day seminar on conflict that I had conducted about three years earlier (I did not remember him). Joshua

came across to me as rigid, angry without owning up
to his anger, and passive-aggressive, whereas Simon
seemed funny, gregarious, and vulnerable. I found it
much easier to communicate with Simon than with
Joshua, and this troubled me, since I *did* communicate
more with Simon (though I told Joshua about the extra
calls). Add to this that I often found Joshua difficult
to understand—he talked in a circular manner, but
one dressed in the linguistic style of deductive logic.
On the other hand, I thought Simon was being a
bit unreasonable in what he was requesting, whereas
Joshua was more reasonable. Joshua was trying to figure
out how to get past this situation, whereas Simon
seemed to think that nothing short of having Joshua's
head delivered to him on a platter would suffice.
Neither seemed to doubt my fairness, and I was able
to dodge Simon's efforts to make me an ally. And I
tried very hard to do right by both of them. They both
appeared to appreciate my work with them and did
arrive at an agreement, although I doubt that their
relationship was significantly improved.

The Dimensions of Advocacy

As with mediation, advocacy is a basic life skill. We all function as
advocates at times, formally and informally. We advocate for our
children, for ourselves, for a particular point of view, for clients, for
a cause, or for a particular course of action. Hospitals have patient
advocates. Children's advocates are formal participants in many
child-protection proceedings. We speak of the "devil's advocate"
when we refer to taking a point of view that may (or may not) be
contrary to our own in order to consider different sides of an issue.
We often equate advocacy with representation, and specifically

with legal representation. The one commonality among all these usages is that advocacy means promoting something or someone.

Advocacy as a Role

The role most commonly associated with advocacy is that of the lawyer, whom we often refer to as an advocate. In many countries (e.g., India, France, Scandinavia, and Holland) the term "advocate" (*avocat, advokat, advocaat*) actually means lawyer or barrister. Because of the identification of advocacy with legal representation, we often equate advocacy with protecting a client's rights. However, advocates perform a wide range of roles. For example, social workers are also expected to advocate for their clients, and advocacy is seen as a key guiding principle in the practice of social work:

> The original mission of social work had much to do with championing the rights of society's most vulnerable members, from children to homeless people to the physically disabled. That mission remains the same over 100 years later. (National Association of Social Workers, 2014)

Many other professions, including nurses, educators, real estate agents, accountants, and psychologists, assume responsibility to advocate for clients. But in all of these roles, the professional is also expected to be mindful of the larger social good and to bring a professional perspective to the situation, which can be understood as a degree of impartiality. All of us, regardless of our professional role, also often act informally as advocates, guided by our personal ethical sense and worldview rather than any particular professional obligations or expectations.

The type of expertise we require to be an effective advocate in different professional contexts varies greatly, particularly in terms of the substantive knowledge needed. The specific roles we play as advocates also vary depending on our profession or the context within which we offer our services. For example, advocates may represent people or causes in negotiations or decision-making forums (lawyers, lobbyists, and real estate agents). They may coach people to advocate better for themselves (therapists, collaborative practitioners, and community organizers). They may provide assistance in formulating an argument, a campaign, or a programmatic initiative (executive coaches, political advisers, and public relations consultants). Or they may provide the personal support people need to help sustain them as they contend with conflict (counselors, friends, and self-help groups).

Conflict specialists have had an easier time embracing some activities that may be associated with an advocacy function—such as coaching, assisting with negotiations, offering strategic advice—rather than accepting the broader context of the advocacy role itself. Advocacy seems to many conflict practitioners to be antithetical to acting as an effective third party. But constructive conflict intervention requires effective advocacy. I have urged that the conflict field embrace the formal role of an advocate, and not just informal advocacy activities, as an essential part of what we offer people in conflict. Advocates are the professionals people in conflict are most likely to turn to for assistance (Mayer 2004). This does not mean that we can act in the formal role of a neutral and advocate on the same case, however, but both roles are essential to assisting people in engaging in conflict constructively and effectively.

Advocacy as a Set of Attitudes

Our focus on advocacy as a role has sometimes obscured the way we function as advocates in almost everything we do as conflict interveners. So it is helpful to look at advocacy not only as a role, but also as a set of attitudes and a range of skills. Here, too, the image many have about what it means to be an advocate is based on the approach articulated by the legal profession. Lawyers are ethically bound to be "zealous advocates" according to the American Bar Association model standards for lawyers (2014). Specifically, these standards say: "As advocate, a lawyer zealously asserts the client's position under the rules of the adversary system. As negotiator, a lawyer seeks a result advantageous to the client but consistent with requirements of honest dealings with others."

Although we can interpret zealous advocacy in widely different ways, it sounds unfortunately close to being a zealot—a term that implies being unreasonable and quite the opposite of neutral or objective. Another interpretation, probably closer to the intentions of this statement, is that advocates should be energetic in their commitment to promoting their clients' interests, but "honest in their dealing with others." As conflict specialists know, disputes are rarely (if ever) purely distributive, and given that cooperation and competition are so closely intertwined (see chapter 2), effectively advocating for our own clients generally means finding a way of meeting their opponents' needs as well. This requires taking an impartial look at the situation. The tension between these interpretations is an expression of the tension between a distributive and an integrative approach to advocacy.

A purely distributive approach, often associated with the concept of zealous advocacy, is likely to be highly adversarial in nature. It also tends to view the outcome in terms of how well one's clients have done compared to how well others have done. Distributively oriented advocates are not likely to think in terms of what helps the entire system of disputants or participants. Suggestions to such an advocate that a prolonged struggle is not in anyone's interests (say, in a divorce) may fall on deaf ears.

On the other hand, advocacy that has an integrative orientation is characterized by efforts to promote the goals of a client or cause through working cooperatively with others—trying to figure out what needs to be done for one party so that the other party's needs are also likely to be met. The attitude here is less adversarial and more problem-solving in nature. The more advocates adopt this attitude, the more likely they are to look for cooperative opportunities. People who are deeply embroiled in conflict may not believe that someone with an integrative orientation is entirely on their side. Of course, in practice, advocates can never take a purely distributive or integrative approach, but must use a combination of both.

In discussing how legal practice is changing, Julie Macfarlane, a law professor who has written extensively about dispute resolution, has put forward the concept of conflict resolution advocacy (2008):

> Conflict resolution advocacy means working with clients to anticipate, raise, strategize, and negotiate over conflict and, if possible, to implement jointly agreed outcomes... Advocacy as conflict resolution places the constructive and creative promotion of partisan outcomes at the centre of the advocate's role and sees this goal as entirely compatible with working with the other side—in fact, this goal can only be achieved by working with the other side. (p. 109)

The Goals of Advocates

Advocates and advocacy efforts vary considerably in their goals and focus. Some may be more attuned to immediate results, while others are more concerned about building power for their cause or clients over a longer time frame. Advocacy efforts intended to promote fundamental social change can be derailed if they fail to focus on changing power dynamics over time and instead direct their attention to obtaining immediate or short-term victories.

In an analysis of the work of the Industrial Areas Foundation, a network of community organizations in the Southwestern United States with a focus on advocating for disadvantaged and underserved communities, labor economist Paul Osterman (2002) summarized the strategy and impact of the group in terms of its capacity to change not only power dynamics but also the political discourse itself:

> Politics itself [has become] increasingly procedural and distant, focused more on legal rights and formal representation than on participation. The solution is a revival of community, stronger associations and groups, and a shift in politics toward more opportunities for citizens to deliberate and decide (p.178).
>
> At its base the IAF wants to alter what it views as an imbalance in power, and it assumes and accepts that as part of its efforts it will encourage and engage in political conflict (p. 179).

Advocates may be personally committed to the work they do, or they may view their activities more dispassionately as part of their professional responsibility. They may take a narrow view of advocacy (I am here to advocate for you to get a good deal in this negotiation) or a broad view (I am here to help you get to where you want to be in your life).

When we act as advocates, we may consciously make decisions about these variables. Or we may be unaware that we are making any choices at all—and, of course, we seldom adhere strictly to any one approach.

The Advocate's Skills

Advocates need and employ the same general skills used by all conflict interveners. They need to be effective communicators and competent conflict analysts, be familiar with a broad range of conflict intervention processes, be knowledgeable about the substantive arenas in which are working, and be excellent negotiators. They also need to be able to understand and work with the power issues, cultural complexities, and systems dynamics at play in a conflict. These are requirements for any effective conflict intervention, but as advocates, certain aspects of these skills become especially important, particularly in the area of strategic thinking, communication, and emotional management.

I suspect that training for advocates in most arenas of practice emphasizes strategic skills (for example, how to craft an argument, analyze a conflict, look at power dynamics, prepare for a negotiation, develop a campaign for change). Some training also emphasizes communication skills, but in my experience, there is not much training regarding the emotional skills necessary for effective advocacy. So we will start by looking at these.

Emotional Skills

Advocates should be able to separate their needs and goals from those of their clients. For example, I may want to end sexual harassment in an organization, and I may believe that the more frequently incidents of harassment are raised and the more corrective action is taken, the more likely cultural norms around harassment will change. But if I am an advocate for individual victims, I will frequently find that they want a quiet way out of the situation and are not ready to make a public charge. There is good reason for this, given how often victims become revictimized by the formal procedures for requesting redress. I must, therefore, be conscious of my commitment both to the larger cause and to my individual client, and I must remain clear that my primary obligation is to my client. This means that I need to be ready to manage my own disappointment if a complaint is not brought forward.

Similarly, an advocate should be able to recognize the tensions in his or her own responsibilities. For example, a patient's advocate in a hospital may genuinely want to support each patient in having his or her concerns addressed, but in the end, the advocate still works for the hospital or health care organization. A desire to help a patient or family who is hurting might prompt an advocate to mislead them about what can actually be done.

In addition, advocates should use their emotions and passions effectively in service of their client or cause. However, they also need to be able to manage these so that their own emotional needs do not take over from those of the clients or cloud their capacity to act strategically. I suspect most people who have worked as advocates have at some point led clients down unproductive paths—with the best of intentions—because they have become too emotionally involved in the conflict.

Advocates also need to establish appropriate boundaries with their clients. To be effective, advocates have to connect personally and emotionally with their clients (and they may have a prior relationship with them). But to provide the wisdom and perspective a client needs, an advocate must be able to establish appropriate boundaries as well. It is not helpful to succumb to "rescue fantasies" or to completely buy into clients' narratives or emotionality. On the other hand, too much distance can also create problems. Effective advocates are empathic with their clients and care about them, and they are not focused solely on the issue or the cause, but they do not try to take on their clients' pain, anger, or fear. Finding and maintaining appropriate boundaries is a challenge for all professionals, but advocates have a unique challenge: they are supposed to take on the cause of their clients without losing their perspective (which is one reason impartiality is essential to advocacy).

What I have labeled as emotional skills may also be viewed through an ethical lens. How we handle our emotions in conflict, whether in an advocate or neutral role, has significant ethical implications. But at root, these skills are emotional in nature. If we can recognize and manage the emotional challenges, we will find that the related ethical problems can be more readily addressed.

Communication Skills

No matter what role we play as conflict specialists (and perhaps in life), communications skills are essential. If we do not practice good listening, either with our own clients or with others involved in a conflict, we cannot be effective advocates. We also need to be able to speak to others in an appropriate and effective way. This requires being aware of how others are responding to what we are saying and modifying our communication appropriately. These are challenges for all of us, but there are specific challenges related to the advocacy function.

Effective advocates should be able to frame issues constructively and wisely. The most effective advocates are not those who can martial the best arguments in support of a cause, but those who can frame the issue so that that the arguments in support of their point of view flow from the very definition they have put forward. (For example, is the immigration issue in the United States about protecting our borders and insuring that jobs go to Americans rather than illegal immigrants? Or is it about making the American dream available to everyone, as it was for our parents and grandparents?) But it is also important that advocates define issues in a way that does not exclude others' concerns.

Advocates also need to raise difficult issues clearly and with sensitivity. One of the main reasons people rely on advocates is because they are reluctant to raise conflict or to deal directly with those they are in conflict with. Advocates help with this by delivering bad news to their own clients and raising divisive issues with others. In doing so, they have to be aware of the tendency we all have to avoid conflict by overstating it or being overly positional as we raise it. We have discussed the tension between avoidance and engagement in chapter 3. Advocates need an effective approach to handling this paradox.

Finally, advocates are educators. The most effective advocate helps an individual, group, or community develop the knowledge and skills to be their own best advocates. The best union organizers, for example, are those who recognize and nurture the natural leadership within the workplace they are organizing.

Strategic Skills

Effective advocates have to be able to work with clients on developing a sound strategy for how to approach a conflict or issue.

Advocates should also understand the essential sources of power of the individual, group, or cause they are promoting. This means understanding where the potential for real power lies and the limitations on this power. They also need to understand the essential sources of power of those on the other side of the issue.

Advocates need to take a long view of their clients' needs and goals, even if the advocates are involved for only a short period of time. The most important conflicts in people's lives usually have an enduring element that won't be resolved simply or quickly (Mayer 2009). Although an advocate may be engaged to help deal with an immediate manifestation of the conflict or to achieve a short-term goal (e.g., a satisfactory resolution to a grievance in a highly conflicted workplace), they should do so with a clear view of how this fits into the long-term needs of their client. Related to this is the capacity to separate nonessential concerns or conflicts from those that are truly important to the client.

Advocates should also be able to plan for how to intervene in complex systems. They therefore need the ability to develop a campaign or long-term change effort, to mobilize support, to work with multiple overlapping and contradictory interests, and to build an effective organization or advocacy group. This requires understanding systems and particularly the system in which the conflict is taking place—be it a community, workplace, political entity, family, organization, or nation.

Advocates and Third Parties

Though certainly not an exhaustive list, the skills discussed in the preceding sections cross over many types of advocacy. Although I have not specifically discussed negotiation skills, which are critical to effective advocacy, the advocate's emotional, communication, and strategic skills form the foundation for effective negotiation.

I have presented these skills from an advocate's perspective, but they are also essential to those operating as third parties. And any skill that is useful to someone operating from a neutral stance—say, framing issues as mutual problems to be mutually solved—is useful to an advocate as well. That is because neutrality and advocacy are inseparable, except in the sense of the formal role we play at any given time. The skills that advocates develop are immensely valuable to third parties; similarly, the skills of third parties are very useful to advocates.

In addition, the skills, roles, and attitudes of advocates and third parties often meld together in practice. Although this connection can be extremely useful, it can sometimes lead to frustration on the part of both the advocate and the people or groups whose interests they are supporting. I became aware of just how frustrating several years ago when my wife and I used the services of a patient advocate:

> Going through chemotherapy under the best of circumstances is awful, and my wife, Julie, was having very harsh reactions to the regime she was on. But when the chemo missed her vein entirely, the upshot was terrible. Despite the frequent ringing of the alarm on the infusion apparatus, warning that there was a problem, we were repeatedly assured that all was OK. At the end of the session, we noticed a swelling around the injection site. Not to worry, we were told; although the vein was clearly missed, the swelling was caused by saline solution that was injected at the end of each treatment. It would be absorbed the next day and all would be well. At no point during this event was a doctor asked to examine the swelling.

When Julie's arm turned red a few days later, we went to the emergency room at our local hospital. We were told that this was the worst point of the reaction and that the irritation would soon subside. So I took off on a business trip to Alaska the next day. That is when what we later realized was a third-degree chemical burn—extending from her wrist to her upper arm—really flared. For the next two weeks, the pain was horrible. Eventually, the burns healed, although the inside of Julie's arm is numb to this day and probably always will be.

From this point on, the medical system treated the clinical problem, but no one from the cancer center talked to us about what had happened. At a subsequent appointment, I pulled aside a nurse who I felt had been very attentive to us in the past and said that I thought it would be a good idea for someone from the hospital or the cancer center to contact us about this. She right away suggested that she put the patient representative in touch with us. We were about to experience what it was like to be on the other side of the table—my wife, Julie Macfarlane, is a law professor and mediator.

The patient representative called several days later, and we had a frank discussion in which we described our experiences. We said what we most wanted was some acknowledgment about what had happened and a commitment to address the problem so it did not occur again for another patient. She said that she would talk to the medical staff and get back to us.

About a month later, she called to report back. She had talked to everyone involved, she said, and could assure us that "all procedures were correctly followed." Now we were angry, and I actually thought of contacting a lawyer. I told the representative in no uncertain terms that if they followed their procedures and this still happened, then there was something seriously wrong with the procedures. I then suggested her job wasn't to ascertain whether the hospital had screwed up but to convene a discussion among the responsible medical staff and us. So that is what she did.

At the meeting, the patient representative introduced everyone and then sat back. Several of the medical staff were quite defensive, but two key individuals, the medical director and the supervising nurse of the unit that delivered the chemotherapy, really stepped up to the plate. The medical director listened to our experience, acknowledged what had happened to us, and said that there were obviously flaws in their procedures that needed to be corrected. Then—and this was the critical event in this meeting—the supervising nurse produced a new information document for patients that showed how they were going to alter their procedures. She said they had already introduced this new document and had implemented the new procedure. We were satisfied, thanked them for responding to our concerns, and there we left it.

The hospital website describes the role of the patient representative in terms that clearly demonstrate the overlap between neutrality and advocacy and the dual responsibility of the advocate to represent the patient and the hospital:

The Patient Representative works to support the patient and their family during your stay or visit to the hospital. The Patient Relations program exists to strengthen, personalize and enhance the relationship among patients, their families and the health care team. The Patient Representative provides a way to ensure that conflicts may be resolved in a manner that supports the patients, family members and staff members. The Patient Representative acts as an unbiased resource for patients/clients/residents and families when dealing with services delivered at any campus of [the hospital].

In the end, we did feel supported by the patient representative. She heard us, acted on what we said, and made sure that the meeting that needed to occur did occur. She said very little at the meeting, but what she said was intended to make sure that our concerns were heard. Her initial report back to us showed the complexity of her dual role as patient representative and hospital employee. When we got upset with this, she quickly backed off and adjusted her approach.

Aside from the part of this that involved my coaching her on what she needed to do (patronizing, no doubt, but, I felt, necessary), I doubt that our experience of working with an advocate was very unusual. Her effectiveness was part procedural, setting up the meeting, discussing how it might proceed; part advisory, informing us about who had decision-making power, how the system worked, who needed to be at the meeting; and part supportive, listening, empathizing, and, perhaps most importantly, believing us. However, as essential as it was that she was a staff member of the hospital—because this gave her the capacity to make something happen—it also limited the degree to which she could be an effective advocate. Her neutrality was essential to her ability to advocate, and yet it limited her in this regard as well. Perhaps with more experience, she will be able to integrate the two aspects of her role more effectively, as ombudsmen all over the world have learned to do. But no matter how skilled, advocates will always find this a challenge.

Susskind and Stulberg: A Classic Debate on Neutrality and Advocacy

Conflict specialists have long struggled with the ethics of neutrality. On the one hand, we make a commitment to being fair and impartial. On the other, how can we be neutral in the face of evil, or when dealing with severe power differentials? If our intervention itself contributes to a significant power differential, and we do nothing to correct for this, then in the guise of being neutral we are actually favoring the more powerful party. This is not an abstract concern; it happens every day. For example, unless mediators in child-protection proceedings take special steps to make certain that parents are prepared for mediation and that the session is conducted in a way that ensures that they have a voice and will not be marginalized by professionals and professional jargon, then mediation can easily become one more way in which the parents are disempowered.

These are examples of a neutral advocating for an empowering process, but what about advocating for a just outcome? Do conflict specialists acting as neutrals have an obligation to ensure that the processes they have helped to organize and conduct not only provide a fair voice for all participants but also result in good outcomes? A classic debate about this was conducted in the pages of the *Vermont Law Review* in 1981 by Larry Susskind, a professor at MIT and the former director of the Program on Negotiation at Harvard; and Josh Stulberg, a law professor, now at Ohio State University. They returned to this issue at a forum at Marquette University in 2011, taking much the same positions that they took earlier (Stulberg 1981; Susskind 1981; Susskind, Stulberg, Mayer, and Lande 2012).

Susskind, who has worked extensively as a mediator on public policy issues, argues that our credibility depends on our ability to construct and conduct dispute resolution processes that result in socially desirable outcomes—that is, outcomes that are fair, efficient, stable, and wise. If we don't take some responsibility for this, Susskind believes, we will lose legitimacy, and it will not help us to hide behind the guise of neutrality. Stulberg, another very experienced mediator who works in a variety of arenas, argues that mediators have no responsibility for achieving just outcomes, and that even if they did, they do not have the power to do so. Trying to take on this burden, Stulberg believes, would undercut a mediator's essential capacity to provide a socially useful service.

Another interesting view of the tension between our commitment to promoting social justice and to remaining neutral comes from Guy and Heidi Burgess (1996), directors of the Conflict Resolution Consortium at the University of Colorado:

> One of the most difficult challenges facing the conflict resolution and peacemaking fields is the justice problem. This problem arises because the ultimate objective of our efforts is wise and just decision-making—not merely the resolution of conflicts for the sake of resolution. If the power distribution between contending parties is nearly equal, then conflict resolution processes are generally just. However, in cases where power is inequitably distributed, neutral intervention often simply sugar-coats the domination of one group by another, leading to an unjust result. In response to this problem, the dispute resolution field has struggled to find a way to add empowerment responsibilities to the role of the neutral intervener. Unfortunately, as the neutral's empowerment efforts expand, his or her ability to successfully carry out the neutral role diminishes. (para. 1)

What is interesting to me is the way the dilemma articulated in the Stulberg–Susskind debate as well as in the Burgess' formulation continues to resonate with conflict specialists. At the

2011 Marquette Symposium (in which I participated), the issue originally articulated thirty years earlier continued to engage practitioners. I believe that this debate still speaks to us because it strikes at a core issue that we face as conflict interveners, one that is not resolvable in any neat or tidy way, precisely because neutrality and advocacy are so enmeshed.

As I suggested earlier, we can be neutral in the sense that we do not intentionally act to further one party's interests at the expense of another's, but we are advocating at every step of the process, and not just about process. We advocate for disputants to address key interests, for agreements to be flexible and adaptable to changing circumstances, and for people to frame their proposals in a way that is more likely to result in an equitable solution. Because process and outcome are intertwined, whenever we advocate in one area, it has implications for the other. (For example, when we advocate for widening participation in a mediation, we are doing so in part because of the impact this will have on the outcome.)

On the other hand, if we abandon our commitment to providing a perspective characterized by some reflective distance and an appreciation for the importance of addressing the essential concerns of all parties, we also lose an important element of the potential value we bring to a conflict—including our capacity to advocate effectively. And any action that we take must respect the limits on our power as well as the genuine influence we have. If Susskind overemphasized the capacity we have as conflict interveners to insure a just outcome (and the limit of our capacity to influence outcome is an important part of why people are willing to place some trust in us), Stulberg may not fully appreciate the many ways in which we inevitably advocate for just outcomes.

How exactly we join our responsibilities for both neutrality and advocacy depends on our role, the context, and our own style and preferences, but join them we must. How we do so is challenging, and Susskind and Stulberg have offered us a potent dialogue as to why (Mayer 2013).

The Advocate Neutral

So how do we bring advocacy into a neutral role and a commitment to impartiality into advocacy? Let's unpack this process by looking at some specific interventions. We can examine almost any inter-action and see these two strands running through it.

CASE 1: We start by returning to the case of Simon and Joshua. A phone call with Simon prior to the first meeting went like this:

Simon: Before I am willing to meet with Joshua, I need an apology from him for the things he said that led to all this trouble.

Bernie: Why is it important that this happen before the meeting?

Simon: Because otherwise it's just going to be the same old, same old.

Bernie: I get it, but I am not sure Joshua is ready to offer an apology before the meeting. I can ask. I am also not sure that would be as effective as a face-to-face statement.

In fact, I knew that Joshua felt that he, too, was owed an apology and that he also regretted a couple of things he'd said, but he did not want to be "bullied into apologizing when it did not feel genuine." When I asked Simon if there was anything he wanted to apologize for, he resisted; but I pushed him on this and he came up with a couple of things he could have done differently. I then suggested that we might need a joint discussion during which each could decide if and how he wanted to apologize and what each wanted to ask from the other. I was trying to help both of them, but I also felt that it would be difficult to make progress if I could not get Simon to give up at least some of his claim to the moral high ground. What made this work was that I had clearly demonstrated my commit-ment to helping both of them. In other words, neutrality does not mean passivity—far from it. Seeing that I was committed to helping them both afforded me the credibility to advocate for an approach that was different from the one Simon initially wanted to take.

CASE 2: Sheila was the informal leader of a professional organization whose members had retained a lawyer and were threatening to sue the board over alleged misuse of funds. The members were concerned, however, that the organization would fold if they were to bring a lawsuit. I had a private conversation with Sheila:

Sheila: Bernie, I believe we need to settle this, but our lawyer says we can win if we go to court, and we are not sure what to do.
Bernie: Does he share your concerns about the fate of the association?
Sheila: He is minimizing the danger, and he is very sure we can get significant refunds on members' dues.
Bernie: Do you agree?
Sheila: Not really, but he is being very assertive.
Bernie: Well, Sheila, remember that he works for your group; you don't work for him.

True enough, but tricky: You don't interfere with a relationship between lawyers and their clients without taking serious risks. But I thought Sheila's instincts were correct and the lawyer was not listening to his clients. I built on what she said, but I supported her in her concerns about having the lawyer drive the agenda. Shortly thereafter, her group decided to settle. This could easily have gone badly, but I believed that she was asking for some independent advice, and to fail to give it would also have been taking a stand. I based my approach on her own concerns and encouraged her to use her own best judgment, but the impact of my statement was significant.

CASE 3: The following exchange took place during a private conversation with the co-owner of a successful business who was consulting me about negotiating a (unwelcome) buyout of his partner.

Jean: I think I should say to Pietro, "Either you buy me out at the price I am proposing, or I will buy you out at that price." He can't afford the price or run the company without me, and he won't have a choice, other than to let me buy him out or watch the company go under.

Bernie: Maybe so, and I don't know Pietro, but how will this seem to him? Will he feel manipulated? Will he resist, even if it means hurting the company? In the long run, isn't it better to work out an approach that will allow him to walk away feeling OK about how this ended?

Jean: Pietro helped a great deal at the beginning of our business, but he has not been pulling his weight in the last few years. He doesn't deserve more.

Bernie: You have to handle this so it feels OK to you, but you should also try to make it easy, rather than difficult, for Pietro to do what you want.

In this situation, I was Jean's ally and was trying to help her be an effective negotiator, but what she also needed from me was the perspective of a neutral.

CASE 4: During a mediation of a dispute about an inheritance between two siblings, Joel and Grace, the conversation became quite tense. Grace was the executor of the estate.

Joel: Grace tells me nothing about what is happening. I don't know exactly what's in the estate or how the assets are being handled. For all I know, she could be selling things off and never reporting it.

Grace: Joel, you are so full of s***. You never did anything to help out, and now you want to look over my shoulder. Well you can go to hell.

Joel: See, Bernie. That is what I mean. I just want to know what is happening and all I get back is this crap. It's like when we were kids.

Bernie: So, Grace, regardless of how you feel about each other at the moment, what would you want to know if Joel were the executor?

My question may seem innocent enough, asked from a neutral stance. But it pushes the conversation in a decided direction. Grace can avoid the question—for example, she could say that she would trust the process, or she could argue that Joel was not named as the executor precisely because he is not trustworthy. But the question implicitly asks her to consider Joel's request as potentially reasonable. Without entirely realizing it, I was advocating for Joel's concerns about transparency to be taken very seriously. In fact that is what Grace did, and it led to an agreement and, over time, a better relationship. I could as easily have asked Joel to consider Grace's point of view, but I didn't, because my first advocacy instinct was to ask Grace to take seriously Joel's need for more information.

I brought advocacy and neutrality together in each of these interchanges. Although I was not consciously trying to do this, each situation called for it. I did this by maintaining a commitment to addressing each party's concerns and a perspective on how the situation might appear to each, including those whom I had never met or who were not present. But I was also willing to commit myself to a point of view about what direction the interaction should take. If my perspective and understanding were shaped by an impartial approach, my actions were at times more those of an advocate.

Third-party interveners are inevitably required to function in an impartial manner, yet we must act as advocates. How we do this is in part a function of our approach to intervention. Perhaps an evaluative mediator is much more open and at ease with the role of an advocate, while a transformative mediator is more committed to avoiding any actions that smack of advocacy. But regardless of our approach to mediation, or whether we are acting as third parties or allies, we are always pulled by the dual requirements of impartiality and advocacy. The art of our trade is how we handle these—and it is also a core source of our value to disputants. The neutrality–advocacy paradox is the source of some of the most interesting practice developments in recent years—for example, the rise of the collaborative practice movement in which a multidisciplinary team works with disputants (primarily in divorce) to provide legal representation, counseling services, and financial advice for the purposes of assisting people in settling their disputes, but not litigating. This movement essentially offers services that combine the values and perspectives of advocates and neutrals.

(Further) Reflections from Practice and Life

My father used to enjoy recounting how he was once introduced, "This is Fritz Mayer, who is neutral about nothing!" This was a source of pride for him, and I grew up feeling that being neutral was a sign of weakness, somewhat akin to the sentiment expressed in the Elie Wiesel quote at the start of this chapter. Perhaps that is not surprising, since my parents were Holocaust survivors, and the importance of "speaking truth to power" was paramount in my family's value system. So it naturally raised some eyebrows among my friends and family when I found myself making my way as a professional third-party neutral. But I never saw this as contradicting my commitment to social justice or as compromising my essential values.

Perhaps I was deceiving myself, had surpassed that untrustworthy age of thirty, or no longer held the same values. But I don't think so. I think I always sensed this was a false dichotomy. Underlying the role of the neutral are some important values that define our work. These include what we have sometimes referred to as "deep democracy"—citizen empowerment, respect for self-determination, and a belief in the capacity of communities and individuals to make good decisions for themselves if given the opportunity.

There is an anti-hierarchical, anti-authoritarian mindset to conflict intervention, a belief in nonviolence, and a commitment to equal treatment of all people. I am not saying that these principles are unequivocal, universally held, or consistently applied, but they are implied by the nature of the work we do and the commitments we make. We advocate for these in almost every move we make. Of course, as with any field of practice, we also act as agents of society and social stability. And we need to make a living—so there are many mitigating factors that can impede on our ability to pursue these values.

But these beliefs are nonetheless essential to the field and to who we are as practitioners, and our commitment to them is a source of strength—but a limitation as well. It is a source of strength because it means that we are motivated by a strong belief in what we do and that we have a commitment that goes beyond self-interest. This is important to people's willingness to put their faith in us. However, it is also a limitation. We often assume that our clients share our values, but this is not necessarily the case. As a group, we are not representative of the broad range of beliefs or values that exist in our society. In advocating for neutrality, we are also representing a point of view. There may be a few Tea Party activists who are also mediators, but my guess is that this is a small group.

Sometimes, the tension between neutrality and advocacy is more obvious than at other times. And sometimes, my faith that I am always acting in accordance with my values as a conflict intervener is put to the test. Occasionally I have declined to work on a conflict (such as a negotiation about what to do with a decommissioned nuclear weapons plant that in hindsight was a very valuable process). There have been some cases in which I decided to participate but which were very challenging to my sense of who I was and even seemed at times to be in opposition to important values. One interesting instance of this came when I was asked to advise a university about how to deal with student demonstrations:

I had worked with the university on a variety of different issues, such as how to deal with a dysfunctional department and how to help department chairs deal with disputes among faculty. Now I was being asked to consult about how to manage a wave of student protests, mostly involving issues related to globalization and working conditions in factories that produced university-branded clothing. I was in a quandary about this. In principle, it seemed legitimate for me to work with the university regarding how to take a transparent, open approach in dealing with students. In practice, it seemed like I was selling out. After all, when I thought back to my days as a student activist, I am quite sure I would not have approved of someone doing what I was now proposing to do. The twenty-one-year-old Bernie would not have liked what the fifty-two-year-old Bernie was doing. But I was no longer twenty-one, and the times were different.

So I talked with a friend—a long-term activist who was likely to share my misgivings. That's what I was expecting, almost hoping for. Instead, he said, "I think this is a great idea. Someone needs to tell them how to deal with this or people are going to get hurt." Now I had no excuse but to face up to this dilemma. I told the university that I would work with them on this—not to silence the protests but to find a legitimate way for them to go forward, even if that involved civil disobedience. They agreed, as long as I agreed to keep our conversations confidential. The officials involved knew of my activist background, and that was all the more reason they wanted my help. In the course of my work, I observed demonstrations, listened to speakers, and worked with administrators about how they could prepare for the demonstrations and negotiate with the leaders of the protests before and during the actions.

The most challenging moment for me came when the university received word that a small group who identified themselves as anarchists were not willing to abide by the collective decision of the main organizers and were planning acts of sabotage and vandalism. I participated in meetings with the chief of the campus police, police officials from the town, and university leadership. They were preparing to have a security force nearby, but we also worked out how their contingency plans could be discussed in general terms with the protest leaders. No significant violence occurred, and the demonstrations took place with considerable publicity, but no arrests. Perhaps my intervention helped. Perhaps the organizers would have liked less predictability so that even greater publicity might have ensued.

In the end I felt neither totally compromised nor totally comfortable about this work. What was I advocating for? How did this fit with my essential values? Was I misusing my experience as a protest organizer? As a neutral? Or did I play a constructive role that made it more likely that political actions could take place effectively and sustainably? These are all important questions that I continue to ponder. The tension between our role as advocates and neutrals is a creative tension, but not one we can neatly resolve.

I have often thought about the distinction between what we offer people in conflict and what they want. I suggested in *Beyond Neutrality* (2004) that what people generally seek in conflict is voice, validation, vindication, procedural justice, safety, and impact. All conflict interveners have to address these fundamental needs in some way, but how we do so varies tremendously depending on context and our specific role. Just as with advocacy and neutrality, these needs are often in conflict with one another.

Focusing on vindication, for example, may blunt our impact. Voice and safety may work against each other. And the more some disputants are able to meet their needs, the harder it may be for others to meet theirs. The tension between what we offer and what people want pulls us toward both advocacy and neutrality.

Each of us experiences these tensions in our own conflicts. I have often asked conflict professionals to think about whom they first approach for help when in conflict, and whom next. The answer, almost always, is that the first person we go to is someone who will take our side, agree with us, and support us—usually a friend of family member. Then we may go to someone who will advise us, advocate for us, or empower us in some way. After we have secured this type of support, we may be open to and even appreciate someone who can help us take a broader view, consider the perspective of those we are in conflict with, and think twice before we escalate a conflict. Or we may want no such moderating influence. But that doesn't mean we don't *need* it.

Turning to a third-party neutral is not something we do very often or very readily—at least in the formal sense. And even when we are ready to work with more intentionally neutral interveners, we still want to believe that in some significant way, they understand us and are advocating for us. We expect them to have opinions and views; we just want them to mirror ours (or keep them hidden). In other words, at times we want our allies to be impartial and our neutrals to be advocates. This isn't really a contradiction; it is reasonable and even wise. As interveners, no matter our role, we always face the challenge of addressing both of these needs. Our effectiveness and credibility depend on it.

chapter eight

community and autonomy

I know there is strength in the differences between us. I know there is comfort, where we overlap.

Ani DiFranco, "Overlap," from Out of Range

The autonomy of the individual appears to be complemented and enhanced by the movement of the group; while the effectiveness of the group seems to depend on the freedom of the individual.

Hakim Bey, The Lemonade Ocean and Modern Times

The seventh and final paradox is defined by community and autonomy, which we can also understand as affiliation and individuation. Our need for affiliation, connection, and a sense of belonging is a central feature of human existence, as is our need for independence, autonomy, and a sense of individuality. Coping with the complex interaction between these needs defines a basic struggle of human development and civilization. It is also an essential aspect of human conflict. We can understand every move someone makes during conflict as, in part, a response to the demands of community and the need for autonomy. For example, when we choose to reach an accommodation of some sort with adversaries, we are usually choosing to strengthen our community of interest with them, even as we are trying to make sure we do not do this at the cost of our own autonomy. But at the same time, we may be asserting our autonomy from the community that has been reinforcing the conflict and sustaining us as we have engaged in it. And sometimes, the conflict itself is what binds a community together, and the decision to reach an agreement results in weakening our links to that community while reinforcing our autonomy from it. So while our actions in conflict can have several sometimes contradictory implications for how we experience community and autonomy, they always affect and are affected by these fundamental needs.

The challenge of reconciling this polarity both inhibits and motivates our developmental progress—and the more mature we become, the more able we are to experience a rich sense of both community and autonomy. As with all the paradoxes we have explored, community and autonomy depend on each other. We cannot have a rich experience of community without a secure sense of autonomy, and we can't truly achieve autonomy without the positive influence of community. Both of these are essential elements of our identities.

Identity, Community, Autonomy

Our sense of community and experience of personal autonomy are foundations of our identity—our sense of who we are. It is precisely because community and autonomy—or, more broadly, our feeling of connectedness to others and our sense of ourselves as separate and individual—are essential to our identity that they exert such a powerful pull on us as we engage in conflict.

Identity refers to our sense of ourselves. It is defined by the personality traits that we exhibit, the affiliations that we embrace, our sense of continuity, and our beliefs about what sets us apart from others. Identity as a psychological concept was most prominently described by psychoanalyst Erik Erikson, who differentiated himself from Freud by his focus on the ego. His most famous work, *Childhood and Society* (1950), discussed child, adolescent, and adult development in terms of a series of struggles and tasks presented at different developmental stages in our lives.

Erikson outlined eight stages, from birth to old age, characterizing the adolescent stage (number five in his model), in particular, as a struggle between identity and confusion. Erikson believes that identity is formed by learning to trust our place in the world, to accept the influence of our parents, and then to differentiate ourselves from that influence. He defined ego identity as "the awareness of . . . self-sameness and continuity" and "the style of one's individuality [that] coincides with the sameness and continuity of one's meaning for others in the immediate community" (1968, p. 50).

We can also think of identity in terms of the group memberships that are essential to our sense of who we are. For example, we may define ourselves by our national or geographical connections (e.g., as American, Canadian, Coloradan, or Ontarian, to use a few of my sometimes contradictory but important sources of identity); or by our ethnic, racial, or religious affiliation; sexual orientation; or political or professional associations. In his classic book on identity conflicts, Jay Rothman (1997) describes these affiliations as being "deeply rooted in the underlying human needs and values that together constitute people's social identities, particularly in the context of group affiliations, loyalties, and solidarity" (p. 6).

I have previously suggested that identity needs are one of the three core drivers of conflict (along with interests and survival needs). I defined identity needs as "the needs we all have to preserve a sense of who we are and our place in the world" (Mayer, 2012a, p. 25). I have suggested four essential elements of identity: meaning, community, autonomy, and intimacy.

As we can see from each of these descriptions—and this is true of most discussions of identity—the concepts of identity and identity formation are based in considerations of connection and separation, attachment and individuation, or community and autonomy—the focus of this chapter. These dichotomies are not identical, but they are related. The tension between the pull toward affiliation and the need to define ourselves as different is a central fact of human existence. How we handle it is essential to our sense of who we are, our place in the world, and our purpose in life—in other words, our identity.

Community, as I am using the term, refers to the constellation of social connections we have established that are important to us. These can involve formal or informal group affiliations. My community may involve my friends, family, neighbors, church, workplace, softball team, poker group, or fellow vegetarians. The formal connections are not as important as whom we consider to be a significant part of our network—that is, those with whom we have a relationship and who we feel recognize us. In *Dynamics of Conflict* (2012a), I described community as "not simply about feeling part of a group, it is about having a social home in an impersonal world—a home in which people feel safe, connected, recognized as individuals, and appreciated" (p. 26).

Community is an essential human need. We cannot develop as individuals in isolation. Our first essential community is our family; for most of us, this remains the foundational community of our lives. But to develop fully as individuals, we have to establish a wider range of communities. This is both how we are drawn into the wider world as well as how we establish ourselves as autonomous individuals with an existence separate from our families. Communitarian philosopher Sean Sayers (1999) describes how children form their identity through experiencing conflict between their community of origin—namely their family—and the wider community into which they enter:

> Beliefs and values from the wider world inevitably impinge on the growing child; and this leads to fundamental conflicts for it between the values of its upbringing and those of the surrounding world. . . .

In and through the particular way in which the emerging self assumes and lives the different and conflicting roles which the surrounding world presents, affirming some, resisting others, its identity forms and develops. Just because these frameworks are contradictory, the developing self, striving to identify with them and form its own identity in relation to them, is forced to seek a resolution among the conflicting pressures because these frameworks are contradictory.... In the process, it gradually develops the ability to reflect upon them and to exercise a degree of conscious choice and autonomy with respect to them (p.155).

Though community implies group affiliation, we mostly experience community through a series of interpersonal or small group interactions. For me, the conflict intervention field is an important community affiliation, and although I sometimes experience it at large conferences or seminars, I experience it mostly through one-to-one or small group interactions. That is also how most of us experience our connection to our ethnicity, our family, or our geographical community. Larger group interactions are important, as are other symbolic ways we experience community (e.g., we all celebrate the same holidays at the same time with similar rituals, or in Canadian schools each morning everyone stands and sings "Oh Canada" together). But although these form the superstructure of community, the interpersonal interactions are what flesh out this structure. In this sense, community is related to interpersonal connectedness, and our ability to form interpersonal attachments is a critical aspect of our capacity to experience community.

Although attachment, intimacy, and community are not the same, they all involve connecting to others, the element of human needs that is a pull toward affiliation as opposed to an urge for separateness and individuality. Although all elements of the pull toward affiliation may be important in our work in conflict, the pull toward community seems especially essential because it is always there, no matter where we are in our lives. Every step we make toward accommodating others' needs, entering into an agreement with them, or simply being willing to listen to their point of view and their story in an empathic way is a step toward community. As I mentioned earlier, a step toward one community may be a step away from another, because communities are sometimes defined as much by what people are against or whom they have excluded as by what they are for. And stepping away from one community toward another is an assertion of autonomy as well.

Autonomy refers to the degree to which we can act, think, and feel independently. So although others may *influence* us, they do not *control* us. Our autonomy can be curtailed directly or indirectly. For example, you can limit my capacity to act independently by the control or influence you have over me (e.g., parent over a child, boss over employee, guard over prisoner, priest over parishioner). Or you can limit my capacity to act because of the way I react to you. If I have to behave in a particular way to differentiate myself from you and therefore cannot make a truly independent determination of what I want to do, I am also under your control. Teenagers often feel buffeted between being controlled by their parents directly and indirectly—and finding that sweet spot of autonomy can be very difficult.

We face the same challenge in conflict. Can I truly evaluate whether an offer made by someone I dislike or am in conflict with is reasonable, or will I be subject to "reactive devaluation" (i.e., whatever my enemy proposes has to be bad, whom they like I must dislike, and my enemy's enemy must be my friend)?

We often deal with this as conflict interveners when we find people rejecting an idea that they might otherwise have liked because they are in conflict with the person who put it forward. This was the challenge I faced in working with a dispute over public housing:

Patricia was the president of a homeowners' association whose members were concerned about a plan to build public housing on a vacant lot in her neighborhood. She had been meeting with public officials about her organization's concerns, but these meetings had not gone well. In an appearance before the city council, Patricia had accused the city of "high-handed, insensitive government overreach" and had received quite a bit of media attention as a result. Proponents of public housing responded that the opposition to this project was "elitist, uncaring, and probably racist." That is the point at which I was brought in to conduct a series of meetings about this.

The public housing authority said that although it was not willing to abandon the project, it *was* willing to modify it—to look at the community's specific concerns and to try to address them. Patricia said that she was willing to talk to public housing officials and housing advocates, as long as they did not attack her or her neighbors personally, but she would also pursue her request that the project be moved.

During the course of the meetings, Patricia said the size of the proposed development was too big, the design totally out of keeping with the character of the neighborhood, and the location too close (one block) from a local school. At one point, Patricia said, "I can show you five better locations within one mile of this one. Why don't we agree on criteria to assess whether these are not in fact better, and if an independent evaluator agrees that one of them is, you will agree to move the project? If the evaluator does not think an alternative location works better, we can then consider how best to make it work in the proposed location."

The housing department was not so eager to do this, because it seemed like considering a move would

244 THE CONFLICT PARADOX

be the beginning of a slippery slope toward abandoning
the project (possibly Patricia's intention in making the
proposal) and because it seemed to give an outsider
control. On the other hand, the department was taking
a lot of criticism. After a couple additional sessions, the
head of the department essentially agreed to Patricia's
proposal. He said, "If we can agree on criteria and on
the independent evaluator, and if we can identify at
least three potentially available sites within a mile, we
are amenable to your plan."

Patricia seemed unable to take yes for an answer,
however. She did not believe the department head
really meant what he said. Then she thought she was
being manipulated and that there must be a hidden
trick. She accused the officials of "parsing words" and
of being untrustworthy. But she could not reject the
offer out of hand. I did not believe there was any
hidden poison pill in the offer, but I did think that the
"devil was in the details"—that agreeing on criteria,
sites to look at, and an independent assessor would
be difficult. We decided to proceed first by discussing
the criteria. This actually put Patricia in a difficult
spot, because if the criteria were too strict, it would be
difficult to identify another location; if they were too
lenient, her objections to the current location would
be undercut. In the end, she rejected this approach
and settled on a plan for the proposed location that
addressed many (but not all) of the community's
concerns about size, design, management, traffic, and
community involvement.

Patricia found herself in the uncomfortable position of having
others agree to a proposal she had made that she never expected
them to accept. Moreover, she was obligating herself to work much
more intimately with an entity she had labeled as the enemy. Her

opposition to this project had brought her much closer to her neighbors, and their interactions around this issue had essentially turned
the neighborhood into a community. By agreeing to work with the
department—first on criteria for site evaluation, and then on modi-
fication of the plans—she was building an interactional group with
the city and with proponents of public housing. She did not abandon
her neighbors by doing this, but the boundaries around her neighborhood group—its *autonomy*, if you will—were weakened. At the
same time, her connection with those she had sought to differentiate
herself from became stronger. Though some of the other neighbors
went through a similar process, hers was the most dramatic.

The housing department staff experienced some of this as well.
They were part of a community of interest with other proponents of
public housing—a community that was strengthened by their unity
in opposition to Patricia and her group. Accepting her proposal,
which it appears they did in good faith, required that they loosen the
boundaries around their community and move toward establishing
a different kind of connection with Patricia and her community.

As with conflict itself, autonomy has behavioral, emotional, and
cognitive components that influence each other but can be considered separately. We are most likely to think of our independence
in terms of our freedom to act. But a more pernicious threat to
our autonomy may derive from circumstances or relationships that
impede our capacity to formulate our own thoughts, understand our
situation on our own terms, or even experience our own emotions
independently of the emotional prescriptions and prohibitions of
others. We may be totally unaware of this, but we have all seen it
in others—those who seem to think whatever a group or another
individual thinks, or, by opposition, whatever they do not think. I
still remember an experience of this as a ten-year-old child:

> For reasons having nothing to do with our virtue and
> having everything to do with the power of my father
> in the family system (and maybe that we were not
> local), my brother and I were favored by certain of our

relatives. One year, when I was about ten years old, we were visiting an aunt who lived in a simple but pleasant apartment in New York City. She had a beautiful old radio, and I looked at it and played with the dials. About thirty minutes later, she got very angry at one of my New York cousins for changing the station on the radio (evidently, it was hard to get it just right). When I realized what the fuss was about, I owned responsibility. My aunt (who was usually very soft-spoken and kind) had a look of consternation on her face that I will never forget. She felt OK about being angry at my cousin, but not at me. Somehow, she went through an on-the-spot emotional adjustment and the anger evaporated. She didn't even make an excuse or give a reason; she just said, "Oh, OK." That was the end of it (except my cousin was not so happy with me).

All families exhibit patterns like this. I was the beneficiary in this scenario, but I have also been on the other side. Although there were many dimensions to this interchange, an important one was my aunt's lack of emotional autonomy. She was acting in accordance with a prescription that the family system had created for her, and it was not just her actions that were limited, but her thinking and feeling as well. Every one of us is subject to similar challenges to our autonomy, and our approach to conflict is often constrained by limits on our capacity to arrive at independent judgments or to experience emotions in a genuinely autonomous manner.

One influential framework for understanding the nature and development of autonomy comes from the work of Murray Bowen and his associates at the Georgetown Family Center in Washington, DC. Bowen, a family systems theorist, developed the concept of differentiation of self, which he described in *Family Therapy and Clinical Practice* (1985). He believed that the essential challenge we face as we mature is to differentiate ourselves from others, particularly our families. Differentiation requires that we are comfortable with our own identity and not overly dependent on others' approval, but also not overly reactive to others. We face two primary challenges in achieving differentiation. Emotional fusion occurs when we are so emotionally involved with someone else that we cannot accept our own needs as independent of the other's (or vice versa). Emotional cutoffs occur when we cannot handle the pressure of differences, and we respond by cutting off the relationship, at least on an emotional level. A differentiated self can remain connected and independent at the same time. In *Family Evaluation: An Approach Based on Bowen Theory* (1988), Bowen and Kerr say, "The more differentiated a self, the more a person can be an individual while in emotional contact with the group" (p. 94).

On the other hand, the Bowen Center (https://www .thebowencenter.org/pages/conceptds.html) explains,

> People with a poorly differentiated "self" depend so heavily on the acceptance and approval of others that either they quickly adjust what they think, say, and do to please others or they dogmatically proclaim what others should be like and pressure them to conform. Bullies depend on approval and acceptance as much as chameleons, but bullies push others to agree with them rather than their agreeing with others. Disagreement threatens a bully as much as it threatens a chameleon. An extreme rebel is a poorly differentiated person too, but he pretends to be a "self" by routinely opposing the positions of others.

Bowen's ideas are by no means unique. They are similar to Minuchin's concept of enmeshment (1974) and that of codependence. Studies of early childhood development have long focused on the process of separation and individuation (Mahler 1969, 1975). The struggle for autonomy is in many respects a lifelong challenge, and an essential task of parenting is to nurture the emerging autonomy of our children. Establishing our autonomy and adapting to that of others is part of every significant human interaction, and especially conflictual ones, because in conflict, we are constantly working to establish appropriate boundaries with other disputants.

It is not really possible to understand independence without understanding attachment, or community without autonomy. It is the search for the experience of both that defines our sense of self and our identity.

Integrating Community and Autonomy: The Challenge for Conflict Interveners

Community and autonomy are not only wrapped up in each other, but one *requires* the other. We establish our independence by having a healthy attachment to others, and we can become truly autonomous only if we have a healthy network of social relationships. This is implied in every discussion about these concepts that I have referred to.

Studies from the animal world show this as well. One study, for example, looked at the social life of spiders (Angier 2014) and found that most spiders live fairly solitary lives. Some species, however, are more social, and the more social the species, the more strongly differentiated their individual personality traits. For example, spiders that live longer in the same social grouping are more likely to show greater variance in boldness, aggressiveness, or caution from one another. The researcher concluded that the collectivity of the spider's lifestyle does not promote uniformity but rather stronger and more differentiated personalities. Similar results were found with fish and other animals. This is somewhat counterintuitive. We tend to think that individuality is associated with individualism, and independence with aloneness; but living in community while putting limits on acceptable behavior can also provide the structure to support a wide variety of personality types.

The close relationship between community and autonomy has significant implications for conflict practitioners. Disputants often believe that they have two choices: they either have to "stick to their guns," maintain in-group solidarity, "take one for the team," and be clear about who their friends are and who are their enemies; or they have to be open to compromise, reach out to adversaries, and be willing to "go the extra mile." I have discussed this in previous chapters in terms of competition and cooperation, principle and compromise, and avoidance and engagement. With community and autonomy, we are facing the very basic level of people's sense of self. Perhaps more than any other polarity, this one is at the heart of enduring conflicts. Working on this, therefore, is at the core of the intervener's challenge.

In particular, conflict interveners face three essential challenges in dealing with this paradox:

- To help people grapple with their fear of losing their autonomy as they reach out to adversaries

- To help disputants maintain connection with others as they either withdraw from engagement or escalate a conflict

- To work with people to handle the contradictory pulls of multiple different communities as they try to find their way through conflict

Staying with Autonomy

Autonomy may always be in play in conflict, but it is seldom truly *at stake*. If we have a stabilized self-image, the moves we make in conflict are not going to threaten it. They may contribute or give expression to an evolving sense of who we are, and they may be an important response to a change in our identity brought on by changing circumstances—divorce, termination of employment, or immigration, for example. If I enter into a divorce agreement, it might feel like I am taking a step that will have a major impact on my autonomy, self-image, and community. And although the act of agreeing itself will have some effect on my identity, this impact is secondary to the larger impact of the divorce and the circumstances that led to it. I may be taking a step toward autonomy, but the divorce agreement is an actualization of this rather than a major cause of it. However, my sense of autonomy—my emotional or psychological sense of independence or connection—may be very much in play, at least for a while.

We often feel like we are protecting something very fundamental about who we are; but more often what is at stake is the image we present to the world and to ourselves. We really have two tasks to accomplish with regard to our sense of autonomy as we make significant moves in conflict: we have to stay in touch with our sense of self, and we have to come to terms with how we are changing. Conflict interveners work with disputants on both tasks. Some of the ways we do this include

- *Asking disputants to revisit how a decision reflects their values, their goals, their hopes, and their fears.* By walking people through the thinking that undergirds their decisions, we provide an opportunity for them to remember who they are and how they are maintaining a "sameness of self," despite the significant steps they are taking. Even during intense conflicts, helping disputants remember these basic beliefs can help move negotiations forward. During the difficult Camp David Accords in 1978, for example, after days of stalemates were threatening to end the negotiations, then-president Jimmy Carter gave former Israeli Prime Minister Menachem Begin autographed photographs for each of Begin's grandchildren. Carter's intention was to help Begin maintain his sense of who he was as an individual as he was considering how to respond to a draft agreement that seemed to be the last chance to conclude this summit with a peace accord. It was only after receiving

these photographs that Begin could bring himself to
conclude what proved to be a historic agreement with
someone (Egyptian President Anwar Sadat) he considered
a profound enemy.

- *Giving disputants permission to stay in conflict.* This is one of
  the most difficult but most powerful things we can do as
  interveners. For example, as interveners, we might say that
  given disputants' views of the circumstances and the
  choices they face, their decision to remain in a conflict, or
  even to escalate it, may be the best choice they can make.
  By doing this, we are in essence asking them to make an
  affirmative decision as to whether to reach out to those
  they are in conflict with, knowing that we will be fully
  supportive should they not do so—and that we may even
  think that staying in conflict makes sense. Somewhat
  paradoxically, this can reinforce disputants' autonomy as
  they consider taking steps that they fear could
  undercut it.

- *Breaking seemingly big decisions into small steps.* A series of
  smaller changes, rather than a few big ones, may pose less of
  a challenge to a disputant's self-image. For example, rather
  than having to change directly from being married parents
  with primary daily parenting responsibilities to co-parents
  sharing parenting equally, some divorcees prefer to make
  the change in gradual steps. They may do this partly
  because they believe this will be better for their children,
  but also because it might help them with the changing
  sense of self that goes along with this change.

- *Helping people develop a rich vision of what big changes would
  look like.* Disputants often cannot imagine what life will be
  like after a major change. If an employee is negotiating a
  severance package for early retirement from a position that

he has held for many years, he will be experiencing a challenge both to his sense of autonomy and his community, and this can be very frightening. He might need help—not just to imagine what the change will be like, but also to experience his "new self." Maybe he needs to spend some time away from the business as he is considering the retirement offer to experience what life away from the organization might be like.

- *Naming the challenge.* As with so much else that we do in conflict, finding an effective way of naming the challenge to disputants' identity that a move under consideration might imply can help people cope with that challenge. For example, naming the identity concerns of the residents of Lucinda was critical when they had to decide whether to become part of an adjacent city:

> Lucinda was a small village adjacent to Mallory, a midsized city. Lucinda residents were proud of their community's small-town ambience, but the surrounding area was experiencing a rapid period of urbanization. Lucinda had entered into an agreement with Mallory, whereby Mallory provided police, fire, water, and wastewater services, but this agreement was nearing its end date, and Mallory officials said it was increasingly costly to service Lucinda in this way. Mallory was proposing to incorporate Lucinda and provide upgraded, permanent services at a rate considerably lower than it would have to charge Lucinda residents and businesses if the town remained an independent entity. Lucinda's leaders were initially very opposed to this because of "the loss of all that Lucinda's residents have cherished

about this village" that would surely follow. But they really had no good alternative.

In a series of negotiations I facilitated, town and city leaders worked out a detailed plan that provided for continuity of zoning, some decentralized decision-making that would maintain a role for Lucinda's council, and a variety of agreements about future land use, traffic planning, and other services. Lucinda's negotiators tentatively agreed to the plan, but they were ambivalent.

I participated in a village meeting on this issue, and I saw that residents were really struggling. Most of them understood that the offer was a good one, but as with the town leaders, it just did not sit right with them. Many were trying to pick the offer apart, but I felt their underlying concern was about a loss of autonomy and community. So I said so:

"No matter how good an agreement you get, in the long run Lucinda is inevitably going to change, and perhaps be more like some of the nearby neighborhoods you have wanted to distinguish yourself from. I understand why this feels bad to you. It may be inevitable no matter what you agree to, but this agreement could hasten it. Also, I have heard the pride you take in being 'Lucindans' and I can understand that this, too, will change. I don't think any tinkering with this agreement is going to help that. Also, if this agreement is executed, you will have a lot less reason to meet as a community than you have had in the past. You have to decide if you can maintain what it is you love about Lucinda if you accept this proposal, and if you can't, then maybe this is not the best agreement for you."

No one challenged this statement, but it wasn't exactly inspiring. In the end, this was the decision they had to face, and they did. Today, Lucinda is part of Mallory. Lucinda has maintained some of its identity, but in other ways, it is just another Mallory neighborhood.

Maintaining Connection

Just as we struggle with maintaining our sense of autonomy as we establish new connections with those with whom we are in conflict, we also may find it difficult to maintain this budding sense of community if we pull back from an agreement or escalate a conflict, as we sometimes must. As a simple example, think about how hard it is to raise a difficult issue with a friend and to continue to experience the connection you have previously felt. And consider how it becomes even harder when your friend's response to this is aggressive or defensive:

Alfred: Mannie, you are my best bud, but I still need to know when I am going to get back the money you owe me.

Mannie: Alfredo, my pal, I told you if you were uncomfortable with the loan I would just cash in my life insurance. You said, "No problem." I can do that now if you need the money, but otherwise, I need to wait until I can sell that boat.

Alfred: Mannie, I understand, but I lent you that money over a year ago, and I thought it was only going to be a matter of a few months. I don't want to make you go into your insurance, but I would like a realistic idea of when you can pay me back.

Mannie: Look, if you are going to be all over my case about this, I am just going to go cash in the policy. Can we talk about something else?

So maybe the lesson is "neither a borrower nor a lender be." But haven't we all found ourselves part of such an interchange in some way? Alfred faces a decision here, which is in part about avoidance and engagement but also about his autonomy from and connection to Mannie. Alfred can try again, work on his framing, let it go—or he could escalate the conflict. If Mannie responds in a way that helps maintain their connection, then any of these choices might work, but from Alfred's point of view, it might seem that he either has to prioritize his connection with Mannie and back off or assert his own concerns and hang in there. Either way, it is very likely that Alfred—probably both men—will feel a period of strain in their interaction, and possibly long-term damage to their relationship will ensue.

This same dynamic can easily exist between groups. Conflict interveners are often called upon to help disputants retain sometimes fragile connections to each other as they decide to raise a difficult issue, call off a negotiation, undertake a legal action, or withdraw an offer. Sometimes, relationship damage is inevitable and our major challenge is to contain the loss. These moments are critical for the long-term course of conflict. Consider the following examples:

- The failure of a negotiation effort, such as between the Palestinians and the Israelis in 2014

- A decision to take a parenting disagreement to court

- A decision to take a grievance to arbitration because of a lack of progress in more informal processes

- A citizen group's choice to file a lawsuit in a dispute over land use, even though they are still negotiating with the developer of the site in dispute

In these circumstances, our work is not over just because disputants opt for something other than a consensus process. We have an obligation to at least consider how we might help maintain the potential for further constructive interaction, and often we will find we can do considerably more than that. For example, we may do the following:

- Help people figure out how to frame and present their decisions to each other in a constructive way.

- Facilitate this interchange, or sometimes deliver the message ourselves.

- Work with disputants to maintain ongoing channels of communication even as they choose to end collaborative decision-making processes.

- Discuss with disputants how to contain a dispute, even as they choose to escalate it.

- Provide ongoing coaching or support for disputants as they escalate a dispute or raise a difficult issue.

- Continue to act as a vehicle for exchanging information.

- Monitor the situation and engage in periodic (or ongoing) discussions with parties to determine when a renewed cooperative effort might be possible.

- Identify elements of a conflict that can be negotiated even as other elements might not be off the table.

Our goals are to help contain a conflict, to keep the door open for future interactions, to support people in the decision to step away from an engagement effort for the moment, and in general to provide a perspective to parties that can assist them in their decision making. In this process, we can help disputants grapple with their needs for autonomy from other disputants as well as affiliation with them as they pursue a conflictual interaction.

Dealing with Multiple Communities and Attachments

Disputants often face difficult choices about how best to honor their loyalties and commitments. Maintaining in-group solidarity often requires keeping strict boundaries with groups with which we are in conflict. Worse than being an enemy, sometimes, is to be seen as being weak to our supporters in our determination to stand up to an enemy—and even worse yet, to be seen as a traitor to our own group. And often, we have conflicting loyalties to the multiple groups to which we belong. As I have described, our identity is wrapped up in our connection to multiple communities, and as the pattern of those connections change, so does our identity. Dealing with conflict almost always requires that we attend to the pattern of our affiliations, as in the following examples:

- Ralph and Luella are in the midst of a very contentious divorce. Each has turned to friends and family for support. Some friends have chosen primary loyalties; others have tried to be supportive of both. Ralph has been very vocal in telling everyone who will listen how awful Luella is. Some of his friends and family have encouraged him to stand firm in his quest for equal parenting time with their children. He has assured them that he would do just that. Luella has been more overtly needy than Ralph and has seemed willing to accommodate Ralph's demands, but her siblings have urged her not to let Ralph bully her.

- A group of high school teachers are unhappy with the approach of their principal, who has seemed arrogant and demanding. They tried complaining to the area superintendent, who asked that they work this out with their principal. Now one of the teachers has been passed over for promotion to department chair in a move that some have seen as retaliatory. She has filed a complaint and mediation has been scheduled. Her colleagues want her to stand firm in demanding that the principal be held to account for this action.

- The membership of a machinists' union in a large company are facing significant downsizing. They are very concerned about job security. The company is threatening to shut down entire plants unless the union agrees to a considerable decrease in benefits. The sides are meeting to renegotiate the contract. Many believe this is the best opportunity for the union to strike a deal with the company, but this means different things to different members. Some want to demand that there be no downsizing at all. Others think that would be overreaching and instead want to push to minimize layoffs, relying instead on attrition, and agreeing on a generous severance package.

In each of these fairly typical scenarios, disputants are part of multiple groups, and any move they make in conflict, including doing nothing whatsoever, will strengthen some of these connections and weaken others.

For example, as Ralph begins to enter into negotiations with Luella, he might strengthen his association with "Team Ralph"—his most fervent supporters—or he might connect more strongly to those friends who are trying to remain connected to both Luella and him. Or he might move toward a more collaborative parenting relationship with Luella. Even if all members of "Team Ralph" continue to support him, the more he relaxes his demands with Luella, the weaker the bonds to this group may become. Luella will experience a comparable dynamic with her own support groups. And, of course, these groups overlap and have an impact on each other. The teacher who is filing a complaint may well be able to arrive at a reasonable settlement, and in so doing, solidify her relationship with the administration.

However, she will weaken the group solidarity of the anti-principal group and may even foment rifts in that group.

Conflict interveners often work at a time when group affiliations are shifting and unstable. Conflict is a mechanism for maintaining the strength of certain alliances and changing adherence to others. Disputants and interveners may not be aware of these dynamics, yet they have a significant impact on the course of a conflict. As interveners, we face the challenge of helping people at all steps of our intervention. We do so by working on the challenges of autonomy and community that disputants' multiple affiliations pose. Strategies we use include

- *Mapping the matrix of associations.* Sometimes this requires a formal process that engages the participants; sometimes we do it informally. When disputants can see and understand their different communities, they can become more aware of the strategic choices they face.

- *Coaching disputants about how to handle the array of group pressures they face.* For example, we may help a divorcing parent rehearse how to tell her own, sometimes overly zealous, supporting parents that she is planning on compromising with her ex-spouse about parenting time.

- *Encouraging disputants to stay in appropriate contact with certain key communities of support* as they are seeking to establish a stronger connection with those with which they are in conflict. We sometimes have to lean a bit on disputants to make sure they bring along the groups they represent, or at least keep them informed about what is going on in a negotiation.

- *Acting as an internal mediator* or facilitator within certain subgroups.

- *Bringing potentially competing communities together* so that the burden of dealing with the complexities of cross-group loyalties can be faced as a group. This, for example, is one of the purposes of family-group decision making in child welfare, in which the extended family system is brought together with parents to work out a plan for the care of children in protective custody.

Reflections from Practice (and Life)

In this chapter, I have used "community" as a specific term within the broader concept of attachment and affiliation. Community represents the ties we have with people to whom we may not have close or intimate connections, but whom we recognize as part of our circle of associates and whom we feel recognize us. Most communities have porous boundaries, because all communities overlap with other communities. Furthermore, most communities are not self-aware or deliberately constructed as communities. But some are. I learned a great deal about conflict from my personal experience with collective living. In the sixties and seventies, the establishment of "intentional communities" became an important feature of the "counterculture." The nature of these communities varied greatly, from collective living arrangements to "hippie communes" to religious communities to political collectives.

There is a scene in the 1974 movie *Harry and Tonto*, when Art Carney picks up a hitchhiker, an adolescent girl, who says she is running away from home to live on a commune in Boulder, Colorado. As it happened, when I watched this, I was a living on a communal farm in Boulder, Colorado (this line got a huge response when I saw it in a movie theater there). It seemed almost iconic—the stereotypical destination for children of the sixties looking for a place to provide a sense of meaning and community. I guess I fit that stereotype, at least to a degree (that particular farm, however, was owned by two tenured professors at the University of Colorado). For almost thirty years, starting at that time, I lived in one form of collective living arrangement or another.

Actually, I lived most of my prior life in intentional communities. I grew up at a residential treatment center in Cleveland, Ohio, where my father was director (we had a house on campus). Though hardly a commune, it was an intentional community. About 150 people—children and adults—lived and worked there with a common purpose and clearly defined community norms. This community could be a challenging place for the son of the director at times, but never for a moment did I regret growing up in that setting. I felt surrounded by people who were living and working together for a purpose that seemed both idealistic and realistic, and it was a source of autonomy for me as well—a means of differentiating myself from the surrounding suburban community where my friends lived. In college I was part of a cooperative living and eating arrangement for three years. For the thirty years I worked as a partner at CDR Associates, I was a member of another very intense community, one in which all essential decisions were made by consensus.

Clearly, community has been a very important part of my life, and my experience in community is one of the foundations of my approach to conflict. I have come to understand that conflict work is in large part about helping build and maintain a sense of community in a world in which many forces are trying to atomize us and disrupt the functioning of the natural communities in which we live. Our natural way of being in the world is essentially communal. And of course, our most basic community during most of the years of our lives is our family. Communities exert much of their influence on us as individuals through our families, and families in turn are very dependent on communities. Our work with our own families on autonomy and community is the foundation of our approach to this challenge throughout our lives in all the social settings in which we travel. Whether we are working on family, organizational, community, international, or business conflict, we are dealing with the challenge of maintaining both a healthy relationship to community and personal autonomy.

My years of living in intentional communities have provided some important lessons about conflict, and particularly how to deal with the challenge of autonomy and community as it expresses itself in conflict. Four lessons stand out:

- *Boundaries are important.* Communal living feeds an important need for connection and affiliation, but unless it also provides for our need for autonomy, genuine community is not possible. To do this, the community has to take into account the norms we grow up with, even if we may be trying to reject many of these. The sixties ideal of community was often naive in this regard. Sharing income, personal possessions, and parenting with others is not supported by most of our cultural experiences or by the social structures in which we live (while it make take a village to raise a child, child rearing is still a parental responsibility, for example). Many of the more ideologically driven communities that did not establish effective culturally appropriate boundaries were either unstable or dependent on authoritarian and often exploitive leaders.

- *When people need to withdraw, that should be supported—and when they are ready to reengage, that, too, should be supported.* This is related to boundaries, but it is also about flexibility. At different times in our lives—or even our day, our week, or our year—our needs for community and autonomy change, and we often can't predict how. Community relations need to be renegotiated just like marriages or friendships sometimes do. Communities often organize themselves around norms of interaction that people cannot always maintain. And while withdrawal is sometimes healthy, many communities do not readily accept this and make reentry difficult in the process. Sometimes, communities need to cease to exist—or at least change their nature. The communal farm I lived on, for example, eventually changed its formal organization to that very middle-class American structure—a condominium complex.

- *Both formal and informal rituals of coming together are also important.* Communities need a means of experiencing themselves as communities. Holidays, celebrations, meetings, or sports events often play this role. Once a year, around Christmas, my wife and I host a party for our neighbors on our street. We originally did this out of guilt that our dogs seemed to be playing havoc with our neighbors' yards, but over the past twelve years, this event has become very important and we dare not skip it. It symbolizes that in some way we are a community and not just a block.

- *Communities need an effective way to deal with conflict.* Communities need to find a way for members to raise important issues with each other, or the vitality of the community will diminish. Communities, however, also need to be able to recognize conflicts that can't be resolved.

Our capacity to put these principles into operation was critical to the functioning of the most durable of the living groups I was affiliated with, the "Juniper Street Collective":

The community that I settled into for more than twenty-five years, the Juniper Street Collective, was in many ways a variation of an extended family unit. For most of its existence, it consisted of two adjacent houses on a quiet street in Boulder. My brother and his family lived in one of these, and I lived with my family in the other. Usually, there were one or two additional members living in one house or the other. We ate together five days a week, rotating cooking and cleaning duties, and we also purchased our food out of joint funds. When our children were young, we shared after-school childcare. We also met weekly, shared a garden, and engaged in many other joint activities. But our houses were still our houses, children were the primary responsibility of their parents, and our financial resources were separate. After the first fifteen years, we changed from eating together five times a week to doing so once a week.

Several times a year, we hosted big events for our larger community as well. For example, we had big feasts on Christmas Eve, Passover, and Thanksgiving. Years after the Juniper Street Collective ceased to exist, some of these still take place and continue to provide an essential sense of community. And, of course, we had our share of conflicts over the years as well. One occurred over assigned seats at the dinner table. After a few too many arguments among our children about who got to sit where at dinner, the suggestion was made that we have assigned seats—for everyone. This violated my sense of individual freedom, and I objected that I didn't want an assigned seat. After what seems in retrospect prolonged discussions, we decided that the children would have assigned seats and adults who wanted one also would, but those who didn't could sit in any unassigned seat. "Those who didn't" proved to be me and no one else. So every night I was free to sit at any unassigned seat—of which there was only one. I let it go at that. There is no perfect integration of our need for autonomy and community.

Over the years of working on conflict, I have applied the lessons I've learned from living in intentional communities over and over again. To function well, families, organizations, communities, unions, and all the other groups I have worked with in conflict need to establish effective boundaries, allow for people to vary in their commitment, have rituals, and be able to deal with conflict. These seem to be essential tasks in almost all conflict, and our capacity to assist people with these is an essential element of what we have to offer to disputants. By working on these tasks, we help people cope with the pulls toward community and autonomy that both fuel conflict and guide people through it.

chapter nine

the conflict
dialectic
Better Paradoxes, Better Conflict

Conflict resolution is dialectics as a practice.

Ken Cloke, The Dance of Opposites

In this book, I have discussed seven key paradoxes that collectively define the challenge conflict presents to interveners and disputants. Three things may have become clear as you were reading about this:

- This is not an exclusive list.

- There is considerable overlap among the paradoxes.

- The underlying approach used in considering these seeming contradictions is itself an important part of the message of this book.

In this chapter, I discuss paradox as a method and consider several additional paradoxes that conflict presents. In order to examine the overlap and synergies among the key paradoxes, I apply each of them to the same conflict, which involves two brothers who co-owned a business. I then turn to the essential paradoxes of democracy, peacemaking, social change, and conflict intervention—the effort to achieve a society that is peaceful, secure, just, free, and equal—and conclude with some final reflections.

Paradox as a Method

The bifurcated view with which most of us approach disputes is often the very thing that keeps us mired in conflict. When we are embroiled in an intense dispute, we tend to believe that one side is right and the other is wrong, that there is a single truth, that we have to choose between holding the line or giving in, or that that we must either take on a conflict or avoid it. The essential challenge we face is to understand that not only do we not have to come down on one side or the other of these polarities, but that in fact they are *not really polarities*. When we understand that we are truly dealing with a paradox, we can approach conflict in a more powerful, sustainable, and constructive way.

A paradox is a seemingly contradictory reality that in fact contains an important truth. For example, I have often noticed as a mediator that if I want people to listen to me, I have to listen more; if I want them to reveal more, I have to be more revealing. I have also observed that the more rigidly someone adheres to a position, the less sure of that position they often are. Other examples of paradox are "less is more," "slower is faster," "vulnerability is power." David Hoffman (2003) has suggested that a willingness to accept the paradoxical nature of our work is essential to being effective in what we do. He explains that being an effective mediator requires "a high tolerance for ambiguity . . . and a willingness to accept the possibility that reality is riddled with paradox" (p. 168).

Each of the polarities I have described in this book is a paradox in the sense that each seems to imply a choice. But it's not only unnecessary for us to choose one approach over the other, but impossible, because each element of the paradox is dependent on the other. Effective cooperation requires competition, principle is meaningless without compromise, and every time we choose to engage in conflict, we are making avoidance decisions as well.

But when we go beyond that and delve more deeply into these paradoxes—when we reflect on our practical experience and recognize how they manifest themselves—we realize that they are not really separable and that each element is part of a larger truth. When we find the underlying unity in each polarity, we take a leap forward in our capacity to engage in conflict effectively and constructively. This is not easy to do, but it is the essence of what effective conflict work is about. Embracing paradox is a core method for dealing with conflict.

When we step outside the polarity and embrace the apparently contradictory elements as true and necessary to each other, we move a conflict forward and open up new ways of thinking and acting that can lead us to more constructive engagement. Consider a few examples of paradoxes at work in conflict:

- Disputants present different stories, different facts, and different truths, and they bolster these by accusing each other of dishonesty, distortion, and fabrication. The intervener's job is to work with all parties to discover the larger truth, the narrative they can create that incorporates the essential elements of each of their seemingly contradictory stories. I have always treasured the moment when one party in a mediation tells me his or her version of what has happened in such a persuasive way that it is hard to imagine what the other side's perspective might be. I treasure it because I know I am about to find out, and that in doing so, I will be challenged to move beyond my own desire to decide who is right and who is wrong.

- Serious efforts to arrive at a resolution of a conflict take place against a backdrop of preparing for the eventuality that no agreement will be reached. Rather than seeing these preparations as a sign of bad faith (and interveners often do just that), we need to help people view the whole system of interaction—both the effort to resolve and the preparation for escalation—as part of an overall effort to handle conflict responsibly. Parties to serious conflict really do have to prepare for both peace and war at the same time. And although we must make decisions about how much effort to put into each, the underlying challenge is not about whether to compete or cooperate, to compromise or to escalate, but how to be effective, constructive, and wise in approaching conflict.

- The most important conflicts that we face do not end easily or through reaching agreements about the presenting issues. They almost always have an enduring element. We have to understand the agreements we are seeking in this context. The point of agreement is most often not to end a conflict but to take it to its next stage—to provide a platform for ongoing struggle.

- Disputants often experience considerable tension because they do not trust, respect, or like the person with whom they are in conflict. Sometimes, they are locked into a relationship that they cannot easily walk away from—with siblings, business partners, or neighbors. Interveners often need to help disputants realize that disliking and mistrusting someone does not mean that you can't have a productive and even friendly relationship. Often the best way to improve such a relationship is to acknowledge how bad it is. For example, when I have said to disputants, "You two don't seem to like each other or trust each other, but you don't have to in order to work together or to have a cordial relationship," the tension level has often diminished. This is not about putting relationships aside and just agreeing on substantive or procedural next steps. In fact, it is about *building* relationships.

Another way of understanding how we work with paradox is to think of it as a *dialectical* process. The concept of dialectics is an ancient one, but its two most famous modern proponents are Georg Wilhelm Friederich Hegel and Karl Marx (Hegel 2003; Marx 1977). Hegel's dialectic was based on our awareness of the nature of our own existence; for example, an awareness of our being leads to the opposite awareness of nothingness, which leads to a concept of becoming. Marx argued for a dialectic based on the material conditions of human existence—in particular, on the contradiction between the means of production and the ownership of production. The dialectical method assumes that a given state of awareness or existence (thesis) breeds its own negation or contradiction (antithesis). The struggle or tension between these two leads to a new awareness or condition (synthesis), which then produces its own negation.

I have not posed the polarities I have described in this manner, because I am not suggesting that one element exists prior to the other or that we ever reach a full synthesis. But there are elements of this analytical approach that are useful for understanding paradoxes. Most importantly, a dialectical process suggests that each element implies its opposite and that we make progress as we develop an ever-greater ability to understand how the two elements come together and pose new strategic challenges. Ken Cloke (2013) describes it this way:

> Dialectics in conflict resolution can be regarded as a theory of the ways of transforming polarity into unity, and how mediators can turn two antagonistic, hostile, or contradictory ideas, forces, perspectives, or positions into one. (p. 355)

Achieving this transformation in practice is not easy, but it is also natural for us to try. For example, when divorcing parents argue for a very different approach to parenting—with one advocating for a clear primary residence and the other for equal time with each parent—we are presented with an apparent polarity. Finding the essential unity is not so easy. But mediators try, usually by beginning with the principle that both parents want to do what is best for the long-term adjustment of their children—true, but general. They often then suggest (or elicit) that the goal is to arrive at stable parenting arrangements that provide for rich and meaningful time with each parent. This "both-and" approach is a step toward unity, but it is still more a statement about balance than a true integration. Only when parents recognize that each of them is really fighting for something that the other also believes in and that the struggle itself is a sign of their commitment to the children do we even begin to achieve an integrated perspective. This is truly difficult to come by in highly contested divorces, but the effort itself is important.

Each of the seven paradoxes I have suggested offers an avenue for moving people beyond a polarized view, but finding the unity beyond the polarity is always challenging. There is no universal formulation that we can easily take across all conflicts. But an underlying unity exists, and the challenge we face is to discover how it manifests itself in any particular conflict.

Consider, for example, how each of the seven paradoxes might be expressed as an integrated whole with the divorcing couple:

- **Competition and cooperation.** Learning how best to influence and be influenced by each other

- **Optimism and realism.** Facing the challenges of shared parenting with wisdom and energy

- **Avoidance and engagement.** Focusing on the differences that are most important to work on to promote effective parenting

- **Principle and compromise.** Finding a principled way of being an effective co-parent

- **Emotions and logic.** Bringing one's whole self to decision making

- **Neutrality and advocacy.** Advocating for one's children in a way that respects the different needs and values of each parent

- **Community and autonomy.** Maintaining the boundaries and the communication that will promote good parenting (or "good fences make good co-parents")

Whether these particular formulations work is, of course, dependent on the players and the circumstances. But the paradoxical approach is clear. No matter which element we start with, we will inevitably have to deal with its counterpart, and if we can move beyond the polarity, we can reach a more nuanced and useful understanding of the challenges and the choices we face.

Other Paradoxes

There is nothing magical about the number seven (although it seems to have worked pretty well for Steven Covey, Snow White, and Sinbad the Sailor), and I do not mean to suggest that these seven paradoxes are the *only* appropriate ones on which to focus. I urge readers to consider other potential paradoxes or different ways of formulating those I have presented that may fit better into your way of viewing conflict. I have chosen these because they seem critical to the challenges that I have observed as a student of conflict and as a conflict intervener. Collectively, they paint a comprehensive and rich picture of conflict and of the pitfalls we all face as we engage or intervene in conflict.

But other paradoxes are also prevalent, and some might view these as more essential. Let's briefly consider three: process and substance, relationship and substance, and outcome and transformation.

Process and Substance

This paradox is almost as commonly addressed as competition and cooperation. I have often heard mediators refer to themselves as "in charge of" process, not substance. The problem with this, however, is that it's really not possible to separate the two. The procedural moves we make affect the substance of a conflict, and substantive developments inevitably affect the process used to deal with the conflict. Furthermore, disputants have a large procedural voice, and mediators inevitably have a substantive impact. So we might look upon this as a critical paradox. I believe it is largely expressed by other polarities I have discussed, but interveners and disputants do have to deal with this throughout the life of a conflict.

Substance and Relationship

Disputants and interveners constantly juggle the apparent contradiction between whether to focus on the substance of a conflict or the relationships of those involved. Conflicts that rise to the level of requests for intervention are usually presented as disagreements over action and are often couched in terms of rights and obligations. But frequently, the driving force behind a conflict is a disrupted or destructive relationship. Formal systems of intervention are not often designed to deal with relationship issues, so disputants find a way to frame their disputes in terms of legal rights, contractual obligations, or company policy. They can hope to get redress on this basis, and at least they can imagine an outcome that will satisfy their concerns about substantive specifics. It is hard to imagine a ruling on a grievance, for example, that would have a significant impact on trust, respect, or collegiality. But these concerns are often the most painful driving forces behind conflict.

If we are to aid disputants effectively in uncovering and facing the roots of their conflict, we need to understand the interplay of the substantive and relational aspects. This can be a very difficult challenge, because the systems we work in tend to promote a "rational," rights-based, problem-solving orientation, and relational issues do not easily fit this outlook. But we are also working on relationship issues as we work on substantive differences, and we usually can't make much progress in one area if we ignore the concerns people have in the other.

Outcome and Transformation

Most cogently argued by Bush and Folger in *The Promise of Mediation* (2005), there is tension between focusing on a desired outcome versus working to provide the opportunity for a genuine growth experience for disputants. The more focused disputants and interveners are on the potential for reaching an agreement, the more likely they are to miss the opportunities for parties to feel heard on a deeper level and to recognize each other as something other than enemies. In a different but related vein, John Paul Lederach (2003, 2005) has written eloquently about the transformation of conflict from a destructive to a creative endeavor. If we see this as a paradox and not a choice, we understand that it is not a matter of deciding whether to focus on outcome or transformation, but of understanding that these two are inextricably interdependent. Transformation without a satisfactory outcome is unlikely to be durable, as is an acceptable outcome without the genuine change that is necessary to sustain it.

All three paradoxes are intertwined with each other. Furthermore, they are reflected in the polarities I have discussed in previous chapters. For example, the tension between community and autonomy is a defining element of our own identity formation, and the most profound transformations we undergo are identity-related. We can therefore understand some of the dynamics of transformation and its relationship to outcome by looking at the pulls for community and autonomy.

And Still More

Other paradoxes that influence our understanding and approach to conflict include

- Focusing on systemic forces or individual needs
- Personal and structural power
- Analysis and instinct
- Cultural particulars and universal truths
- Objectivity and involvement
- Equality and leadership
- Short-term and long-term focus
- A relational approach versus an individual focus

And, of course, the list can go on. (For a consideration of additional paradoxes specifically related to the work of mediators, see "Paradoxes of Mediation," by Hoffman [2003].) Over time, we each develop our own analytic framework that gets expressed in how we handle conflict (our "theory in action" [Schön 1983]). Part of that framework inevitably involves how we understand these (and other) polarities and how we use them in conflict.

Overlaps and Synergies

Each of the polarities provides a lens that we can use to understand a conflict. They can give us insight into an individual's struggles, problems disputants have in interacting with each other, challenges for interveners, and the nature of the conflict itself. But they are not entirely separate lenses. For example, when we talk about competition and cooperation, we also examine compromise and principle; when we look at avoidance and engagement, we are considering optimism and realism as well. There is value in employing multiple lenses to understand a conflict, even though—or because—they overlap. Consider the following example involving solar energy and sibling rivalry:

> Jacob and Stan were brothers and partners in a company that installed solar energy systems in houses and apartment buildings. They jointly purchased this business with money they had received from their mother after their father died. At fifty-five, Jacob was the oldest of five siblings and had recently left a position as the CFO of a private university. Stan was the youngest of the siblings, at forty-one. Six months prior to the start of their partnership, Stan had been laid off when the automobile plant he had been working at for twenty years was shut down. Stan had been a mechanic, a millwright, and a tool and die maker at the plant.
>
> They purchased this business thinking that Jacob could provide the business expertise and Stan the technical know-how. Because of their age difference, they had interacted only infrequently prior to the start of this partnership. Jacob had lived in a different community and had only recently moved back to his hometown. While the brothers had maintained a cordial relationship, they had never been close. Jacob was divorced; Stan was married and had three young children. Stan's wife worked as an emergency room nurse on a rotating schedule.
>
> Although they were ostensibly equal partners, Jacob ran the show in most respects, which created problems from the beginning. Stan supervised installation and repair crews, but everything else—for example, budgeting, fee structures, payment schedules, marketing—was Jacob's purview. There were numerous little issues between the brothers around

hiring decisions, shop location, suppliers, allocation of resources, and other things, but these were all secondary to the tension that developed about compensation and hours. Jacob felt that they needed to maximize the reinvestment of their profits in the business to build its capacity and create a more durable foundation for future growth. Stan needed a steady and reliable source of income to support his family. This mattered less to Jacob, whose one child was grown and who had significantly greater financial resources than Stan. Also, Stan wanted flexible working hours due to his wife's schedule, whereas Jacob felt that the business could not accommodate this and questioned how many hours Stan was actually working.

All this came to a head when the economy took a plunge, and their business did as well. Jacob felt that unless they "tightened their belt" and increased their efficiency, they would go under, and he insisted that they both take a 50 percent cut in pay. Stan did not agree to this, and a conversation about this had degenerated into a shouting match with some shoving and lots of swearing. That's when I was brought into the picture.

Jacob confided in me that the only reason he had agreed to go into this business was to help his brother, and that his mother had made it clear to him that she thought Stan would need the family's support after being laid off. He now considered the business partnership to be a huge mistake, because Stan had shown himself to be both irresponsible and incompetent. Jacob said, "Either I buy him out—and there is not much equity in the business at this point—or he can buy me out. But he can't afford to, and even if he could, the business would not last ten minutes under his management."

Stan thought Jacob was just being a jerk and claimed that this was why no one else in the family, including Jacob's own daughter, could stand him. "My sister warned me that Jacob would be a problem, and so did my wife, but Jacob and I seemed to have a clear understanding about how we wanted to do this, so I thought it would be OK. Was I ever wrong." Stan thought he should sell his share to Jacob, but he also thought the company was worth considerably more than Jacob did. He wanted to walk away from the partnership, but he did not want to be fleeced or to upset his mother or anyone else in the family.

Let's look at this example through the lenses of each of the seven paradoxes.

Competition and Cooperation

Jacob and Stan were engaged in a power struggle that may well have been rooted in the roles they each played in the family system. But they also really needed each other in order for the business to succeed. Jacob was the eldest in the family and seemed to expect that he would hold the most power, an attitude that Stan resented. He thought Jacob was a bully and believed he needed to stand up to his older brother or they would never be able to work together. Jacob thought it was time to "stop babying" Stan (interesting words—Stan was the "baby of the family") and to put it to him straight. In another words, both of them were acting as if they had cooperated enough and that the time had come to compete, in this case by exercising their power in a coercive manner. But, of course, they had been quietly competitive all along, and the real problem was that they had not brought their different visions, needs, and styles of working into the open.

Engaging in more competitive interchanges early on might have opened the door to a more genuinely cooperative approach. Now that they were being more openly competitive, they were also in some sense being more openly cooperative as well—that is, they were actually cooperating to figure out how to end the partnership—and although they were very angry at each other, they were closing in on a very similar view about how to negotiate an end to their joint venture. Their failure as partners was very much related to their inability either to cooperate or compete in an effective manner. They believed that they could succeed only by cooperating. If they could not cooperate, they would have to end the partnership, but they had not been able to cooperate, because they could not appropriately compete.

Optimism and Realism

When I met Stan and Jacob, both were claiming the mantle of realism, and neither was expressing optimism about either the business or their personal relationship. However, both had been optimistic when they started the enterprise, even while others suggested they were not being realistic. Their initial optimism was brittle, because it was not informed by realism. Jacob's positive outlook was based on his faith in his management ability and on a reliance on his traditional familial role as the "alpha male" among the siblings. He may also have felt that he did not really have much to lose and approached the business almost as a hobby. Stan, on the other hand, assumed that everything would be OK because he wanted it to be, needed it to be, and was therefore not looking at the potential for problems. His lack of bad experiences with Jacob prompted him to assume that everything would go well. Had each been more realistic about the challenges that all new businesses face, their different visions and needs, and the challenges of forging a new kind of relationship between them, their optimism about their capacity to deal with these issues would have led to a more meaningful and sustaining dynamic.

When things began to fall apart, Stan in particular abandoned all elements of optimism and felt that he needed to get out, with as much money as possible, and minimize all future interactions with Jacob. However, this perspective was not so realistic in the sense that the quick, clean break he was envisioning could happen only if the two could work together closely to make it happen, which they were not able to do. In a sense, Stan flipped from being optimistic that the partnership would work out to being optimistic that it could be ended relatively painlessly. Jacob, on the other hand, played the realistic card with a heavy hand. He couched almost everything in terms of having to be realistic—which, for him, meant seeing things his way. He thought he could force his reality on Stan (in that sense he was optimistic), and discounted everything Stan said as being unrealistic. But of course, that was not realistic, either. The challenge was how to engage enough of their optimism so that they could recognize that addressing each other's most fundamental concerns, whether they chose to stay together or not, was the most realistic way of moving forward.

Avoidance and Engagement

Stan and Jacob both used multiple approaches to avoiding their real differences. They colluded in avoiding a clear discussion of decision-making and management styles, how they wanted to deal with conflict, or the risks they were taking—not just business risks—by entering into a partnership. Furthermore, they did not spend much time getting to know each other. When differences began to emerge, they either avoided talking about them or did so in vague terms. They found a way of working out, on a month-to-month basis, what they would each be paid, but these discussions were superficial. Jacob would say that they needed to reinvest a certain amount, Stan would argue for a lower amount, and they would quickly compromise somewhere in the middle. But they would never really delve into *why* they had these differences or what were their underlying concerns. Had they raised these issues earlier, they might have arrived at some different arrangements. Or they might have concluded that this business partnership was not such a great idea at a time when they could have extracted themselves from it in a less costly way, financially and personally.

Instead, they raised peripheral differences. For example, they fought over whether to continue using a particular subcontractor, which became a surrogate for their power struggle. It may also have represented their misgivings about being partners at all. While this involved a heated interaction, they worked their way through it without ever raising their more basic concerns.

When the more fundamental issues arose, they again avoided a genuine discussion by escalating the argument—that is, by quickly going from avoiding the topic by ignoring it to avoiding it by fighting in a manner that shut down genuine communication. Then they both quickly staked out positions about how to end the partnership. Because I sensed that they were rushing to this position in part as an avoidance mechanism, I suggested that we look more carefully at their different visions about how to run the business before we focused on how to dissolve their partnership. But as I discuss next, I did not push this conversation very far.

Principle and Compromise

In fact, Stan and Jacob had been able to compromise pretty well throughout the course of the business. However, they had done so without a clear view of the underlying principles involved, which led to short-term and fragile compromises. They then arrived at a point where each felt that they were violating their principles by even trying to accommodate the other's needs. Standing up to Jacob and "not letting him bully me anymore" had become a matter of principle to Stan—perhaps even more important than having the business succeed. For Jacob, principle and realism were deeply enmeshed. He had come to feel that being a "hard-headed businessman" and not giving in to Stan's lack of realism was a matter of principle not to be compromised. Also as a matter of principle, Jacob felt that he should not continue to compromise the business's needs so that he could take care of his dependent and needy younger brother. So if principle was grounded in the competition and cooperation paradox for Stan, it was grounded in Jacob's sense of realism and optimism.

I sensed that Jacob, while seeming to be more focused on making good business decisions, might have been more trapped in a rigid view of how to be principled than Stan. Jacob was willing to sacrifice a lot to maintain a principled stance. Stan, while wanting to stand up to Jacob, was ready to let this go if it allowed him out of the partnership and away from Jacob, whom he really saw as a malign force in his life.

Emotions and Logic

Jacob appeared to me to be a very emotional man. Underneath his rational, realistic front, he seemed quite angry. I suspect this was a pattern that ran through much of his life and not one with which he had come to terms. He presented his stance as all about logic, and in fact accused Stan of being too emotional in his decision making. But because Jacob was not in touch with his anger, he was not always very logical.

Stan was more overtly emotional—a bit angry, obviously anxious about what was in store for him, and also hurt by the way Jacob seemed to question his competence and commitment. He did not need to develop the logic behind his thinking–feeling. When he said he wanted out, Stan just "knew" that was the right thing to do. Yet there was an implied logic. Working with Jacob was unpleasant, did not meet his financial needs, and undermined his self-confidence. It was time to move on. Stan's comfort with the role emotions were playing in his thinking was actually a source of strength.

We can see how the emotion–logic paradox was tied into realism and optimism in this conflict. Jacob could not integrate the logical and emotional dimensions of his thinking, and this led him to a more rigid approach—ostensibly realistic, but only within a narrow framework. Emotional information fed Stan's sense of what was realistic and made him both more optimistic that leaving was the right thing to do and would make things better and pessimistic that things would never improve in this partnership or with his brother. In general, Stan was better able to integrate the different elements of the paradoxes he faced than Jacob was. Jacob was more tenacious and perhaps a better businessman, but he was much less creative and flexible in approaching this conflict.

Neutrality and Advocacy

This mediation presented some interesting challenges in relationship to this paradox. I had to ensure that the brothers perceived me as fair and committed to helping, but they each set this up as a situation in which I was either for them or against them. Jacob tried very hard to convince me how incompetent, unrealistic, emotionally driven, and uncooperative Stan was, and he almost demanded that I agree with him. I would try my best to validate his concerns without indicating that I concurred with his judgment. Stan seemed to assume that I was on Jacob's side, and the only way I could break through this was to act as an advocate for him—by trying to help him state his point of view as forcefully as possible. But I felt throughout the time I worked with them that Stan assumed I would take Jacob's side. I sensed some sibling dynamics at play with my relationship with them, as I felt Stan treated me as if I were a parent figure, while Jacob saw me as a sibling.

Ironically, as perhaps apparent from some of my previous comments, I felt more sympathetic to Stan in many ways and thought he was actually the more grounded, if less effective as a business man, of the two. Throughout this mediation, I felt I had to suppress some of my reactions to Jacob, who could be very abrasive. Yet Jacob treated me as an ally, whereas Stan doubted that I was. Maybe I was overcompensating by being more attentive to Jacob, despite my attempts not to do so.

I wanted to push them to consider whether they could maintain the partnership if they clarified expectations, renegotiated the partner agreement, and set up some protocols for decision making and communication. But neither of them was interested in doing this, and they were the ones who knew the situation best and were going to have to live with the outcome. So I suppressed this instinct in the name of being neutral.

In the end, I wondered if it might have been wise to push it a little further—even if only to help them make a more affirmative and less negative decision to go their own ways. By advocating for this a bit more, I might also have helped them to work on some of the other paradoxes more effectively. For example, they might have been better able to understand the principled basis of the compromises they were going to have to make to end the business arrangement if they considered more thoroughly the compromises they would have to make to stay together. They might also have approached that decision with a clearer sense of what they were sacrificing by ending the relationship. But given what they were saying, I felt that pushing for a discussion of what it would take to stay together would interfere with my credibility as a neutral.

Community and Autonomy

This was the most painful and intense element of the conflict, as it often is, because it was so closely connected to their sense of themselves. The family system that they were part of was a significant presence in this dispute. Jacob saw his entry into the partnership as a step toward community—in this case, with the family and with Stan. Although the oldest of his generation and accustomed to being deferred to, Jacob had been the most distant from the rest of the family. He had lived in another state for most of his life, whereas his parents and siblings all lived in the same community. Now he was returning after a marriage that had ended acrimoniously and was taking a step that he saw as offering something positive to his family. "Rescuing Stan" (how he saw the situation) was his way of giving his family a gift and taking a step toward community. But this was also about establishing who he was after so much else that defined him had changed—his marriage, his job, his geographical community, and perhaps much more.

This realignment of identity involved a step away from one community and a step toward another, but it also was a change in the nature of his autonomy. Jacob had previously worked in a large organization in which he had a great deal of authority but also had to work cooperatively with many others. Now he was working as a supposed equal with his sibling, but in fact he was operating much more autonomously than he had before. It seemed to me that Jacob was trying very hard to forge a new path, but the result of this was alienation from his family, further isolation, and, I suspect, a greater challenge both to his sense of community and his autonomy than he would have experienced had he not entered into this partnership.

Stan's sense of identity was also at stake. He had lost one important element of his sense of self when he was laid off, both because of the work itself and because of the loss of capacity to support his family. He also had lost the sense of community that his work provided. He had remained close to his extended family, but his work had provided boundaries to keep him from becoming too enmeshed. When that ended, his family seemed to pull him back into a dependency relationship. This was intensified by his business relationship with his brother, especially when Jacob started treating him like an incompetent dependent. I think one reason Stan was so clear he had to leave was that he sensed he could not work out the community-autonomy dynamic in this partnership, no matter how well he and Jacob could get along. One element in the conflict's escalation may have been that Stan needed a dispute to motivate him to leave a situation that did not feel healthy to him.

In the end, Stan and Jacob dissolved the partnership. Stan found another job. They agreed on a buyout agreement that would allow Jacob to become the sole owner over time and that could be altered based on an outsider's evaluation of the worth of the company. Jacob took over the company's management and promoted one of the installation team members to be the director of operations. While Jacob and Stan said some constructive things to affirm their caring for each other as family members, I sensed that at best their relationship would be distant—cordial at family affairs and not much more.

Each of the paradoxes provides a useful lens on this case. Clearly they overlap, and taken together, they offer interesting additional insights. I find it useful to consider them separately, but also together. In this case, some paradoxes particularly call out for joint consideration. Emotions and logic, principle and compromise, and optimism and realism were very intertwined, as they often are. And competition and cooperation overlapped with avoidance and engagement. As is usually the case, each of these paradoxes provided a way to consider the same overall set of challenges.

Society's Essential Paradoxes

Freedom or security? Justice or peace? Equality or freedom? Some would say we have to choose; others argue that we must have it all. The paradoxical approach suggests that we can't have one without the other, even though they sometimes seem in opposition. These paradoxes define some of the most significant social struggles of our time—actually, of any time. Just as we make progress through conflict by arriving at ever-more-sophisticated ways of understanding the conflict paradox, we also make progress as societies by growing our capacity to work with these societal paradoxes. And what we learn in conflict informs our understanding of these broader societal challenges.

In the United States, after the terrorist attacks of 9/11 and because of the trauma those events inflicted, we reverted to a more primitive understanding of the tension between freedom and security. In my opinion, we lost sight of just how much our freedom and our reputation as a model of a free society are essential to our security. We had to make adjustments in how we dealt with this paradox. Increased security checks, for example, made sense. But as our thinking became increasingly polarized, we sacrificed a great deal of our civil liberties, and in the process, it seems that we have indeed become *less* secure. I hope and believe we are slowly working our way back to a more mature view of this, but it has been slow going, and we have lost much in the process.

In negotiating the end of South African apartheid in the early 1990s, Nelson Mandela and his associates went counter to the demand of many of their followers for justice in the hopes of securing peace. Some think they went too far, and in the process sowed the long-term seeds for social unrest. Others feel this was a necessary exchange, because there could ultimately be no justice without peace. But without justice, peace could be ephemeral. The Truth and Reconciliation Commission was an effort to deal with this by, in a sense, redefining justice. Instead of jail, perpetrators of the crimes of apartheid could face the commission and own up to their misdeeds, and restitution for the victims could then be offered. But restitution has been minimal, and many of the perpetrators continue to lead very comfortable lives, while many of the victims struggle with poverty. Clearly some tradeoff between peace and justice had to be made, or there would be neither. But this story is far from over.

As we face the growing gap in our society between the very wealthy and the very poor, many believe that something is amiss. Full equality is not a realistic goal—not if we are to maintain a modicum of prosperity and freedom. But the level of inequality that exists threatens both our prosperity and freedom—and it is getting worse. We need to do a much better job of figuring this out. As with all paradoxes, we must commit to both elements and develop our capacity to embrace both as essentially one.

Like the conflict paradoxes, these social dilemmas overlap and define each other. A paradoxical view provides a lens for looking at essential societal challenges, just as it does for interpersonal conflicts. We can better understand conflicts around health care, drug abuse, nuclear proliferation, violent crime, or immigration in terms of the polarities that define them. In this book, I have used examples that range from global conflict to small group and interpersonal disputes to illustrate the full range of issues that a paradoxical view can illuminate. As individuals and as a society, we experience conflicts in our everyday lives, in our communities, in our organizations, and in our society, and these provide us the opportunity to increase our capacity to work with paradoxes and to view them in a nuanced and sophisticated way. The work we do on any level of conflict or social problem affects our work on every level. That is what makes conflict work so interesting—and so vital.

Final Reflections (and a Final Paradox)

Why paradox? Why focus on how we see the unity behind the polarity? I could have discussed these in terms of *balance* (a word I have avoided throughout this book), compromise, or finding a middle way, for example. After all, in conflict, both cooperation and competition play a role, so isn't it really a matter of finding the right balance? Why delve into the more complex concept of seeing them as integrated concepts, where you need one to have the other?

I have no doubt that it makes more sense for many to think in terms of balance rather than integration; if so, that will be the most useful approach for them. For me, the value of taking the paradoxical approach lies in the final paradox I want to mention—complexity and clarity. To develop our capacity to engage and intervene in conflict constructively, courageously, wisely, and effectively, our thinking needs to become more complex, and yet clearer. Often the first step is to give up a simplistic clarity, thereby increasing our confusion (and sometimes temporarily diminishing our effectiveness), but in the process deepening our capacity to consider the true complexity of conflict.

290 THE CONFLICT PARADOX

This can then lead to a new and more profound clarity. Clarity without complexity is simplistic and therefore cloudy (not clear), and complexity without clarity is confusion. We often respond to this confusion by trying to force clarity, which leads to less complex thinking—and less genuine clarity. Clarity therefore requires complexity, and complexity clarity.

How do we find clarity from complexity? In large part, we do this through developing metaphors that provide the anchors that help both to complicate and clarify our thinking. Paradox is such a metaphor. The idea that seemingly contradictory ideas are both true and that one requires the other to make sense is a metaphor that leads us to more complex thinking, but it also provides an anchor for clarity. Consider some of the metaphors that conflict specialists have relied on over the past thirty years to help us understand conflict:

- Positions and interests

- Power over and power with

- Win/win

- Conflict dynamics

- Neutrality and bias

- Transformation

- Third parties

Each of these helps illustrate underlying ideas that, when first developed, were intended to challenge old clarities, to encourage a more complex approach to conflict, or to provide an anchor (another metaphor) to simplify complexity in a more sophisticated way. Because something is a metaphor does not diminish its conceptual integrity. All concepts are communicated through metaphors. In fact, we can't communicate or think except through the use of metaphors. Cognitive linguists George Lakoff and Mark Johnson (1980) argue that "our ordinary conceptual system, in terms of which we both think and act, is fundamentally metaphorical in nature" (p. 3).

The challenge we face in advancing our thinking—and in advancing the complexity and clarity of our understanding of our world—is to build ever-better metaphors, and in the process to let some old ones go. I think we may be ready to move beyond positions and interests, win/win, and neutrality, for example. And I believe it is high time for us to move beyond balance as a pervasive metaphor. I have argued that balance of power is a misleading concept (Mayer 2012a), and I think balancing the interests of each party, taking a balanced approach to conflict, being balanced in our use of language, and so forth, while an advance over a purely adversarial mindset, has actually limited our thinking. I believe a better metaphor, and therefore a better conceptual framework, is paradox. It provides a useful anchor for the complexity with which we need to approach conflict. It induces a more systemic approach to understanding conflict, whereas systems thinking is often difficult to grasp in practical terms, and mirrors our most essential challenge in conflict: to help people understand that there can be two seemingly contradictory truths that are both still truths.

Finding the underlying unity beyond seeming opposites has been a challenge that I have long found intriguing. It was an important element of what attracted me to mediation in the first place. But there is also something slightly troubling for me about this. Being an activist for social change has been an important part of my identity, and I have wondered if my desire to find unity in the face of polarity might in fact undercut my effectiveness in advancing causes that are important to me. Do I always see truth in the views of those whose beliefs I am struggling against, and, if so, does that undercut my effectiveness? More to the point—since my personal effectiveness is probably less the issue—does taking the paradoxical approach make it harder to struggle against social evil and for social good (however we define that)? I am sure there are many who would argue that, in fact, it does.

There may be times when a paradoxical view makes it more difficult to build a movement for change, but in the long term, I believe quite the opposite. Understanding the truth in the views of those who take a stance that I consider wrong, and even immoral, does not over time undercut my ability to take a strong stand, and I certainly seem to have maintained the capacity to do that (just ask my friends and family). A paradoxical view challenges us to move beyond simplistic formulations that may have provided effective and perhaps comforting rallying cries but that are not sustainable in the long run. We need to find new rallying cries that reflect a more sophisticated view, and that in time will be rejected as the dialectical process of paradox formation proceeds. The United States is no doubt an imperialist country, but is that a useful metaphor for the time we live in? Class and the metaphors that go with it (e.g., class consciousness, class struggle, ruling class, bourgeoisie, proletariat) may have passed their sell-by dates. To confront the serious problems of inequity in our society, we need new metaphors, new paradoxical formulations, and thereby new understandings of the challenges we face.

The slogan, common in the sixties—and probably originating at the Free Speech Movement at the University of California (Weinberg 2000)—advising, "don't trust anyone over thirty," in part referenced how we become compromised by the demands of family, career, and lifestyle as we get older, but it also reflected a sense of what happens cognitively as we mature—our thinking becomes too complex to hold to simple truths (or as Bob Dylan sang in 1965's "Subterranean Homesick Blues," "You don't need a weather man to know which way the wind blows"). I would argue that you need all ages (and more generally, diversity) to create the complexity that leads to clarity and new simplicities. You can't trust people over thirty *on their own* to run the world. You can't trust *any* group *on their own.*

We need diversity, we need complexity, we need clarity, and we need simplicity. We also need the courage to advocate fiercely for social change and for particular policies that we believe will contribute to that change, even as we grapple with the limits of our understanding. Being clear and yet open to our confusion is essential to our survival. This requires a growing capacity to act with certainty while being aware of our doubts, to be committed to our principles and aware of their limitations, to act with the intellectual clarity that only our emotions can achieve, and to be committed to the community of change while we maintain our autonomy of doubt. As conflict interveners and as citizens of this planet, this requires that we increase our capacity to embrace paradox. And that has been the goal of this book.

references

Allred, K. G. "Anger and Retaliation in Conflict: The Role of Attribution," in *The Handbook of Conflict Resolution: Theory and Practice*, ed. P. T. Coleman, M. Deutsch, and E. C. Marcus, 236–255. San Francisco: Jossey-Bass, 2000.

American Arbitration Association, American Bar Association, and Association for Conflict Resolution. *Model Standards of Conduct for Mediators*, 2005. Accessed April 22, 2014. http://www.acrnet.org/uploadedFiles/Practitioner/ModelStandardsof ConductforMediatorsfinal05%281%29%281%29.pdf.

American Bar Association Center for Professional Responsibility. *The Model Rules of Professional Conduct, 2014 Edition*. Chicago: ABA Publishing, 2014.

Angier, N. "The Lives of Sociable Spiders." *New York Times*, May 11, 2014.

Aubert, V. "Competition and Dissensus." *Journal of Conflict Resolution* 7, no. 1 (March 1963): 26–42.

Axelrod, R. *The Complexity of Cooperation: Agent-Based Models of Competition and Collaboration*. Princeton, NJ: Princeton University Press, 1997.

———. *The Evolution of Cooperation*. New York: Basic Books, 1984.

Bey, H. *The Lemonade Ocean and Modern Times: A Position Paper by Hakim Bey*, 1991. Accessed May 24, 2014. http://hermetic.com/bey/lemonade.html.

Blake, R., and J. S. Mouton. *Corporate Excellence Through Grid Organization Development*. Houston: Gulf Publishing, 1968.

The Bowen Center. *Differentiation of Self*. Accessed May 14, 2013. https://www.thebowencenter.org/pages/conceptds.html.

Bowen, M. *Family Therapy and Clinical Practice*. Lanham, MD: Rowman and Littlefield Publishers, 1985.

Bowen, M., and M. Kerr. *Family Evaluation: An Approach Based on Bowen Theory*. New York: Norton, 1988.

Bowling, D., and D. A. Hoffman. *Bringing Peace into the Room: How the Personal Qualities of the Mediator Impact the Process of Conflict Resolution*. San Francisco: Jossey-Bass, 2003.

Brock, S., and E. Mares. *Realism and Anti-Realism*. Durham, UK: Acumen Publishing, 2007.

Burgess, G., and H. Burgess. *Advocacy Advisors and the Neutrality/ Empowerment Problem*. Boulder, CO: The Conflict Resolution Consortium, 1996. Accessed from http://www.colorado.edu/conflict/hwltap4.htm.

Burnell, P. *The Augustinian Person*. Washington, DC: Catholic University of America Press, 2005.

Bush, R., and J. Folger. *The Promise of Mediation: Responding to Conflict Through Empowerment and Recognition*. San Francisco: Jossey-Bass, 2005.

Chesterton, G. K. "Puritan and Anglican." *The Speaker*, December 15, 1900.

Churchill, W. S. *The End of the Beginning*. London: Cassell, 1943.

Cloke, K. *The Dance of Opposites: Explorations in Mediation, Dialogue and Conflict Resolution Systems Design*. Dallas: Goodmedia Press, 2013.

Cooks, L. M., and C. L. Hale. "The Construction of Ethics in Mediation." *Mediation Quarterly* 12, no. 1 (1994): 55–76.

Copleston, F. A. *History of Philosophy, Volume I: Greece and Rome*. New York: Image Books, 1985.

Coser, L. A. *The Functions of Social Conflict*. New York: The Free Press, 1956.

Costa, P. T., R. R. McCrae, and Resources Inc. *NEO Personality Inventory-Revised (NEO PI-R)*. Odessa, FL: Psychological Assessment Resources, 1992.

Crane, T., and S. Patterson. *History of the Mind-Body Problem* (London Studies in the History of Philosophy). London: Routledge, 2000.

Damasio, A. *Descartes' Error: Emotion, Reason, and the Human Brain*. New York: Penguin Books, 2005. First published in 1994 by G. P. Putnam's Sons.

————. *Looking for Spinoza: Joy, Sorrow and the Feeling Brain*. San Diego, CA: Harcourt, 2003.

Danner, M. "In the Darkness of Dick Cheney." *New York Review of Books* 61 no. 4, (March 6, 2014): 49–53.

Dawkins, R. *The Selfish Gene*. New York: Oxford University Press, 1976.

de Sousa, R. *The Rationality of Emotion*. Cambridge, MA: Massachusetts Institute of Technology Press, 1987.

Descartes, R. *Meditations on First Philosophy: With Selections from the Objections and Replies*, trans. Michael Moriarity. New York: Oxford University Press, 2008.

Deutsch, M. "Cooperation and Competition," in *The Handbook of Conflict Resolution: Theory and Practice*, ed. P. T. Coleman, M. Deutsch, and E. C. Marcus, 23–42. San Francisco: Jossey-Bass, 2006.

DiFranco, A. "Overlap," from *Out of Range*. Righteous Babe Records, 1994, compact disc.

Dylan, B. "Subterranean Homesick Blues," from *Bringing It All Back Home*. Columbia Recording Studios, 1965, LP.

Editorial. "The First Historic Steps to Real Middle East Peace." *The Record* (Woodland Park, NJ) Sept. 12, 1993.

Ekman, P. "Universal and Cultural Differences in Facial Expressions of Emotion," in *Nebraska Symposium on Motivation, 1971,*

Vol. 19, ed. J. Cole, 207–282. Lincoln, NE: University of Nebraska Press, 1972.

Elster, J. *Alchemies of the Mind: Rationality and the Emotions.* New York: Cambridge University Press, 1999.

Erikson, E. *Childhood and Society.* New York: W. W. Norton and Company, 1950.

———. *Identity and the Life Cycle.* New York: W. W. Norton and Company, 1980.

———. *Identity: Youth and Crisis.* New York: W. W. Norton and Company, 1968.

Federal Bureau of Investigation (FBI). *Forcible Rape, Uniform Crime Reports: Crime in the United States 1996.* Washington, DC: US Department of Justice, Federal Bureau of Investigation, 1997. http://www.fbi.gov/about-us/cjis/ucr/crime-in-the-u.s/1996/96sec2.pdf.

Felstiner, W., R. Abel, and A. Sarat. "The Emergence and Transformation of Disputes: Naming, Blaming, Claiming . . ." *Law and Society Review* 15, no. 3–4 (1980–1981): 631–654.

Fer, B., D. Batchelor, and P. Wood. *Realism, Rationalism, Surrealism: Art Between the Wars.* New Haven, CT: Yale University Press, 1993.

Fisher, R., W. Ury, and B. Patton. *Getting to Yes: Negotiating Agreement Without Giving In.* 2nd ed. New York: Houghton Mifflin, 1981.

Fitzgerald, F. S. "The Crack-Up," *Esquire Magazine*, February 1936.

Follett, M. P. *Dynamic Administration: The Collected Papers of Mary Parker Follett*, ed. H. C. Metcalf and L. Urwick. New York: Harper & Brothers Publishers, 1942.

Freud, S. *Civilization and Its Discontents.* London: Penguin, 2002.

Gandhi, M. K. *Satyagraha in South Africa.* Ahmedabad, India: Navajivan Publishing House, 2008.

Gibson, K., L. Thompson, and M. H. Bazerman. "Shortcomings of Neutrality in Mediation: Solutions Based on Rationality," *Negotiation Journal* 12, no. 1 (1996): 69–80.

Gibson, M. "Cate Blanchett and Alec Baldwin Respond to Woody Allen Abuse Claims." *Time*, last modified February 3, 2014. http://entertainment.time.com/2014/02/03/cate-blanchett-and-alec-baldwin-respond-to-woody-allen-abuse-claims/.

Gilligan, C. *In a Different Voice: Psychological Theory and Women's Development*. Cambridge, MA: Harvard University Press, 1982.

Gladwell, M. *Blink*. Boston: Back Bay Books, 2007.

Goleman, D. *The Brain and Emotional Intelligence: New Insights*. Northampton, MA: More Than Sound LLC, 2011.

———. *Emotional Intelligence: Why It Can Matter More than IQ*. New York: Bantam Books, 2005.

Gramsci, Antonio. *Letters from Prison, Volume 1*, ed. F. Rosengarten, trans. R. Rosenthal. New York: Columbia University Press, 1994.

Hale, K. "The Language of Cooperation: Negotiation Frames." *Mediation Quarterly* 16, no. 2 (Winter 1998): 147–162.

Haley, J. *Problem Solving Therapy*. San Francisco: Jossey-Bass, 1987.

Hardin, G. "The Tragedy of the Commons." *Science* 162, no. 3859 (1968): 1243–1248.

Hathaway, S. R., and J. C. McKinley. *MMPI-2: Minnesota Multiphasic Personality Inventory-2: Manual for Administration and Scoring*. Minneapolis: University of Minnesota Press, 1989.

Hegel, G.W.F. *The Phenomenology of Mind*, trans. J. B. Baillie. Mineola, NY: Dover Publications, 2003. First published in 1899 by The Colonial Press.

———. *The Philosophy of History*, trans. J. Sibree. Minneola, NY: Dover Publications, Inc., 2004. First published in 1956.

Hoffman, D. A. "Paradoxes of Mediation," in *Bringing Peace Into the Room: How the Personal Qualities of the Mediator Impact the Process of Conflict Resolution*, ed. D. Bowling and D. A. Hoffman, 167–182. San Francisco: Jossey-Bass, 2003.

Izard, C. E. *The Face of Emotion*. New York: Appleton-Century-Crofts, 1971.

Jefferson, T. *The Works of Thomas Jefferson, Vol. 12*, ed. P. L. Ford. New York: The Knickerbocker Press, 1905.

Jung, C. G. *Psychological Types (The Collected Works of C. G. Jung) Vol. 6*, ed. R. F. C. Hull, trans. H. G. Baynes. Princeton, NJ: Princeton University Press, 1976.

Kahneman, D. *Thinking Fast and Slow*. New York: Farrar, Straus and Giroux, 2011.

Karafyllis, N. C., and G. Ulshöfer. *Sexualized Brains: Scientific Modeling of Emotional Intelligence from a Cultural Perspective*. Cambridge, MA: Massachusetts Institute of Technology Press, 2008.

Kegan, R. *In Over Our Heads: The Mental Demands of Modern Life*. Cambridge, MA: Harvard University Press, 1994.

Kennedy, J. F. "Remarks in Bonn at the Signing of a Charter Establishing the German Peace Corps (258)," June 24, 1963. *Public Papers of the Presidents: John F. Kennedy, 1963*. Washington, DC: US Government Printing Office, 1964.

Kenny, A. *Aquinas on Mind*, Topics in Medieval Philosophy Series. New York: Routledge, 1994.

King, M. L. Jr. "Where Do We Go From Here?" Presidential address, The Southern Christian Leadership Conference, Atlanta, GA, August 16, 1967.

Kohlberg, L. *The Philosophy of Moral Development: Moral Stages and the Idea of Justice (Essays on Moral Development, Volume 1)*. New York: Harper and Row, 1981.

Kuttner, R. "The Wave/Particle Tension in Negotiation." *Harvard Negotiation Law Review* 16 (2011): 331.

Lakoff, G., and M. Johnson. *Metaphors We Live By*. Chicago: University of Chicago Press, 1980.

Lang, M. D., and A. Taylor. *The Making of a Mediator: Developing Artistry in Practice*. San Francisco: Jossey-Bass, 2000.

Lax, D., and J. Sebenius. *3-D Negotiation*. Boston: Harvard Business School Press, 2006.

——. *The Manager as Negotiator*. New York: The Free Press, 1987.

Lederach, J. P. *The Little Book of Conflict Transformation*. Intercourse, PA: Good Books, 2003.

———. *The Moral Imagination: The Art and Soul of Building Peace*. New York: Oxford University Press, 2005.

Lindley, D. *Uncertainty: Einstein, Heisenberg, Bohr and the Struggle for the Soul of Science*. New York: Doubleday, 2007.

Locke, E. A. "Why emotional intelligence is an invalid concept." *Journal of Organizational Behavior* 26, no. 4 (2005): 425–431.

Lonsway, K. A., J. Archambault, and D. Lisak. "False Reports: Moving Beyond the Issue to Successfully Investigate and Prosecute Non-Stranger Sexual Assault." *The Voice* 3, no. 1 (2009), publication of The National Center for the Prosecution of Violence Against Women, American Prosecutors Research Institute.

Macfarlane, J. *The New Lawyer: How Settlement Is Transforming the Practice of Law*. Vancouver, BC: The University of British Columbia Press, 2008.

Marx, K. *Capital: A Critique of Political Economy, Vol. 1*, trans. Ben Fowkes. New York: Vintage Books, 1977.

Marx, K., and F. Engels. *The Marx–Engels Reader*, ed. R. C. Tucker. New York: Norton, 1972.

Mahler, M. *On Human Symbiosis and the Vicissitudes of Individuation*. New York: International Universities Press, 1969.

Mahler, M., F. Pine, and A. Bergman. *The Psychological Birth of the Human Infant: Symbiosis and Individuation*. New York: Basic Books, 1975.

May, R. *Power and Innocence: A Search for the Sources of Violence*. New York: Norton, 1972.

Mayer, B. *Beyond Neutrality: Confronting the Crisis in Conflict Resolution*. San Francisco: Jossey-Bass, 2004.

———. *The Dynamics of Conflict: A Guide to Engagement and Intervention*, 2nd ed. San Francisco: Jossey-Bass, 2012a.

———. "Mediation: 50 Years of Creative Conflict." *Family Court Review, 50th Anniversary Issue* 50, no. 1, January, 2013.

————. *Staying with Conflict: A Strategic Approach to Ongoing Disputes*. San Francisco: Jossey-Bass, 2009.

————. "What We Talk About When We Talk About Neutrality: A Commentary on the Susskind–Stulberg Debate, 2011 Edition." *Marquette Law Review* 95, no. 3, 2012b.

Mayer, B., S. Wildau, and R. Valchev. "*Promoting Multi-Cultural Consensus-Building in Bulgaria.*" *Cultural Survival Quarterly*, Fall 1995.

Miller, A. "Realism," in *Stanford Encyclopedia of Philosophy*. Stanford University, April 2010. Article first published July 2002. http://plato.stanford.edu/entries/realism/.

Minuchin, S. *Families and Family Therapy*. Cambridge, MA: Harvard University Press, 1974.

Mnookin, R. *Bargaining with the Devil: When to Negotiate, When to Fight*. New York: Simon and Schuster, 2010.

Moore, C. *The Mediation Process: Practical Strategies for Resolving Conflict*, 3rd ed. San Francisco: Jossey-Bass, 2003.

Moore, C., and P. Woodrow. *Handbook of Global and Multicultural Negotiation*. San Francisco: Jossey-Bass, 2010.

Moore, R. E. *Niels Bohr: The Man, His Science, & the World They Changed*. New York: Knopf, 1966.

Morris, P. *Realism*. New York: Routledge, 2003.

Murray, M. "McCain Fires Back on Foreign Policy." NBCnews.com, May 21, 2008.

Myers, I. B. *Manual: The Myers-Briggs Type Indicator*. Princeton, NJ: Educational Testing Service, 1962.

Myers, I. B., M. H. McCaulley, N. Quenk, and A. Hammer. *MBTI Handbook: A Guide to the Development and Use of the Myers-Briggs Type Indicator*, 3rd ed. Palo Alto, CA: Consulting Psychologists Press, 1998.

Myerson, R. *Game Theory: Analysis of Conflict*. Cambridge, MA: Harvard University Press, 1997.

National Association of Social Workers. *Advocacy and Organizing*. Accessed April 25, 2014. https://www.socialworkers.org/pressroom/features/issue/advocacy.asp.

Nietzsche, F. *The Portable Nietzsche*, ed. and trans. Walter Kaufmann. New York: Penguin Books, 1954.

Nowak, M. "Why We Help: The Evolution of Cooperation." *Scientific American* 307, no. 1 (July 2012).

Nowak, M., and R. Highfield. *Supercooperators: Altruism, Evolution, and Why We Need Each Other to Succeed*. New York: Free Press, 2011.

Obama, B. "Remarks by the President to the United Nations General Assembly." United Nations Headquarters, New York, September 23, 2009.

Osterman, P. *Gathering Power: The Future of Progressive Politics in America*. Boston: Beacon Press, 2002.

Piaget, J. *The Psychology of Intelligence*, trans. M. Piercy and D. E. Berlyne. New York and London: Routledge Classics, 2001.

Pink, D. *Drive: The Surprising Truth About What Motivates Us*. New York: Riverhead Books, 2009.

Pittenger, D. "Measuring the MBTI ... And Coming Up Short." *Journal of Career Planning and Employment* 54, no. 1 (1993): 48–52.

Porter, E. H. *Strength Deployment Inventory*. Pacific Palisades, CA: Personal Strengths Assessment Service, 1971.

Quenk, N. L. *Essential of Myers-Briggs Type Indicator Assessment*. Hoboken, NJ: John Wiley & Sons, 2009.

Rapoport, A. *Two-Person Game Theory: The Essential Ideas*. Ann Arbor, MI: University of Michigan Press, 1966.

Rapoport, A., and A. Chammah. *Prisoner's Dilemma*. Ann Arbor, MI: University of Michigan Press, 1965.

Reagan, R. Address at Commencement Exercises at Eureka College, Eureka, IL, May 9, 1982.

Rifkin, J., J. Millen, and S. Cobb. "Toward a New Discourse for Mediation: A Critique of Neutrality," *Mediation Quarterly* 9, no. 2 (1991): 151–164.

Rothman, J. *Resolving Identity Based Conflict in Nations, Organizations, and Communities.* San Francisco: Jossey-Bass, 1997.

Rubin, J. Z., D. G. Pruitt, and S. H. Kim. *Social Conflict: Escalation, Stalemate and Settlement,* 2nd ed. New York: McGraw-Hill, 1994.

Sayers, S. "Identity and Community." *Journal of Social Philosophy* 30, no. 1 (1999): 147–160.

Schelling, T. *Strategy of Conflict.* Cambridge, MA: Harvard University Press, 1960.

Schön, A. *The Reflective Practitioner: How Professionals Think in Action.* New York: Basic Books, 1983.

Schwarts, S. "The Evolution of Eriksonian and Neo-Eriksonian Identity Theory and Research: A Review and Integration." *Identity: An International Journal of Theory and Research* 1, no. 1 (2001): 7–58.

Seligman, M. *Learned Optimism: How to Change Your Mind and Life.* New York: Vintage Books, 2005. First published in 1991 by Alfred Knopf.

Shri Purohit Swami (trans.) *The Bhagavad Gita.* Seattle: Pacific Publishing Studio, 2010.

Simmel, G. *Conflict and the Web of Group Affiliations,* trans. K. H. Wolff and R. Bendix. New York: The Free Press, 1955.

Smith, S. B. "A Lincoln for Our Time." Review of *Lincoln's Tragic Pragmatism,* by John Burt. *New York Times Sunday Book Review,* New York, February 14, 2013.

Spinoza, B. "Ethics," in *The Collected Works of Spinoza, Volume 1,* trans. Edwin Curley. Princeton, NJ: Princeton University Press, 1985.

Starmer, K. "False allegations of rape and domestic violence are few and far between," *The Guardian* (London, UK), March 13 2013.

Stinehart, M., S. Scott, and B. Barfield. "Reactive Attachment Disorder in Adopted and Foster Care Children: Implications for Mental Health Professionals." *The Family Journal: Counseling and Therapy for Couples and Families* 20, no. 4 (2012): 355–360.

Stricker, L. J., and J. Ross. "An Assessment of Some Structural Properties of the Jungian Personality Typology." *Journal of Abnormal and Social Psychology* 68 (1964): 62–71.

————. *A Description and Evaluation of the Myers-Briggs Type Indicator*, Research Bulletin #RB-62-6. Princeton, NJ: Educational Testing Service, 1962.

Strijker, J., E. J. Knorth, and J. Knot-Dickscheit. "Placement history of foster children: A study of placement history and outcomes in long-term family foster care." *Child Welfare* 87, no. 5 (2008): 107–124.

Stulberg, J.B. "The Theory and Practice of Mediation: A Reply to Professor Susskind." *The Vermont Law Review* 6, no. 1 (1981): 85–117.

Susskind, L. "Environmental Mediation and the Accountability Problem." *The Vermont Law Review* 6, no. 1 (1981): 85–117.

Susskind, L., J. B. Stulberg, B. Mayer, and J. Lande. "Core Values of Dispute Resolution: Is Neutrality Necessary?" Transcript of the Opening Plenary Session of Symposium on Court Based Mediation, Marquette University Law School, September 23, 2011.

Tannen, D. *That's Not What I Meant: How Conversational Style Makes or Breaks Relationships.* New York: Ballantine Books, 1986.

————. *You Just Don't Understand: Women and Men in Conversation.* New York: William Morrow Paperbacks, 2007.

Thomas, K. W. "Conflict and Negotiation Processes in Organizations," in *Handbook of Industrial and Organizational Psychology, Vol. 3*, ed. M. Dunnette and L. Hough, 651–717. Palo Alto, CA: Consulting Psychologists Press, 1992.

Thomas, K. W., and R. H. Kilmann. *Profile and Interpretive Report*. Accessed March 15, 2014. https://www.cpp.com/pdfs/smp248248.pdf.

———. *Thomas-Kilmann Conflict Mode Instrument*. Sterling, NY: Xicom Inc., 1974.

Thompson, D., as quoted in J. Ungerleider,"Conflict," in *Effective Multicultural Teams: Theory and Practice*, ed. C. B. Halverson and S. A. Tirmizi, 211–238. New York: Springer, 2008.

"Treaty on Principles Governing the Activities of States in the Exploration and Use of Outer Space, Including the Moon and Other Celestial Bodies." *International Legal Materials* 6, no. 2 (March 1967): 386–390.

Twain, M. *Pudd'nhead Wilson*. Mineola: Dover Publications, 1999. First published in 1893–94 in *The Century Magazine*.

Ury, W. *Getting Past No: Negotiating in Difficult Situations*. New York: Bantam Books, 1993.

Ver Steegh, N., and C. Dalton. "Report from the Wingspread Conference and Domestic Violence and Family Courts." *Family Court Review* 46, 2008: 454–475.

Voltaire . *La Bégueule: Conte Moral*. Charleston, SC: Nabu Press, 2010. First published in 1772.

Weinberg, J., as quoted in "Don't Trust Anyone Over 30, Unless It's Jack Weinberg." *The Berkeley Daily Planet*, Berkeley, CA, April 6, 2000. http://www.berkeleydailyplanet.com/issue/2000–04–06/article/759?headline=Don-t-trust-anyone-over-30-unless-it-s-Jack-Weinberg—Daily-Planet-Staff.

Wiesel, E. The Nobel Acceptance Speech, Oslo, Norway, December 10, 1986.

Williams, P., and J. Denney. *How to Be Like Walt: Capturing the Disney Magic Every Day in Your Life*. Deerfield Beach, FL: Health Communications Inc., 2004.

Yule, S. A. B., and M. S. Keene. *More Borrowings*. San Francisco: C. A. Murdoch & Co., 1891.

index

A

Abel, R., 104
Absolute commitments, 137
Accommodation, 12
Advocacy, dimensions of, 211–216
Advocate neutral, the, 228–232
Advocates: skills of, 216–220; and third parties, 220–224
Affordable Care Act (ACA), 137, 148, 149
Allen, W., 120
Allred, K. G., 14, 22, 41
Angier, N., 248
Arafat, Y., 157
Archambault, J., 120
Aristotle, 11
Aspirational neutrality, 209
Assimilation, 12
Attribution theory, 22
Aubert, V., 152
Autonomy and community: in conflict paradox, 5; and identity, 238–248; integrating, 248–260; need for both, 237–238; reflections from practice, 260–265
Avoidance and engagement: attitudinal aspects of, 112–115; behavioral elements of, 100–108; in conflict paradox, 5, 95–99; and conflict specialist's challenge, 121–123; dimensions of, 99–100; emotional elements of, 108–111; ethical challenge of, 119–121; example illustrating, 281–282; and prevention and escalation, 116–119; reflections from practice, 123–130
Axelrod, R., 32, 35, 36, 41, 42, 43, 45, 46, 48, 50

B

Baldwin, A., 120
Barfield, B., 135
Bargaining with the Devil, 157
Bazerman, M. H., 201
Begin, M., 250
Behavioral neutrality, 206–207
Berra, Y., 199
Bey, H., 237
Beyond Neutrality, 235
Blake, R., 25
Blink, 172
Bohr, N., 267
Boundaries, importance of, 262
Bowen, M., 51, 101, 246, 247
Bowling, D., 171
Burgess, G., 226
Burgess, H., 226
Burnell, P., 11
Bush, R., 186, 275

C

Carney, A., 260
Carter, J., 250
Chamberlain, N., 155
Cheerful pessimists, 69–70
Cheney, D., 131
Churchill, W., 90, 156
Cloke, K., 267, 271
Closet optimist, 70

Cobb, S., 202
Cognitive dissonance, 21
Cognitive neutrality, 208
Collaborating, defined, 29
Community and autonomy: in conflict paradox, 5; example illustrating, 285–287; and identity, 238–248; integrating, 248–260; need for both, 237–238; reflections from practice, 260–265
Competition, description of, 28
Competition and cooperation: in conflict paradox, 4; and evolution of cooperation, 35–45; example, 279–280; influential approaches to, 28–35; six responses to, 51–52
Complex thinking, promoting, 16–18
Complexity and clarity, as final paradox, 289–293
Compromise and principle: compromising with evil, 155–159; in conflict paradox, 5; example illustrating, 282–283; importance of, 131–132; power of, 148–151; principle without compromise, 133–142; reflections from practice, 159–166. See also Values, interests, and resources
Conflict: as driving force, 9–10; and simpler thinking, 14–16
Conflict interveners, and five essential elements, 2
Conflict paradox: defined, 3; and other paradoxes, 273–276; paradox as a method, 268–273; and seven essential dilemmas, 4–6
Conflict prevention, 116–118
Conflict resolution advocacy, 215
Connection, maintaining, 254–256
Contradictions, role of, 9–12
Cooks, L. M., 202
Cooper, G., 69
Cooperation, evolution of, 35–45. See also Competition and cooperation
Copleston, F. A., 11
Costa, P. T., 187

Covey, S., 273
Crane, T., 11

D

Dalton, C., 93
Damasio, A., 11, 167, 168, 171, 175, 176
Darwin, C., 45
Dawkins, R., 25, 45
Decision making, and emotions and logic, 171–176
Deferring, as intervention strategy, 89
Descartes, R., 11
Deutsch, M., 25
Developmental psychology, 12–13
Dialectical process, paradox as, 271
Differentiation, 101, 246–247
DiFranco, A., 237
Discourse, 204
Disney, W., 61
Distributive power, 150
Domestic violence, victims of, 136
Dualistic thinking, 21, 23
Dylan, B., 292
Dynamics of Conflict, The, 2, 31

E

Ekman, P., 193
Emotional elements of avoidance and engagement, 108–111
Emotional intelligence, 175–176
Emotional neutrality, 207
Emotional skills of advocates, 217–218
Emotional well-being of children, 136
Emotions and logic: in conflict paradox, 5; in conflict work, 176–180; and decision making, 171–176; example of, 283–284; feelings about thoughts, 181–183; and gender, 191–195; in narratives, 183–184; as opposites, 167–168; reflections from practice, 195–199; response of conflict specialists to, 168–171

Engagement and avoidance:
   attitudinal aspects of, 112–115;
   behavioral elements of, 100–108; in
   conflict paradox, 5, 95–99; and
   conflict specialist's challenge,
   121–123; dimensions of, 99–100;
   emotional elements of, 108–111;
   ethical challenge of, 119–121;
   example illustrating, 281–282; and
   prevention and escalation,
   116–119; reflections from practice,
   123–130
Engels, F., 11
Enmeshment, 247
Equidistance, 204
Ericson, E., 238, 239
Escalation, conflict, 116, 118–119
Evil, compromising with, 155–159
Evolution of Cooperation, The, 32

F

Farrow, D., 120, 121
Fast thinking, 172–173, 174, 175
Feeling and thinking: identifying, 185;
   integrating, 186–191; language of,
   181. *See also* Emotions and logic
Feelings about thoughts, 181–183
Felstiner, W., 104
Fisher, R., 25, 31, 143, 195
Fitzgerald, F. S., 1
Folger, J., 186, 275
Follett, M. P., 25
Forgiveness, 36, 41–43
Free Speech Movement, 292
Freud, S., 239

G

Gandhi, M., 148
Getting to Yes, 143
Gibson, K., 201, 204
Gibson, M., 69, 120
Gilligan, C., 12
Gladwell, M., 171, 172, 176
Goleman, D., 175, 176, 185, 192
Gramsci, A., 71

H

Hale, C. L., 202
Hathaway, S. R., 187
Hegel, G., 11, 271
Highfield, R., 46, 47, 50
Hitler, A., 156
Hoffman, D., 171, 268, 276
Hopelessness: safety through, 68–69;
   as self-fulfilling prophecy, 94

I

Identity: and autonomy, 242–248; and
   community, 240–242; defined,
   238–239
Ignoring, as intervention strategy, 89–90
Impartiality, 202, 204
Integrative power, 150
Integrative reframing, 90
Intentional communities, lessons
   from, 262–265
Izard, C. E., 193

J

Jefferson, T., 113, 131
Johnson, M., 291
Jung, C., 187

K

Kahneman, D., 172, 173, 174, 175, 176
Karafyllis, N. C., 192
Kegan, R., 12
Kenny, A., 11
Kerr, M., 51, 101, 247
Kilmann, R., 25, 28, 29
Kim, S. H., 14
King, M. L., 63, 64, 148
Knorth, E. J., 135
Knot-Dickscheit, J., 135
Kohlberg, L., 12
Kuttner, R., 12

L

Lakoff, G., 291
Lande, J., 225

Lax, D., 25, 28, 30, 31, 38, 195
Lederach, J. P., 114, 275
Lindley, D., 12
Lisak, D., 120
Locke, E. A., 176
Lonsway, K. A., 120

M

Macfarlane, J., 215, 222
Mahler, M., 247
Mandela, N., 156, 157, 288
Marx, K., 11, 271
Mayer, B., 14, 59, 94, 99, 110, 118, 126, 195, 204, 213, 220, 225, 227, 239, 291
Mayer, F., 232
McCain, J., 82
McCrae, R. R., 187
McKinley, J. C., 187
Memory, and forgiveness, 42
Millen, J., 202
Miller, A., 65
Minnesota Multiphasic Personality Inventory, 187
Minuchin, S., 51, 101, 247
Mirroring, as intervention strategy, 88
Misogyny, 121
Mnookin, R., 157, 158
Modesty of goals, 43
Mood, group's predominant, 87–88
Moore, C., 144, 152, 153, 160, 193, 195, 202
Mouton, J. S., 25
Murray, M., 82
Myers-Briggs Type Indicator (MBTI), 187, 188

N

Naming, as intervention strategy, 88
Naming, blaming, and claiming, 104–105
Narratives, 183–184
Negotiator's Dilemma, 30
Netanyahu, B., 37

Neutrality and advocacy: advocates and third parties, 220–224; classic debate on, 225–227; in conflict paradox, 5; dimensions of advocacy, 211–216; elements of neutrality, 209–211; example of, 284–285; four cases of both, 228–232; reflections from practice, 232–236; and skills of advocates, 216–220; types of neutrality, 203–209
Niceness, 36, 37–38, 69
Nietzsche, F., 167
Nowak, M., 46, 47, 48, 50

O

Obama, B., 15, 82, 83, 148, 149
Observations, 184
Optimism and realism: in conflict paradox, 4–5; emotional dimension of, 65–71; ethics of, 82–84; example illustrating, 280–281; faces of, 64–65; integrating, 85–90; need for both, 61–64; and uncertainty, 71–82
Osterman, P., 215
Outcome and transformation, 275

P

Paradox, conflict: defined, 3; and other paradoxes, 273–276; paradox as a method, 268–273; and seven essential dilemmas, 4–6
Paradoxes: final reflections on, 289–293; society's essential, 287–289
Paradoxes, seven. See Avoidance and engagement; Community and autonomy; Competition and cooperation; Emotions and logic; Neutrality and advocacy; Optimism and realism; Principle and compromise
Patterson, S., 11
Patton, B., 25, 195
Perceptive neutrality, 208–209

Personality inventories, 187–188
Pessimism: cheerful outlook with, 69–70; as personality trait, 63; realism versus, 63
Piaget, J., 12
Pittenger, D., 188
Plato, 11
Porter, E. H., 187
Prevention of conflict, 116–118
Principle and compromise: compromising with evil, 155–159; in conflict paradox, 5; example illustrating, 282–283; importance of, 131–132; power of, 148–151; principle without compromise, 133–142; reflections from practice, 159–166. See also Values, interests, and resources
Principles: as absolute commitments, 137; as pragmatic, 142–147; several ways to think of, 138–140; standing on, 151
Prisoner's Dilemma: description of, 19, 32–35; innovative application of, 46; limits of, 47–51; real conflict versus, 48
Process and substance, 274
Provocability, 36, 38–41
Pruitt, D. G., 14
Putin, V., 15

Q

Quenk, N. L., 187

R

Rabin, Y., 157
Reagan, R., 113
Realism: as cooler or wiser, 69; pessimism versus, 63
Realism and optimism: in conflict paradox, 4–5; emotional dimension of, 65–71; ethics of, 82–84; example illustrating, 280–281; faces of, 64–65; integrating, 85–90; need for

both, 61–64; and uncertainty, 71–82
Referring, as intervention strategy, 89
Rifkin, J., 202
Rigidity, as weakness, 150
Rituals, and communities, 263
Ross, J., 188
Rothman, J., 239
Rouhani, H., 37
Rubin, J. Z., 14

S

Sadat, A., 37, 251
St. Augustine, 11
St. Thomas Aquinas, 11
Sarat, A., 104
Sayers, S., 240
Schön, A., 276
Scott, S., 135
Sebenius, J., 25, 28, 30, 31, 38, 195
Self-referencing and interrupting, 106, 107
Seligman, M., 63, 79, 80, 81
Seven essential dilemmas, 4–6
Seven paradoxes. See Avoidance and engagement; Community and autonomy; Competition and cooperation; Emotions and logic; Neutrality and advocacy; Optimism and realism; Principle and compromise
Sexual abuse, allegations of, 120–121
Slow thinking, 172, 173, 174, 175
Smith, S. B., 131
Spinoza, B., 11
Starmer, K., 120
Staying with Conflict: A Strategic Approach to Ongoing Disputes, 93
Stinehart, M., 135
Strength Deployment Inventory, 187
Stricker, L. J., 188
Strijker, J., 135
Structural neutrality, 204–206
Stulberg, J. B., 225, 226, 227
Substance and relationship, 274–275
Susskind, L., 225, 226, 227

T

Tannen, D., 49, 101, 192
Tea Party movement, 149
Thinking: and conflict, 14–16; fast
    versus slow, 172–175; promoting
    complex, 16–18
Thin-slicing, 172
Thomas, K., 25, 28, 29
Thomas-Kilmann model, 28–29
Thompson, D., 95, 114
Thompson, L., 201
Transformative moments, 18
Transparency, 36, 43–45
Twain, M., 114

U

Ulshöfer, G., 192
Uncertainty, embracing, 71–82
Ury, W., 25, 31, 143, 195

V

Valchev, R., 94
Value claiming, 30–31
Value creating, 30–31
Values, interests, and resources,
    152–155
Venting, 185
Ver Steegh, N., 93
Voltaire, 65

W

Weinberg, J., 292
Wiesel, E., 201
Wildau, S., 94
Woodrow, P., 193

Z

Zero sum thinking, 14